# Beth's Incredible Journey

Eberly Frazier Mehesy

# Beth's Incredible Journey

Cover Design by CreateSpace, an Amazon.com company

Printed by CreateSpace, an Amazon.com company

Available from Amazon.com, CreateSpace.com, and other retail outlets

ISBN-10:1530949912
ISBN-13:978-1530949915

# Author's Notes

This book is a fictionalized biography of my mother's life, based on the stories which she told me about her childhood and young adult years, and on my own childhood experiences. All of the events in this story actually happened, and all of the characters were real people, with the exception of the events and persons depicted during my mother's stay in the orphanage, the happenings described during my mother's first romance, and the reason for my father's false imprisonment when I was a very small child. These portions of the story, by necessity, are products of my imagination. Also, although most of the characters in this book were real people, I have "fleshed out" their characters and created dialogue when necessary to tell the story more effectively. Some names have been changed to protect the privacy of the individuals involved. However, even the most unbelievable events in this story actually happened! As the old saying goes, "Truth is stranger than fiction!"

# Table of Contents

# <u>Dedication</u>

This book is dedicated to my dear mother, Beth Averne Conrad Frazier, who lived this story, but most of all, it is dedicated to her beloved Savior, the Lord Jesus Christ, Whom she loved passionately, and served faithfully for almost 50 years!

# Chapter 1—A New Name

"Mama! Mama!" Five-year-old Elsie May Rogers sat bolt upright in bed, startled awake by the sound of her own cries. But Mama did not come. Elsie May looked around the room in confusion. The moon was shining outside the window, and she could see the dark outlines of trees through the curtains. She could hear the steady breathing of the girl in the bunk above her own.

Looking across the room, she saw another bunk bed, with two more sleeping girls. "Where am I?" she thought. Then she remembered. She was at the orphanage, and Mama was not here. The horrifying events of the day before, which she had just relived in her nightmare, came flooding back to her mind in vivid detail.

"Elsie May, wake up," Mama had said yesterday morning. "Today we have to go downtown."

Elsie May had been excited. She loved to go to town with Mama. They didn't usually buy very much, but Elsie May loved to look at the interesting things in the store windows, and usually

Mama would buy her a small treat at the grocery store, after she had finished buying food.

But yesterday had been different. After riding on a bus, they had come to a big stone building with a long flight of steps. They had climbed up the stairs into the building, entered a large room, and sat on a hard bench. Facing them was a grumpy-looking man who was wearing a long black robe and sitting behind a desk. Elsie May and Mama had sat for what seemed like hours.

At last, the man had called for Mama to come up to his desk and talk to him. Immediately, a tall, thin woman had walked up and stood beside Mama. She had talked angrily to the man, pointing to Mama as she spoke. Mama had stood there looking at the floor, talking quietly, and shaking her head. Suddenly, the tall woman had turned around, looked directly at Elsie May, and pointed her finger right at her. Without knowing why, Elsie May had shrunk down into her seat, wishing that she could hide from the woman's stern eyes.

Finally, Mama had said, "Elsie May, it's time to go now." Elsie May had been so glad when the long meeting was over.

"Perhaps now Mama will take me someplace more interesting," she had thought.

They had gone out of the building and down the steps to the sidewalk. As they reached the bottom of the steps, the tall, thin woman, who had been walking beside Mama, had suddenly grabbed Elsie May by the hand, yanked her away from Mama, and dragged her toward a shiny black car that was parked at the curb.

"Mama! Mama!" she had screamed in terror, but her cries were soon muffled by the black-gloved hand of the woman. To Elsie May's amazement, Mama had not come to help her, but had just stood motionless, watching while the woman had shoved her into the waiting car and sped away. Looking out the window, she had caught her last glimpse of Mama, standing helplessly on the sidewalk, with tears streaming down her cheeks.

Elsie May had struggled, squirmed, and cried as the car zoomed down the street. "I want my mama! I want my mama!" she sobbed over and over again.

"Hush, child," the woman had said. "Your mama wasn't taking good care of you like she should have done. I'm taking you to a nice place where you will live until we can find a new family to take care of you."

After driving for a long time, the car had stopped in front of a gray stone building. Boys and girls of all different ages were playing in the yard, but Elsie May had hardly glanced at them as the woman led her up the steps and into the building.

"This is the orphanage, Elsie May," the woman had told her. "You will live here until someone adopts you." She hadn't explained what an orphanage was, or what it meant to be adopted. Elsie May had wondered what she meant, but had been too frightened to ask.

They had gone into a room where a kind-looking white-haired lady was sitting behind a desk. She had immediately stood up and walked around the desk to meet them. "Mrs. Foster," the tall, thin woman had said. "This is Elsie May Rogers. She will be staying with you for a while." Then the woman had turned around, walked out the door, and left Elsie May alone with Mrs. Foster.

Mrs. Foster had reached out and taken Elsie May by the hand. "Come with me, Elsie May. I'll show you your room, and you will get to meet the other girls who will be living there with you."

They had walked down a long hall, up a flight of stairs, and into a room that had two bunk beds and a dresser. There were three girls in the room. Two of them were big girls, but one was almost exactly the same size as Elsie May. She had golden curls and blue eyes, and she smiled shyly at Elsie May.

3

"Elsie May, this is Amy." Mrs. Foster had pointed to the little girl. "And this is Millie and this is Fran," she had continued, indicating the bigger girls. "Girls, this is Elsie May. She will be your new roommate. Please help her to feel at home here with us."

As soon as Mrs. Foster had left the room, Elsie May had run into the corner of the room, buried her face in her hands, and begun sobbing quietly. Fran had hurried over to her, taken her into her arms, pulled her onto her lap, and sat softly stroking her hair, until Elsie May had finally calmed down a bit.

Hesitantly, Elsie May had looked up into Fran's face. It was a friendly face, framed by long dark hair. Fran's bright brown eyes smiled down at her. "Don't be scared, Elsie May. They take good care of us here at the orphanage."

Shyly, Elsie May had whispered, "What's an orphanage?"

"It's a home for boys and girls like us who don't have any mamas and papas to take care of us. We live here until we get adopted."

Elsie May had wanted to tell Fran that she <u>had</u> a mama to take care of her, and that she had a papa too, even though he didn't live with them and she had only seen him a few times when he came to visit. However, she had noticed that Fran had just used the other big word that the tall, thin woman had used. "What's 'dopted'?"

"'Adopted' means that you get a <u>new</u> family. They take you away from the orphanage, and you go and live with them and become a part of their family."

"But I don't want a new family! I want my mama!" Elsie May had cried.

Just then a bell had rung. "Come with me, Elsie May." Fran had gently pulled her to her feet. "It's time for supper."

The four girls had walked back down the stairs and into a large room that was filled with boys and girls all sitting at long tables. When Elsie May's food had been brought to her, she hadn't felt hungry, and had just sat looking down at her plate and pushing her food around on it until the meal was finished.

Soon it had been time for bed. Mrs. Foster had brought Elsie May a long white flannel nightgown, and Fran had helped Elsie May to get ready for bed. "You can sleep on the bottom bunk, right under where I sleep, Elsie May."

Now, as Elsie May lay back on her pillow, crying quietly, she could hear Fran's quiet breathing above her. "Dear God," she whispered, "Please help me. I'm scared, and I want my mama." At last she drifted back into a restless sleep.

The loud ringing of a bell jarred Elsie May from sleep. Sunlight was streaming in the window and falling in golden squares on the floor. Just then, there was a gentle knock on the door. The door opened, and Mrs. Foster walked in. She was carrying two dresses and two sets of underwear. "Elsie May, these are for you. Since you came to us with only one set of clothes, you will need something else to wear."

Elsie May, whose eyes had been focused on the floor, sneaked a shy peek at the dresses. One was a dark, somber navy blue, and the other was a drab shade of brown. How she wished that they had been bright colors, like the golden sunlight, or the red maple leaves that she could see through the window of her room.

"Thank you, ma'am," she murmured, in a voice so quiet that Mrs. Foster could barely understand her.

"You're welcome. And now, Elsie May, I need to explain our rules to you. Each morning as soon as the bell rings, you must get up, get dressed, and get ready for breakfast. Then you must make your bed and clean your room. We have room inspection at eight o'clock. When the bell rings again, it will be time for breakfast, and you must not be late. Since you are still too young to go to school, you may play outside until the bell rings for lunch. After lunch, it will be naptime, and you will go to your room and rest for a while. After naptime, you may play again until suppertime. A bell will ring to tell you when it is time to go to supper. When it is time to go to bed, another bell will ring, and you must immediately get into bed and be quiet. Do you have any questions?"

Elsie May, still looking at the cracks in the wooden floor, shyly shook her head. However, she was totally confused. There were so many bells! How would she ever know what to do when they rang?

After Mrs. Foster left the room, Amy smiled at Elsie May and took her hand. "Don't be scared, Elsie May. I'll help you know what to do. Just follow me and do what I do."

At breakfast that morning, hunger overcame Elsie May's loneliness, and she managed to eat a few bites of oatmeal, and part of a piece of toast. When they were finished eating, Amy said, "Let's go outside and play on the playground, Elsie May." Amy led her out into a fenced yard, which had swings, a slide, and a seesaw in it. Bright scarlet leaves were falling from three huge maple trees. Some of the children in the yard were piling them up into heaps and diving into them, or throwing handfuls of leaves at each other.

"Let's play on the seesaw, Elsie May."

Without answering, Elsie May followed Amy to the seesaw and climbed onto one end. Up and down, up and down they went. As she watched some of the other children, who were swinging, a picture flashed into Elsie May's mind. Just last week, she and Mama had gone to a park, and Mama had pushed her high on a swing. There had been puffy white clouds in the sky, and as Elsie May had soared up into the sky, she had felt as if she were almost high enough to touch them with her toes. It had been such fun!

When her end of the seesaw came to the ground, she suddenly jumped off, leaving Amy to hit the ground with a bump. Sobbing, she ran behind the nearest tree, and huddled on the ground, her face in her hands.

Amy recovered from her unexpectedly hard landing, and ran over to find her. "Elsie May, what's the matter?"

"I want my mama!" Elsie May sobbed.

"I miss my mama too. She got sick and died, and that's why I'm here. What happened to your mama?"

"Nothing happened to her. A mean lady grabbed me away from her yesterday, and then brought me here. I don't know why she took me away from my mama," Elsie May cried.

Amy was stunned. Not knowing what else to say, she simply dropped to the ground beside Elsie May and hugged her and patted her as she cried.

As the weeks passed, Amy and Elsie May became inseparable companions. Fran and Millie were busy with school and had little time for the younger girls. Each morning after breakfast, Amy and Elsie May would rush outdoors to play on the playground and act out the imaginary stories that they made up. Elsie May's favorite story was the one that they played about Mama coming to the orphanage to take her back home again. As time went on, Elsie May stopped crying in front of anyone, but each night she quietly sobbed out her sorrow to God until she finally dropped off to sleep on her tear-stained pillow.

One morning when Elsie May awakened and looked out the window, she found that the entire world was blanketed with white, and huge lacy white flakes were drifting lazily down from the cloudy sky. Amy awakened at precisely the same moment, erupted from bed, and ran over to the window with a squeal of delight. "Look, Elsie May! Snow! We can make a snowman, and throw snowballs and make snow angels!"

Elsie May tumbled out of bed and ran to join her friend at the window. They hurriedly dressed and cleaned their room, and as soon as breakfast was over, they ran outside to begin constructing their snowman. After making his body, they began digging under the snow, looking for rocks and pieces of coal that could be used for his eyes, nose, and mouth. Elsie May found two shiny lumps of coal which made beautiful black eyes, and Amy found a pointed rock which made a perfect nose, but they were at a loss to know how to make his mouth until Elsie May said, "I know! Let's break off some twigs from this tree and put them together to make a mouth."

"That's a great idea, Elsie May!" As the girls were working, other children from the orphanage were also making snowmen, but when they were done, Amy and Elsie May agreed that theirs had the brightest eyes and the friendliest smile.

By the time supper came, the girls had worked up a hearty appetite. However, before supper began, Mrs. Foster stood up, her face beaming. "Boys and girls, we are going to have a special treat after supper tonight. Some nice people from the church across the street are coming to visit us. We are going to have a special Christmas celebration."

Elsie May was excited and sad at the same time. She remembered last year when Mama had put up a small tree and she and Mama had popped popcorn and made strings of popcorn and cranberries to hang on the tree. Mama had told her to hang up her stocking, and in the morning, it had been filled with an orange, an apple, several pieces of hard candy, and a pair of warm, red woolen mittens.

Sure enough, after supper, several kind-looking ladies came into the dining hall. One of them went to the piano, which was in the corner of the room and began to play some of the most joyful music that Elsie May had ever heard. As she played, the other ladies sang songs about a Baby Who had been born in a stable and laid in a manger. Elsie May just listened, but many of the other children joined in the singing.

After the singing, one of the ladies began to tell a story, using pictures that seemed to magically stick to a board which was covered with a piece of cloth. There were pictures of a beautiful young lady, a young man, a tiny baby, some angels, some men who were taking care of sheep, a star, and some beautifully dressed men who were riding camels. The lady kept talking about Someone named Jesus, Who she said was the Son of God, and Who was born on the first Christmas Day. Even though Elsie May didn't fully understand it, she was fascinated by the story.

When the story was over, the ladies brought in huge sacks loaded with brightly wrapped presents, and began calling out names. Elsie May and Amy each received a package. In each package was a rag doll. Elsie May squealed with delight when she saw her doll, and then she burst out laughing, as she looked from the doll's face to Amy's face. The doll looked like Amy. It had golden yarn curls and bright blue button eyes. "Her name is Amy," she exclaimed.

Amy looked from her doll to Elsie May's face. "And my doll's name will be Elsie May," she announced, as she gazed at its brown yarn curls and brown button eyes.

From that time on, as Elsie May talked to God each night, she did so with Amy Doll hugged tightly in her arms, and just before she dropped off to sleep she would whisper to her, "No mean lady is ever going to take you away from me, Amy Doll! I'll never let you go, and I'll always take care of you!"

As the months went by, the girls played house with their dolls each day under the maple trees in the yard outside. Gradually, the snow melted, and one morning Elsie May noticed tiny green leaves on the maple branches. Near the building, sunny yellow daffodils and deep purple hyacinths were blooming. The air was warm, and the sun was shining brightly.

Suddenly the door of the orphanage opened, and Mrs. Foster came outside and hurried over to the tree where Elsie May and Amy were playing. She had a big smile on her face. "Hurry and come inside, girls. There are some people here who are interested in adopting a child, and I want you to come and meet them. Perhaps today you will each find a new family to take care of you."

Elsie May trudged across the yard dragging her feet and looking at the light green shoots of grass that were just beginning to poke their way through the soil. "If someone adopts me, then Mama will never be able to find me and take me back home!" she thought in terror.

Mrs. Foster led them into her office, where two men and two women were sitting. "Girls, this is Mr. and Mrs. Vance and Mr. and Mrs. Tremont." Then, turning to the visitors, she continued her introductions. "This is Elsie May, and this is Amy."

Mrs. Vance, who had blond hair and blue eyes like Amy's, turned to her husband, pointed to Amy, and whispered, in a voice loud enough for Elsie May to hear, "Isn't she adorable? Let's take that one."

"Whatever you want, my dear." Then Mr. Vance turned to Amy. "Would you like to come to our house, Amy?"

Amy's blue eyes sparkled, and she nodded her head eagerly. Soon Amy was leaving the office with the Vances. As she walked out the door, she turned to wave goodbye to Elsie May.

Mrs. Tremont smiled at Elsie May. "How would you like to come home with us for a little visit, Elsie May?"

Elsie May just looked at the floor and shook her head. "She's a bit shy," Mrs. Foster explained apologetically. "She has only been with us for a few months, and she still misses her mother terribly."

"Well, let's give it a try anyway," Mr. Tremont said. He had stern-looking dark eyes, and Elsie May felt a bit afraid of him.

Soon Elsie May found herself getting into the back seat of the Tremonts' car, tightly clutching Amy Doll in her arms. Mrs. Tremont turned around to talk to Elsie May. "How old are you, dear?" Instead of answering her, Elsie May merely held up five fingers.

After driving for what seemed like hours, the car stopped in front of a small green house surrounded by a white picket fence. Daffodils and hyacinths were blooming in the yard, there was a swing hanging from a large oak tree, and a black cat with white paws was lying on the doorstep sunning herself.

"Would you like to try out our swing, Elsie May?" Mr. Tremont invited. "I'll push you."

"All right," Elsie May whispered, as she got out of the car. Soon she was in the swing and Mr. Tremont was pushing her higher and higher. The puffy white clouds seemed so close that she felt she could touch them with her toes. Then suddenly the memory of that day in the park with Mama overwhelmed her, and she began sobbing uncontrollably. Quickly, Mr. Tremont stopped the swing and Elsie May jumped off the swing, ran to the corner of the yard, hid her face in her hands and continued crying.

Mrs. Tremont hurried over to her and awkwardly stroked her hair. "Calm down, Elsie May, and tell me what is wrong. Were you scared because Mr. Tremont was pushing you so high?"

"No," Elsie May choked between her sobs. "I want my mama."

"Why don't we go inside and show you our house?" She drew Elsie May to her feet and led her up the steps and through the door. They walked through the living room, up the stairs, and into a small bedroom. "This will be your room while you are visiting us, Elsie May." Elsie May didn't answer, but just fidgeted and looked at the patterns on the rug.

That night at supper, Mr. Tremont said, "Since this is your first night with us, Elsie May, we are having a special dinner—a turkey dinner, just like we have at Thanksgiving time."

"That's right," Mrs. Tremont chimed in happily. "We are so glad to finally have a little girl in our home that we just had to have a celebration!"

However, even though the food looked and smelled delicious, Elsie May only picked at it and ate very little. She just wanted to go back to the orphanage, because as long as she was there, she could still hope that Mama would come and get her. She missed Mama so much, and now she realized that she missed Amy too. Even if she had to stay at the orphanage, at least Amy would be there to keep her company.

After a very long and silent weekend, Mrs. Tremont called Elsie May to her. "Elsie May, I'm sorry, but it looks like it just isn't going to work out for you to stay with us after all. Today we will be taking you back to the orphanage." For the first time since she had been at the Tremonts, Elsie May almost smiled. She felt sure that Amy would be back by this time too, and she could hardly wait to see her again.

Finally the long trip was over, and Elsie May was back at the orphanage again. She raced through the door, up the stairs, and into her room. School was over for the day, and Fran and Millie were busily doing their homework, but Amy was nowhere to be seen. "Where's Amy?" she cried.

Fran got up, laid her book down, came over to Elsie May, and enfolded her in her arms. "Amy isn't here.  She was adopted by the Vance family."

"When is she coming back?" Elsie May cried in panic.

"She's not coming back.  She is going to live with the Vances and be part of their family from now on.  Don't you remember that I told you what being adopted means?"

Elsie May tore herself out of Fran's loving arms and flung herself on her bed, crushing Amy Doll in her arms.  She buried her face in the pillow and her shoulders heaved as she sobbed out her grief.  First she had lost Mama, and now Amy.  "Oh, God, help me," she sobbed.

The month of May came, and Elsie May's sixth birthday passed unnoticed and uncelebrated.  Elsie May still did not find another friend her own age.  Though Fran and Millie were kind and caring and read stories to her every night, Elsie May was very lonely and missed Amy terribly.  Nothing was like it had been when Amy was still there.

One night as the three girls were sitting in their room, Millie spoke up. "You're lucky, Elsie May."

"Why?" Elsie May asked in surprise.

"Because you're still little.  That means you have a good chance of being adopted.  No one wants big girls like Fran and me."

"Millie's right," Fran agreed. "We'll probably have to stay here at the orphanage until we're all grown up." Elsie May shuddered. She hoped that <u>she</u> wouldn't have to stay at the orphanage until she was grown up.

As spring turned into summer, and Mama still didn't come to get her, Elsie May slowly began to realize that Mama was not going to come, and she began to think that perhaps being adopted really would be better than staying in the orphanage.

One day in the middle of summer, as Elsie May sat alone under the maple tree cradling Amy Doll in her arms, Mrs. Foster called to her from her open office window, which overlooked the playground. "Elsie May, please come into my office. There's someone that I want you to meet." Elsie May ran across the yard, up the steps, and into the office. Sitting in two chairs were a man and woman. "Elsie May, this is Dr. and Mrs. Conrad. They want to adopt a little girl, and they would like to take you to their house for a visit."

The Conrads looked very old to her—old enough to be her grandparents. Both of them had gray hair and were wearing glasses, and Dr. Conrad was quite bald. Mrs. Conrad looked quite stern, but Dr. Conrad had a merry twinkle in his eyes, and when he smiled at Elsie May, she liked him instantly.

They took her home to their spacious white house, with its flower-filled yard and spreading oak trees. Mrs. Conrad took her upstairs to the room that would be hers while she was staying with them. "This is where you will sleep, Elsie May. It will be your responsibility to make your bed each morning, and to keep your room clean."

"Yes, Mrs. Conrad," Elsie May whispered shyly, with her eyes on the floor.

"Well, you don't have to act so frightened of me, child!" Mrs. Conrad replied sharply. "I don't bite!"

After Mrs. Conrad left, Elsie May looked around the room. It was bigger than the room that she shared with the other girls at the orphanage, and the bed was covered with a beautiful, flowered bedspread, which matched the curtains at the window. Above the dresser was a mirror, and a door opened into a closet where clothes could be hung. Looking out the window, she saw a brown dog running across the lawn. She began to feel a little bit more at home.

Just then she heard Mrs. Conrad call her. "Elsie May, please come downstairs. We would like you to meet the other member of our family."

Elsie May was surprised. "Who could be the other member of their family?" she wondered. Curious, she hurried downstairs.

Standing beside Dr. Conrad was a short slender young lady with wavy light-brown hair and friendly-looking gray eyes. "Elsie May, this is our daughter Dot," Dr. Conrad said. "She is twenty years old. Most of the time she is away at college, but right now she is home for the summer."

Dot reminded Elsie May of Dr. Conrad, and she felt instantly comfortable with her. "So you are going to be my new little sister!" Dot exclaimed excitedly. "I've been telling Dad and Mother for just ages that I wanted a little brother or sister. We're going to have lots of fun together, Elsie May!" And they did.

That weekend, Dr. and Mrs. Conrad and Dot took Elsie May to their vacation cottage on Green Pond. When they pulled into the driveway, Elsie May looked puzzled. "Is this your house too, Dot? Why do you have two houses?"

"Yes, this is our house too, Elsie May. Our house in town is where we live most of the time, and this one on the lake is where we come on weekends and during the summertime." Then Dot turned to Mrs. Conrad. "I'd like to take Elsie May swimming now. Is that all right, Mother?"

"Certainly."

Dot helped Elsie May change into the pretty pink bathing suit that the Conrads had bought for her, and soon they were running out the back door and down to the shore of the lake. Elsie May had never been swimming before. She dipped one toe in the water and quickly drew it back, shivering. "Brrr! It's cold!"

"Only until you get used to it!" Dot jumped into the water, then turned and held out her hands. "Come to me, Elsie May. You don't have to be scared. I'll hold on to you." Hesitantly, Elsie May ventured out into the water. With Dot holding her hand, they walked out deeper and deeper until the water was up to Elsie May's waist, and she was more used to the temperature. "All right, now it's time for your first swimming lesson. First, just stay right where you are and watch what I do, and then I'll help you know what to do."

Elsie May watched as Dot plunged into the water and smoothly moved her arms and legs in rhythm, propelling herself swiftly through the water. It looked like fun! When she returned to Elsie May's side, she instructed, "I'll hold you up, and I want you to lie down on your tummy in the water and move your arms and legs like you saw me do." Elsie May felt safe with Dot holding her, and even though she got water in her nose a few times, she just blew it out with a giggle and kept trying to learn. She could hardly wait until she could swim as well as Dot.

"That's enough for today," Dot said finally. "Let's get dried off and go for a ride in the rowboat."

Soon Dot and Elsie May were gliding smoothly over the surface of the lake, as Dot pulled at the oars in perfect rhythm. Elsie May looked at the bright blue sky with puffy white clouds sailing by overhead, she felt the warmth of the sun on her face, and she heard the joyous songs of the birds in the trees at the edge of the lake. She felt happier than she had been since the day when she had been taken away from Mama.

After the boat ride was over, Dot said, "Elsie May, I want to show you something special." She went into the kitchen, got two large bowls out of the cupboard and beckoned to Elsie May. "Follow me." They went out the door and around the side of the house. Elsie May saw several short bushes filled with plump blue berries. "These are blueberries, Elsie May. Taste one. They're delicious."

Elsie May picked one and popped it into her mouth. As she bit into it, and tasted the juicy sweetness, a delighted smile lit up her face. "Mmm! That's good!"

"Let's pick enough so that Mother can bake a pie for supper. Blueberries make great pies." Dot and Elsie May worked hard, and soon they had enough to make a pie.

By suppertime, Elsie May had worked up a good appetite, and had no trouble making all of the food on her plate disappear. She especially enjoyed the delicious blueberry pie that Mrs. Conrad had made with the blueberries that she and Dot had picked.


After that first wonderful weekend was over, they returned to the Conrads' house in town. Every day, Dr. Conrad spent many hours in his office, which was attached to their house. "Dr. Conrad," Elsie May asked shyly one day, "Do you help people when they are sick?"

"No, Elsie May. I'm not that kind of doctor. I'm a dentist. I help people when they have toothaches."

That night after supper, Dr. Conrad beckoned to Elsie May. "Come with me." He led her into his workshop, which was filled with tools and pieces of wood. Elsie May saw a hammer, a saw, a screwdriver, and many other tools whose names she didn't know. "Have you seen how many birds we have in our yard, Elsie May?"

Elsie May nodded. She had seen all different colors of beautiful birds—red, blue, black, brown, and yellow.

"How would you like to help me make a birdhouse for some of our bird friends?"

"I'd love to!" Soon she was helping hold the wood as Dr. Conrad measured, sawed, hammered and glued. When the birdhouse was completed, they proudly showed Mrs. Conrad and Dot what they had constructed.

"It's beautiful, Herbert!" Mrs. Conrad exclaimed.

"Well, I couldn't have done it without Elsie May's help." Elsie May felt warm and happy inside. She was beginning to feel like she really belonged here and was part of the Conrad family.

The next Saturday, Mrs. Conrad awakened Elsie May early. "Today we are going to Green Pond again, but before we do, I need you and Dot to help me clean the house. There is a simple rule that has always helped me to keep my house in order, and it will help you too. Never forget it! I always make sure that I have 'a place for everything, and everything in its place'."

"I'll always remember that, Mrs. Conrad," Elsie May promised.

Mrs. Conrad handed Elsie May a broom and asked her to sweep the kitchen while Dot was vacuuming the living room and Mrs. Conrad was cleaning the bathroom. Soon the work was done, and they were on their way to Green Pond for another enjoyable weekend.

As time went by, Elsie May began to hope that she could stay with the Conrads and really become a part of their family. Although she had been with them for several weeks, she kept wondering if they were going to take her back to the orphanage like the Tremonts had done.

When Mrs. Conrad called her into her room one day, and said that she had something important to talk to her about, she was instantly afraid that now Mrs. Conrad would tell her that she must go back to the orphanage. However, Mrs. Conrad had a big smile on her face. "I have something wonderful to tell you, Elsie May. Dr. Conrad, Dot, and I have talked about it, and we all want you to stay here and live with us and be our little girl, and be a part of our family for always. We are going to adopt you."

"Does that mean that I don't have to go back to the orphanage, Mrs. Conrad?" Elsie May asked timidly.

"Yes, that is exactly what it means!" Mrs. Conrad smiled down at Elsie May. "And another thing—from now on, you may call Dr. Conrad and me 'Dad' and 'Mother', just like Dot does."

"And is Dot my big sister now?" Elsie May asked eagerly, her eyes shining with happiness.

"Yes, she certainly is! Now there is just one more thing. We will have to change your name. 'Elsie May' is such a ridiculous-sounding name. It just won't do! It sounds like a cow's name! Now, I will give you a choice between two names, and you may pick which one you would like for your new name. Would you rather be called 'Beth' or 'Margaret'?"

For a moment Elsie May didn't reply, as she pondered this important decision. "'Margaret'—what a lovely name," she thought to herself. Then she whispered softly, "I would like to be called 'Margaret'."

"Very well then, 'Beth' it will be—'Beth Averne Conrad'," Mrs. Conrad concluded, rising and leaving the room.

Elsie May stood rooted to the floor in shocked silence. How could Mrs. Conrad have misunderstood her so terribly? How could she have thought that she had said "Beth", rather than "Margaret"? Being too shy to question or protest, she merely began replying to her new name, without giving any indication of the fact that it was not the one that she had chosen for herself.

That night, as Beth lay snugly tucked into her very own bed in her very own room, hugging Amy Doll close in her arms, she breathed her thanks to God. "Thank You, God, for giving me a new family! And please take care of Mama, wherever she is," she murmured, as she drifted off to sleep.

## Chapter 2—School Days

Summer passed quickly and happily for Beth. One day Mother called her to her side. "Next Monday, school will start, Beth."

"Will I learn to read then, Mother?" she asked excitedly.

"Well, not on the first day, child," Mother laughed, "but I'm sure that it won't take a smart girl like you very long to learn!"

Monday came quickly, and soon Beth found herself seated in Mrs. Taylor's first grade class, listening to her call the roll. She jumped as she heard Mrs. Taylor call a name that was almost, but not quite, like her own. "Elizabeth Conrad."

Beth hesitated. "Why, there must be another girl in my class that has almost exactly the same name as mine," she thought in amazement. She looked around in curiosity to see who it was, but no one answered.

"Elizabeth Conrad," Mrs. Taylor repeated. "Is Elizabeth Conrad here today, or is she absent?"

Timidly, Beth raised her hand. "Yes, what is it?" the teacher asked.

"My name is <u>Beth</u> Conrad," she whispered.

"But Beth is just a nickname," Mrs. Taylor protested. "Your real name <u>must</u> be Elizabeth."

"No, ma'am, it isn't. It's just Beth."

Later that day, at recess, Tommy, a red-haired boy with freckles on his nose, looked at Beth, laughed and started to chant, "Beth, Beth, Bethlehem! Beth, Beth, Bethlehem!" Soon all of the kids formed a circle around Beth, laughing and joining in the chant. Beth's cheeks burned with embarrassment, and she wished that she had never had to come to school.

Several days later, Mrs. Taylor announced, "We are going to have our art period now, class. I will give each of you a paper, pencil, and crayons, and I want each of you to draw whatever you would like to draw."

Beth was excited. She loved to draw, and she could hardly wait to get the pencil and crayons into her hands. "I'll make a picture of Amy. I wonder where she is now. I wish I could see her again!" In her mind's eye, she saw a clear photograph of Amy's laughing blue eyes, bouncing golden curls, and friendly smile. She still missed her friend so much! She drew a picture of Amy sitting under the red maple tree, where she and Beth had played together so often.

When all of the children had turned in their pictures, Mrs. Taylor leafed through them. Suddenly, she selected one from the pile. Beth gasped in astonishment as Mrs. Taylor held it up for the whole class to see. It was her picture of Amy! "Class, I would like you to look at Beth's picture. It is excellent, because it really looks like what she was trying to draw. Who is the girl in this picture, Beth?"

"My friend Amy."

"Well, this is a lovely picture of her. Beth, you certainly do have unusual artistic talent. Perhaps when you grow up, you will be an artist."

"Me--be an artist when I grow up?" Beth thought in amazement. "I would love that!"

At recess time, all of the other kids crowded around Mrs. Taylor's desk to look more closely at Beth's picture, and the chant of "Beth, Beth, Bethlehem" was forgotten. Tommy, who had led the chant, turned to Beth and asked, "Hey, Beth, do you think that you could draw me sometime?"

He was joined by a chorus of other voices requesting, "Me too, Beth! Me too!"

First grade passed happily and uneventfully for Beth. She soon learned to read well, but her favorite subject was still art. The seasons passed quickly, and with fall came a new school year.

When she heard that they were going to have a special art class in second grade, Beth was ecstatic. But her excitement was short-lived. After handing out sheets of clean white paper, Mrs. Clark announced, "I don't want any of you to draw anything yet. First, we must make nice, neat margins on all sides of our papers." By the time that Beth had followed the teacher's directions, measured exactly two inches on each side of her paper, and used her ruler to carefully draw a line on each edge of the paper, her creativity had been stifled, and her mind was as blank as her paper.

"What was it that I wanted to draw?" she wondered. She couldn't think of anything to draw, and finally settled on drawing a picture of her house, with her dog Skipper sitting in the front yard.

Several weeks passed. One day, as Beth was sitting at her desk, trying to work on her arithmetic problems, she suddenly felt terribly hot all over, and her throat began to ache unbearably. She could hardly wait until school was over, so that she could go home.

"Mother," she said, when she trudged into the house that afternoon, "My throat hurts really, really bad, and I feel hot all over."

Mother, who was a nurse, put her hand on Beth's forehead and looked down into her throat. "You're going straight to bed, young lady!" Then Mother hurried to the phone and called Dad's brother, Uncle Edgar, who was a doctor.

Soon Uncle Edgar was at her bedside, peering into her throat, taking her temperature, and listening to her chest. Beth shivered as she felt the cold metal of his stethoscope against her chest. "Well, Beth, it looks like you are going to have a vacation from school for a while," he tried to joke, but as Beth looked into his face, she could see that his eyes weren't smiling. They looked worried.

When he finished the examination, he motioned to Mother, and they stepped outside Beth's room. Beth strained to hear his hushed words through the closed door. "Yes, Mabel, I'm afraid that you are right. It definitely looks like diphtheria to me!"

"Diphtheria!" Beth was terrified. Many kids died of that terrible disease. "Oh, God, I'm scared," she sobbed into her pillow. "Please help me!"

The next few weeks were a blur of pain, fever, and the nightmares that she suffered in her delirium. Once she dreamed that a huge black monster was chasing her. She tried to run away, but her legs wouldn't work. She was sure that it was going to eat her up, and she screamed in terror. "Hush, child. It's only a bad dream," she heard a soothing voice murmur from far away, and she vaguely felt her mother's cool hand stroking her forehead.

Even after she finally started to recover, she was extremely weak. The first time that she tried to climb out of bed, her legs gave way under her, and she promptly fell on her face on the floor. Mother helped her back into bed and called Uncle Edgar. After examining her, he said seriously, "Your muscles are very weak from your being sick and lying in bed for so long, Beth. You will have to do exercises to strengthen them, and you will have to learn to walk all over again. It will be hard work, but you must keep trying. I know that you can do it."

Uncle Edgar was right. It was hard work, but Beth kept trying, and finally her muscles obeyed her commands just as they had done before.

One night, as Beth was lying in bed, she wondered for the first time if she would have died from diphtheria if she had still been with Mama. She knew that Mama had been very poor, and that she would not have had the money to pay for a skilled doctor like Uncle Edgar. "Thank you, God, for taking care of me," she whispered.

One day, shortly after Beth started back to school again, Dad came home waving several tickets in his hand. "Since my little girl is feeling so much better, I thought that we should have a celebration. Tonight, we are all going out to a concert. We're going to hear the Newark Symphony Orchestra." Beth was excited. She had never been to a concert before!

That night, as she was listening to the beautiful music, she noticed the rich, deep tones of the cello. "Dad, what is that instrument called? It's my favorite one!"

Dad smiled at her. "That's a cello, Beth."

"It's beautiful! Dad, I want to learn to play the cello! Could I take cello lessons?"

Dad gave an amused chuckle. "Well, Beth, the cello is a mighty big instrument, and you are still a very small girl. It is also very difficult to learn. I think that you should start with something a bit easier and more practical—like the piano."

"That would be fun! When can I start?"

"As soon as we can find a good teacher for you," Dad promised.

Beth's piano lessons began the very next week. She learned quickly, and one day her teacher called Mother aside before she left. "Beth is extremely talented musically, Mrs. Conrad. She has a wonderful ear for music, and she learns everything that I teach her very quickly. I believe that she can develop into an accomplished pianist if she continues to take lessons and practices faithfully."

Practice! No one had to tell Beth to practice! She loved to play the piano, and many times Mother had to call her away from practicing to wash the dishes or do her other chores .

However, even though Beth enjoyed playing the piano, the cello was still her first love. "Someday I <u>will</u> learn to play the cello," she resolved, "even if I have to pay for the lessons myself!"

The next several years passed happily and uneventfully for Beth, busy with school, music lessons, and vacations at Green Pond. She loved to roam the woods and pick blueberries, to row the boat on the peaceful lake, and to dive into its refreshing wetness, and move swiftly through the water, as she had seen Dot do that first day at Green Pond.

One day, as Beth was gliding along in the boat, her artistic soul drinking in the beauty of the sun, the sky, the trees, and the water, she mused, "God must be very great to make such a beautiful world for us to live in. I wish I knew more about Him. I wonder how I could find out more about God." She pondered a moment and quickly came up with the answer. "I know what I'll do. I'll ask Dad!" With that settled in her mind, she turned around and headed the boat homeward.

As soon as she got to shore, she quickly tied the boat to the dock and ran to find her father. She found him reading a book in a lawn chair near the lakeside. "Dad," Beth began breathlessly, "I have a question. I was just thinking about it when I was out in the boat just now."

Her dad looked up from the book he had been reading and smiled at Beth. "What is it, Honey? You know I always love to answer your questions."

"When I was out on the lake, I started thinking about God. What is God like, Dad?"
Beth was shocked at her dad's response. His cheerful expression suddenly turned to a frown, and he actually snapped at her! "Go ask your mother about that," he said gruffly.

Beth walked quietly into the house and went into the kitchen, where Mother was fixing supper.

"Mother," Beth said hesitantly, "how can I find out more about God? I want to know Him, and I don't know how."

Mother also seemed uncomfortable with Beth's question. "Well, I suppose that it would be all right for you to attend Sunday School and church," she said a bit reluctantly. "There's a Unitarian church right down the street from us. You may go there, if you wish."

The following Sunday, Beth dressed in her very best dress and hurried eagerly down the street to the little brown church, expecting to finally have her questions about God answered. She really enjoyed the interesting Bible story that she heard in Sunday

School. It was about a wise and kind Teacher named Jesus Who had lived and died almost two thousand years ago.

"Jesus is our great Example," her Sunday School teacher said. "We should learn His teachings well, and try to do what He said and treat other people like He did."

Church was a different matter, however. The people all stood to their feet and recited their creed, and then the minister gave a long talk, full of big words that Beth didn't understand.

Each week, Beth faithfully attended Sunday School and church. Though she enjoyed listening to the stories about Jesus, she still didn't feel that she was any closer to knowing God than she had been before she had begun going to church.

As time went by, she finally began to understand the creed that she had learned to repeat with the others each week. However, as she thought about it, she became deeply disturbed as she considered its meaning. "I believe in the Fatherhood of God, the brotherhood of man, and salvation by character," she recited with the rest of the congregation each week.

"Salvation by character…" she mused on the way home one Sunday. "That must mean that the way to please God is to be very, very good—as good as that wonderful Man Jesus was." She thought about her own life. If knowing and pleasing God depended on her goodness, it was hopeless! She tried very hard to be good, but in her heart she knew that she had failed many times. She was sure that it was impossible for her to ever be as good as Jesus had been!

The rapid approach of summer turned Beth's mind away from her puzzling questions about God. This summer she would finally be old enough to go to Girl Scout camp, and she could hardly wait! Finally, the long-awaited day came, and Beth was at Camp Lotawatah.

"Girls," the scout leader announced, "Tomorrow night, we are going to camp out overnight in the woods. We will be sleeping in tents, and we will learn to make campfires and cook our own food."

Beth was so excited that she couldn't get to sleep that night. Finally, she dozed off. She woke with a start the next morning as sunlight streamed into her face. She jumped out of bed hurriedly. All of the other bunks were empty. She had overslept, and the other girls had already gone to breakfast. She jumped into her clothes and ran down the path to the dining hall.

As she slipped into a seat, the scout leader stood up and said, "Here at Camp Lotawatah, we want you girls to learn to be on time to meals. I see that someone is late this morning. Let's show her what happens when people are late, girls."

Suddenly to Beth's amazement, the other campers burst into song. As she listened to the words, her face reddened with embarrassment, and she wished that she could crawl under the table. "You're always behind—just like the old cow's tail!" they sang. "You're always behind—like a ship without a sail!" Beth vowed that she would never be late again!

That afternoon, Beth and the other campers began the long hike to their camping site. As they walked, Beth reveled in the beauty of the summer woods and the clear, sweet songs of the birds.

After they had reached the campground, set up the tents, and gathered wood, the counselor declared, "Now, I will show you the correct way to build a campfire. First, we must make a bare place on the ground, so that the woods won't catch on fire. Then, to build the fire, we put twigs on the bottom like this, then some larger branches on top of them, and last of all, a few logs on top." Soon the fire was cheerily blazing, and the girls began cooking over it. Beth thought it was one of the best meals that she had ever eaten, and that night, as they sat around the dying campfire, gazing up into the starlit heavens and singing songs, she was sure that camp was going to be just as much fun as she had expected.

Later that summer, after Beth had returned from camp, the Conrad family took their yearly vacation at Green Pond. Dot, who had finished college and was now working in a laboratory and living in an apartment in Newark, joined them as often as she could.

One Saturday morning, as they were leisurely enjoying a late breakfast together, Dot turned to Mother. "Would it be all right if I bring a guest with me next weekend, Mother?"

"Of course, Dot. You know that your friends are always welcome."

Dot's cheeks flushed a rosy pink. "Well, this is a little bit different, Mother. This is a very special friend. His name is Leonard Baker."

"Well, it's about time that my girl found herself a young man!" Dad chuckled. "Bring him up next weekend. If he's going out with my daughter, he's got to pass my inspection!"

Beth could hardly wait for next weekend to come. She was bursting with curiosity to see what Leonard was like. Finally, Dot and Leonard arrived. "Mother, Dad, and Beth," Dot announced, her cheeks pink with excitement, "This is my friend Leonard Baker."

"Pleased to me you, Leonard," they all chorused. Beth took a shy peek at him. He was tall and slender, with wavy hair the color of sand and friendly brown eyes. He smiled down at Beth, and she liked him at once.

"It's great to meet you too!" Leonard shook hands with Dad and Mother. "Dot's told me so much about y'all that I feel like I already know you. Please call me 'Bake'. All my friends do. I really don't care much for 'Leonard'." Then he turned to Beth. "So you're the little sister I've heard so much about. You're <u>almost</u> as pretty as your big sister!"

"Oh, Bake," Dot blushed. "Quit flattering me!"

"But it's the truth, ma'am. Nothing but the truth," Bake declared solemnly.

Later, when Dot and Beth were alone, Beth asked, "Dot why does Bake always say 'Sir' and 'Ma'am' when he's talking to Dad and Mother? And why does he sound so different from us when he talks?"

"He's from Texas, Beth. That's the way that they talk down there. Anyway, I'm dying to know what you think of him! How do you like him?"

"I really like him, Dot. I hope that you bring him up to visit often!"

"I'm planning on it!"

As the months went by, Bake was a frequent guest at the Conrad home, and Beth soon felt as comfortable with him as she did with the members of her own family. Since he was so far from home, Dot asked him to have Christmas dinner with them. After they had all finished eating, Dot exclaimed, glowing with happiness, "Listen, everyone! Bake and I have wonderful news. We are going to be married next spring!"

"Congratulations to both of you!" Dad beamed. "And welcome to the family, Son!" he added, giving Bake a hearty handshake.

The next months flew by as Dot made preparations for her wedding. "I want you to be a junior bridesmaid, Beth. I'd like you to wear a rose-colored dress."

"Oh, I'd love that, Dot! I was wishing that I could be in your wedding, but I was afraid that I was too young."

Beth could hardly wait for the wedding, and at last the long-awaited day arrived. Dot was a radiant bride in a lace-covered white satin dress with a long train, and Beth's deep pink dress highlighted the beauty of her long dark curls and wide hazel eyes. As she watched Dot and Bake solemnly pledge their life-long love to each other, she thought to herself, "I hope that when I get married, I'll be as happy as Dot is today."

The next several years passed uneventfully. Then, the fall after Beth turned thirteen, a catastrophe struck the nation. The stock market crashed, and with each day came more sobering news. People's life savings were wiped out, many of Beth's classmates' fathers lost their jobs, and some of them lost their homes. She heard reports on the news that some people were actually jumping out of the windows of the skyscrapers in New York City and committing suicide because they had lost their fortunes overnight.

One night, Beth joined Dad as he was working in his workshop. "Dad, are we going to lose our house and our place at Green Pond?"

"No, Beth. Even though there's a depression going on, I'm sure that people are still going to have toothaches, and when they do, they are going to need a dentist! We're going to be just fine!"

A few weeks later, Dot and Bake joined them for supper, and once again the talk turned to discouraging news reports, which seemed to grow worse with each passing day. Finally Dot said, "I'm tired of talking about all this bad news. Would you like to hear some good news for a change?"

"I sure would!" Mother replied.

"Well, Bake and I have some <u>wonderful</u> news for you! Next April, you are going to be grandparents."

"And that means that I'm going to be an aunt, doesn't it?" Beth exclaimed excitedly.

"It certainly does!" Bake agreed.

The months seemed to crawl by as Beth waited for the arrival of Dot and Bake's baby. Finally, one sunny morning in April, Mother shook her awake. "Beth! Beth! Wake up! The baby was born late last night!"

Beth jumped out of bed. "That's great! Is it a boy or a girl?"

"It's a boy," Mother beamed. "They named him Stuart, but they are already calling him 'Stu'."

As Beth held her new nephew in her arms for the first time a few days later, she marveled at the perfectness of his tiny features. She smoothed the downy blond hair on his head and gazed deep into his wide innocent blue eyes.

"Well, what do you think of your nephew, 'Aunt Beth'?" Dot asked.

"He's <u>beautiful</u>, Dot," Beth breathed in awe. "And anytime you need a babysitter, you know who you can call!"

"We'll be taking you up on that offer!" Bake replied. "I'm sure that my wife and I are going to want to have an evening out together from time to time!"

The fall after Stu was born, Beth started high school. She was thrilled when she found out that one of the courses offered was art. "Imagine," she thought dreamily to herself, "Now I'll get to draw and paint <u>every</u> <u>day</u>, and it's actually part of school!" She could hardly wait for her first art class.

Taking art in high school was all that Beth had hoped it would be. The teacher instructed them in the correct use of many different techniques and materials—sketching with a pencil, doing pen and ink drawings, using pastels and colored pencils, and painting with both oil paints and watercolors. Though Beth enjoyed the variety, she soon found that her favorite means of artistic expression was painting with watercolors.

"The correct use of watercolors is one of the greatest challenges that faces an artist," Mrs. Wilson, the art teacher, said one day. "It takes a great deal of skill and practice to know how to blend the colors correctly without having them run into each other and spoil the picture."

Beth knew that it was a challenge, but she loved it. To her, the paler colors, the subtle shading, and the more transparent effects that she could produce with her palette of watercolors were more appealing than the bold heavy brightness of oil paints. She practiced diligently at blending her colors and learning how to use just the right amount of water on her brush, and eventually she became one of the most talented watercolor artists in her class.

One day, several weeks after school had started, Beth rushed through the door of the art classroom, her arms full of books, papers, and art supplies. As usual, she was late and was trying to get quickly to her seat before the bell rang. Suddenly she collided with another latecomer, and her art pad flew out of her hands, scattering her paintings across the floor. "I'm sorry," the other girl apologized, as she stooped to help Beth retrieve her belongings. "Say! These are <u>really</u> good! Could I look at your artwork after class?"

"Sure, if you will let me see some of your work," Beth responded shyly

.

After class, the other girl was waiting for Beth out in the hall. "We were in such a hurry to get into our seats before the bell rang that I didn't even get to introduce myself. I'm Betty Roth. What's your name?"

"Beth Conrad."

As Beth looked more closely at Betty, she gasped. Her blond curls, sparkling blue eyes, and friendly smile reminded Beth so much of Amy, her friend at the orphanage. Suddenly a wave of loneliness washed over Beth. She realized that although she had been happy with her family, she had never found another close friend in all the years since Amy had left the orphanage and been adopted.

Abruptly, her mind jerked back to the present. Betty was asking her something. "Could I see your pictures now?"

Hesitantly, Beth handed her pad to Betty. Betty turned the pages slowly, admiring the beautiful pictures of flowers and animals that Beth had painted. "These are great, Beth! Have you ever thought about going to art school when you get out of high school? I bet you're good enough to make a living as an artist."

"Yes, I'd love to do that!" Beth's eyes shone. "It's been a dream of mine ever since I was a little kid."

Suddenly Betty burst out laughing in delight as she turned another page in Beth's pad. "Well, I see that art class isn't the only place where you draw, Beth," she teased. "That picture looks just like Mr. Morris, our history teacher, and this is a great picture of Tom Winston, that red-haired boy who sits in the second row in English class."

Beth blushed. Betty had just found out one of her secrets. Often, while sitting in various classes, she would sketch pictures of her teachers and her classmates to pass the time as she listened to a boring lecture.

To change the subject, she asked, "Could I see some of your pictures now, Betty?"

"Sure. Mine are not nearly as good as yours, but you're welcome to look at them."

Beth enjoyed comparing her artwork with Betty's, and soon the two girls were meeting each morning before school, sketchpads in hand, excitedly asking each other, "What did you draw last night? Let me see!"

One day after school, Beth found Betty waiting for her after her last class. "Guess what, Beth! Dad and Mother are giving me a birthday party this Friday night, and they said that I could invite all my special friends. Would you like to come?"

"I'd love to, Betty!"

Beth could hardly wait for Friday night. She dressed in her prettiest dress and hurried to Betty's house. She thoroughly enjoyed the lively game of charades that they played, and the refreshments were delicious. After Betty had blown out her birthday candles and they had eaten their cake and ice cream, she began opening her presents. When she opened Beth's present and found a new set of watercolors, she squealed with delight. "Oh, Beth, how did you know that this is just what I wanted?" Impulsively, she gave Beth a hug. Beth felt a warm glow. For the first time since she had lost Amy, she felt that she had found a true friend.

One thing that disappointed Beth about high school was the fact that they didn't have an orchestra. She was now an accomplished pianist and had also learned to play the organ, and she had hoped that she would be able to be in an orchestra and begin learning to play the cello when she started high school.

However, when she discovered that her high school only had a band, she decided to join the band and learn to play the cornet. "I still want to learn to play the cello someday," she had confided to Dad when she came home from school that first day, "but I think that it will be fun to learn to play the cornet. I love all kinds of musical instruments!"

Dad had smiled at her encouragingly. "You'll be a great cornet player, Beth. It seems like you can learn to play any instrument that you choose to."

Beth learned to play the cornet as quickly as she had mastered the piano. She thoroughly enjoyed being in the band, playing for the school's ball games, and marching in their little town's parades.

One day, during her sophomore year of high school, Mr. Barnett, the band director, stopped her as she was leaving the band room. "Beth, could I talk to you for a moment?"

"Certainly, Mr. Barnett," Beth replied timidly. "Is something wrong?"

"Oh, no! Nothing is wrong. I just wanted to ask you if you could do me a favor."

"What do you want me to do?"

"Well, I've noticed how quickly, and how well, you have learned to play the cornet. That shows you have a real talent for music, and I thought that you might be able to help me with a problem I have. You see, right now I have more cornet players than I need in the band, but I don't have enough French horn players. Would you be interested in switching to French horn? I'm sure that you could easily pick it up."

"I'd love to, Mr. Barnett. It would be interesting to learn to play another instrument!"

Mr. Barnett was right. Beth found that she easily mastered the fingering for the French horn, and by the end of her junior year, she occupied the first chair in the French horn section.

Beth walked into the house one afternoon toward the end of her junior year to find Mother just hanging up the telephone, her face beaming. "That was Bake on the phone. He called to tell us that their new baby has just arrived. It's a little girl, and they named her Nancy. He invited us all to come down to the hospital this evening to see her."

Beth was thrilled. She had enjoyed playing with, and babysitting, her little nephew Stu, and she was overjoyed that she now had a niece too!

That evening, as she cradled little Nancy in her arms and gazed into her wide, unblinking baby eyes, Beth marveled at how much her little niece looked like Dot. Nancy's soft wavy brown hair was exactly the same shade as Dot's, and her tiny nose and mouth seemed to be a carbon copy of her mother's. "She's adorable," Beth breathed, as she carefully handed her to Bake.

"Is that babysitting offer of yours still good, Beth, now that we have two kids for you to baby-sit?" Bake teased.

"Definitely! Now it will be twice the fun!"

One day shortly after summer vacation had begun, Mother approached Beth with an idea. "You're sixteen years old now, Beth, and I was wondering if you would like to have a summer job to make some spending money for yourself."

"I sure would, Mother, but with this depression going on, and work being so hard to find, I didn't think there was much chance of finding one. Have you heard of a job that I could get?"

"Yes. Two of my friends, Miss Emily and Miss Matilda Patton, are planning to open a tearoom soon. I saw them when I was shopping today, and they mentioned that they will be needing waitresses and asked if you would be interested in working for them."

"I'd love to!" Beth replied, but inwardly she was quaking with fear. She desperately wanted a job, and could hardly believe her good fortune in being offered one when jobs were so scarce. However, being a waitress would involve talking to strangers, and Beth still battled daily with extreme shyness.

"Good," she heard Mother reply. "I'll let them know that you want the job."

The next Monday morning found Beth standing in the dining room of the Patton Sisters' tearoom, wearing a neat black dress with a frilly white apron tied over it. She had a slight smile on her face, but her heart was pounding so loudly that she felt sure that it must be clearly audible as she forced herself to walk over to the well-dressed couple sitting at a corner table.

"May I take your order?" she asked shakily.

"Yes, please," the plump, gray-haired woman replied. "I'll have a cup of hot tea, and one of your English muffins with butter and raspberry jelly."

"I'll have the same," the stern-looking bald man echoed.

Beth hurried to the kitchen, poured the tea into the exquisite china cups in which the Patton sisters served all of their guests, brought it to the couple, and hurried back to the kitchen for the muffins. Finding that she was unable to carry the muffins, butter, and jelly all in one trip, she decided to take the muffins and butter to her customers first, and then return later with the jelly.

However, as she was on her way back to the kitchen, a red-faced man, who was seated at a different table, signaled her impatiently. "Miss, I've been sitting here for five minutes trying to get your attention! I would like to order now."

"Yes, sir. I'm sorry I kept you waiting, sir." Beth's face flushed with embarrassment. Quickly, she took the customer's order, walked to the kitchen, and returned with his food. As she was serving him, she suddenly noticed that the man at the corner table was raising his hand and motioning to Miss Matilda to come to their table.

Miss Matilda hurried over to him and listened as he whispered something and pointed in Beth's direction. "Oh, no! I forgot the jelly!" she realized in horror, rooted to the spot.

Before she could move, tall, dignified Miss Matilda frowned, looked in her direction, and indignantly called across the tearoom, "Belly!" Then realizing the blunder that she had made by getting her tongue twisted, her face turned crimson, as she sputtered, "No! I mean—Beth! I mean—jelly!"

Beth rushed to the kitchen and returned with the jelly, but she couldn't suppress a little giggle as she recalled Miss Matilda's red face. "I guess I'm not the only one around here who makes mistakes," she thought in relief, and gradually her fear began to subside.

Summer sped by as Beth worked at the tearoom. As time passed, she learned the skills of being a waitress, and was finally able to approach her customers with a shy smile on her lips, and without having that terrible shaky feeling inside.

# Chapter 3—Discoveries

That fall, when she began her senior year in high school, Beth found herself caught up in a whirlwind of activity. In addition to playing in the band, taking art classes, and spending as much time as possible with her best friend Betty Roth, she worked each weekend at the tearoom. She also continued to attend church each Sunday.

However, although Beth enjoyed her many activities, she began to sense a growing emptiness in the center of her being. Although they were submerged in her busyness, her unanswered questions about God would often surface. Many times at night, she would lie in bed pondering the questions that had troubled her all of her life. "What is God like? How can I know Him?"

One night she cried out to God in her confusion. "Oh, God, I want to know you, but I don't know how. Help me to find out the truth about You!" A few minutes later, she fell into a peaceful sleep.

That Sunday, Beth once again went to church, more out of habit than out of hope of finding any answers to her questions. She had long since realized that she could never be good enough to win God's favor. However, this Sunday she noticed something new at the back of the church. It was a rack filled with little leaflets. "Finding a Faith to Live By," proclaimed the title of one of them. She grabbed one, and thrust it into her purse. "Ah, this is just what I need. Perhaps this will answer my questions about God!"

She hurried home, ran up the stairs to her room, shut the door behind her, eagerly opened the pamphlet and began to read. "People have many different beliefs about God. It doesn't matter what you believe, as long as you are sincere. It doesn't even matter if you believe that God is in that chair over there, as long as you are sincere in what you believe."

Beth shook her head in disgust. "Phooey! That's no help at all! Whoever wrote that doesn't know any more than I do!" Without bothering to read any further, she crumpled the leaflet into a tiny ball and tossed it into her wastebasket.

In discouragement, Beth concluded that going to church was a waste of time. Besides, she had more than enough other activities to keep her busy. Her senior year sped happily by, and soon spring was once again approaching.

One day in March, as she and Betty were walking home from school together, Betty said, "Beth, my family and I just recently started going to church. I've really been enjoying it, and I'd love to have you come with us! Would you like to go this Sunday?"

"Thanks for inviting me, but I'm just too busy to go to church," Beth declined, not wanting to hurt her friend's feelings by revealing that she had decided that church was a waste of time.

However, each week Betty repeated her invitation. Beth continued to maintain that she was too busy, but as Easter approached, she found that Betty just wouldn't take "No" for an answer. "Why don't you come with me just once, Beth? This Sunday is Easter Sunday, and <u>everyone</u> goes to church on Easter!"

"Well, maybe I could—just this once." She started to give in, then suddenly shook her head. "Oh, I can't come! I don't have a hat to wear!"

"That's no problem. I'll lend you one of mine."

On Easter Sunday morning, Beth dressed in her very best dress, put on the hat she had borrowed from Betty, and hurried over to Betty's house to join her friend and her family as they walked to church. Betty had told her that the church that they attended was a Baptist church, but that meant nothing to Beth, and she was too embarrassed to ask any questions and reveal her ignorance.

When they entered the church, Beth was surprised to see a cross on the wall behind the pulpit, and underneath the cross a small window, through which could be seen a little room. "What's that, Betty?"

"It's the baptistery, Beth. Would you like to see it?"

"Yes, I would." Together they walked down the aisle of the church, up onto the platform, and peered through the window. Beth was astonished to find that the room contained a tank filled with water, and that there were steps leading up to the tank and then down into it.

Betty pointed to the tank. "Well, that's the place where people get baptized."

"Yes," Betty's mother added, "But of course you have to be saved before you can be baptized."

The unfamiliar words swirled around in confusion in Beth's head, but she was ashamed to admit that she had absolutely no idea of what they were talking about. "Saved," she puzzled. "I wonder if that has something to do with the Salvation Army. I know that they go around town salvaging old clothes."

Soon the service began, and the song leader got up to lead the singing, a joyful smile on his face. "I'm so glad that we can celebrate the fact that our Lord Jesus Christ arose from the dead on that first Easter Sunday morning so many years ago. I'm so thankful that Jesus is alive and that we serve a living Savior!" Then he led the congregation in a song that Beth had never heard before, "He Lives!"

However, Beth hardly heard the singing of those around her. She sat motionless in shocked amazement. "Jesus is alive?! I thought that He died nearly two thousand years ago. Why, if He is alive, then perhaps He can help me!"

During the pastor's sermon, Beth sat on the edge of her seat, drinking in every word, like a wilted flower receiving life-giving rain. "Some people teach that Jesus was just a great Teacher who lived and died two thousand years ago, but God's Word, the Bible, teaches us that He is God's own Son. He came to earth to show us what God is like, and then He died on the cross to take the punishment that we all deserve for our sins, so that we can know God and go to Heaven. But praise God, Jesus didn't stay in the grave! He arose and is now living in Heaven, and will one day return to this earth again to rule as King!"

As the service closed, the pastor called on a tall white-haired man in the back of the church to close in prayer. "Lord Jesus, if there's any poor lost sinner here today, I pray that he would receive You as his own personal Savior." Instantly, Beth knew that she was the poor lost sinner for whom the man was praying!

As she walked slowly home in the spring sunshine, Beth had a lot to think about. For years, she had known that she was a sinner, who could not measure up to God's standards. However, never in her seventeen years had she heard that Jesus was not just a great Teacher and Example, but God's own Son, Who had died for her sins so that she could be forgiven and know God, just as she had longed to do all of her life. Most wonderful of all was the astounding fact that He had risen from the dead and was a <u>living</u> Savior, able to be with her and help her in her daily life.

As she pondered what she had heard, it seemed almost too good to be true. "How can I know whether what these people said is really true? I guess I'll just have to try it! If it's not true, I'll find out soon enough. But if it is true—then if I receive Christ, I have everything to gain, and nothing to lose!"

Having come to this decision, Beth stopped right in the middle of the sidewalk and bowed her head. "Lord Jesus, if what these people have is real, I want it. I want You to be my Savior!"

The peace, joy, and sense of closeness to God that flooded Beth's heart soon confirmed to her that at last she had found the truth. "Thank You, God, for answering my prayer!" she breathed in adoration.

As she turned onto the street leading to her home, her steps quickened. She could hardly wait to share her wonderful new discovery with her family. Running up the steps and into the house, she found her dad sitting in his favorite chair in the living room, smoking his pipe and reading the Sunday paper. He glanced up as she walked in, and lowered his paper with a smile. "Well, you certainly look happy today, Beth."

"Dad, I just heard the most wonderful news in the world! I just found out that Jesus isn't dead. He arose from the dead after He died on the cross, and God will forgive us for our sins if we believe that Jesus died for us. I just asked God to forgive me, and I know that He did! Wouldn't you like to ask God to forgive you too, Dad?" she asked without even stopping to catch her breath.

Without warning, Dad's loving smile suddenly changed to an angry frown. "I never want to hear any more talk about this from you again, Beth. I heard enough preaching when I was young to last me for the rest of my life, and I don't need to hear any more preaching from you!" With that, he picked up his paper and resumed his reading

In shocked sadness, Beth slowly left the room and walked into the kitchen, where her mother was busily preparing dinner. More hesitantly, Beth tried to share her amazing discovery with her mother. "Mother, when I went to church with Betty this morning, I heard something that I had never heard before in my whole entire life. The pastor taught us that the Bible says that Jesus arose from the dead on the first Easter morning, and he told us that the reason that He had to die was because He had to take the punishment for our sins. Have you ever heard about this?"

Mother smiled condescendingly at Beth. "Yes, Beth, I heard that story often at church when I was growing up, but many years ago, Aunt Harriet, your dad's sister, gave me some fascinating books which teach something completely different about Jesus. They said that Jesus came to show us how to use the great power that we already have within our own minds. I believe that the teaching of these books is far superior to anything that the Bible has to say. Now, could you please set the table for me? Dot and Bake and the kids will be over for dinner soon."

In quiet disappointment, Beth went to the cupboard, got out the dishes, and began setting the table. Just as she was putting the last piece of silverware in place, Dot, Bake, and their family arrived.

Although she always enjoyed the special days when Dot and her family joined them for dinner, Beth hardly said a word during the entire meal. After dinner, as she and Dot were doing the dishes together, Dot turned to her with a smile. "You're mighty quiet today, little sister. Want to tell me what's on your mind?"

"I went to church with my friend Betty today," Beth confided, "and I heard some things that I've never heard before, but when I tried to tell Mother and Dad about them, Dad got upset, and

Mother acted like she just wasn't very interested in hearing about it."

"Tell me! I'd like to hear about it," Dot encouraged. "What were those amazing things that you heard?"

"Well, I'd always heard that Jesus was a great Teacher Who lived and died almost two thousand years ago, but the pastor of Betty's church said that Jesus is alive. He said that if we believe that He died for our sins, God will forgive us, so I asked God to forgive me, and I'm sure that He did!"

Dot stood looking at Beth in silence for a moment, her hands still in the dishwater, and then she said gently, "I hate to have to tell you this, Beth, but I learned in college that the Bible is just a collection of Jewish myths. It isn't literally true, and it can't be taken seriously. To tell you the truth, I'm not even sure if there is a God. Science has proved that life evolved from simple one-celled creatures many millions of years ago."

Before Beth could answer, Bake burst into the kitchen. "Are you girls done yet? Your dad and I are setting up the croquet set for a game." Then, looking from one solemn face to the other, he asked, "Why such long faces? You must be discussing something mighty serious! Care to tell me about it?"

After Beth had repeated her story one more time for Bake's benefit, he eyed her skeptically. "So you're really sure that God heard you and answered your prayer when you asked Him to forgive you, are you?"

"Yes, I certainly am!"

"Well, that's not what I heard when I went to church down in Texas. When I was growing up, my family went to a little 'hard-shell' Baptist church, and they taught that if you were going to be saved, you would be saved, and if you were going to be lost, you would be lost. So I've always figured that it was up to God to decide, and that there was nothing that I could do about it."

"But I'm sure that's not true, Bake," Beth protested. "We each have to choose whether we want to ask God to forgive us or not."

"All I know is that the preacher down in Texas said that was what the Bible teaches, so that has always been my faith for myself and my family. That's the trouble with preachers. They're always contradicting each other, so that you don't know which one is right or what to believe. I would appreciate it if you would just drop this subject and not discuss it with us any further. Religion is a personal matter anyway. Talking about it just causes arguments."

Beth looked questioningly at her sister, who was emptying the dishwater, and saw her nod in agreement. "Bake's right, Beth. I would rather not talk about it anymore either."

That night, as Beth lay in bed, she quietly thanked God once again for answering her prayer, and helping her find the truth. "I don't care what anyone else says, Lord Jesus. I <u>know</u> that You <u>are</u> alive, and that You have forgiven me. Please help Dad and Mother and Dot and Bake to believe in You too."

In the weeks that followed, Beth enthusiastically attended the services of the little white church where she had finally found the truth. Soon she had her own copy of the Bible, which she devoured eagerly, finding the nourishment for which her soul had hungered so many years. She delighted in the wonderful new relationship that she had with her Heavenly Father, and brought all of her needs and concerns confidently to Him, resting in the fact that He cared deeply about even the smallest details of her life.

On a balmy Sunday night in May, she was baptized and joined the church. It was a joyous occasion for Beth, marred only by the fact that none of her family would agree to come and witness her baptism.

Later that same evening, as she lay in bed beseeching her Heavenly Father once again to bring salvation to her family, she suddenly found her thoughts turning to her other family, whom she had lost so long ago—Mama and Papa. Her artistic mind painted a portrait of Mama's face, so like her own—a heart-shaped face, wide hazel eyes fringed with long dark lashes, dark hair curling around her face and down onto her shoulders, and skin whose natural color was like a luxuriant tan. As she pictured Mama, a sudden realization came to her. "Why, she was young! She must have been little more than a girl when I was born!"

Her thoughts turned to Papa. Although she had seen him only two or three times, the image of his face was indelibly etched upon her brain. With his straight blond hair and bright blue eyes, his looks had been a striking contrast to Mama's. And always he had been wearing a soldier's uniform.

Once again, the old unanswered questions surged to the forefront of her mind. "Why did Mama let them take me away?" her heart sobbed. "And where is she now? Oh, if only I could see her again!" This time, however, the old questions were joined with a heart-piercing, new concern. "I wonder if Mama and Papa know Jesus as their Savior. If I could only find them, I could tell them about Him. Surely Mother must know something about Mama, and about why I was put in the orphanage. When Mother and Dad adopted me, the lady at the orphanage must have told them something about my real parents. I think I'll ask Mother about it tomorrow."

The next afternoon, when Beth returned from school, she hurried into the house and found her mother sitting in a comfortable chair in her bedroom, mending one of Dad's shirts. "Mother," she began without preliminaries, "do you know anything about my real parents, and about why my mama gave me up for adoption? I love you and Dad very much, and I appreciate all that you've done for me, but I wish that I could see Mama and Papa again."

A cloud shadowed Mother's face and she shifted uncomfortably in her chair. "I knew that this day would come, Beth, and that you would want to know the truth about your parents and about why you were placed in the orphanage. I'll tell you everything I know about them, but I don't believe that it would be wise for you to try to contact them." She rose from her chair, went to the bureau, opened the bottom drawer, pulled a yellowed envelope out from under a stack of papers, and handed it to Beth. "Here is the information that the orphanage gave us about you. You can read it for yourself."

Her hands trembling with eagerness and apprehension, Beth opened the envelope and drew out a single sheet of paper. Looking at it closely, she realized that it was her birth certificate. "Date of birth—May 8, 1916." She already knew that, of course! "Place of birth—Hampton, Long Island, New York." Her eyes fastened on the spaces left for the names of her father and mother. In both cases, nothing was written in the places reserved for the first names of her parents. They were left blank—to protect their privacy, because of her adoption, she supposed. However, the last names of both of her parents were written in the correct spaces. "Last name of mother—Rogers. Last name of father— Thompson." Her face reddened as a shameful possibility suddenly dawned on her. Slowly she lifted her eyes and met Mother's equally embarrassed gaze. "My parents weren't married, were they, Mother?"

"No, Beth, they weren't married—at least not to each other. From what Mrs. Foster at the orphanage told us, your father <u>was</u> married—to someone else, and he had several children. Your mother was not married. Apparently, your father served in the army, and was stationed near your mother's home. They became involved romantically, and your birth was the result."

"Can you tell me anything else about them?" Beth pleaded. "Do you know why I was taken away from my mother and put in the orphanage?"

"Yes, I know a few more things. Your father was of Scandinavian background. Thompson is a Scandinavian name. Your mother came from a wealthy English family that was well-known for their breeding of fine horses. When her family learned that she was expecting you, they disowned her because of the shame that she had brought upon the family, and she was forced to leave their home. Since she had been reared in a well-to-do family, she probably never had any training that prepared her for getting a job and supporting you adequately. Mrs. Foster told me that a neighbor of your mother's noticed that you appeared to be undernourished and reported it to the state authorities. After an investigation and a court hearing, the state decided that it would be in your best interest for them to take you away from your mother and put you in an orphanage until you could be adopted. Mrs. Foster said that you <u>were</u> malnourished, and that when you came to them, you were suffering from rickets. I'm sure that your mother loved you very much, Beth, and that she wanted to keep you with her, but as you can see, it was best that the state took you away from her. If you had remained with her, you might not have lived to grow up."

Beth stood in silence, absorbing all this overwhelming new information. It was a balm to her broken heart to know that Mama hadn't <u>wanted</u> to give her up. For the first time, she understood the strange combination of Mama's tears and her seeming refusal to do anything to help her as the woman in black had dragged her away from Mama and forced her to get into the car. "It wasn't that she didn't <u>want</u> to help me. She <u>couldn't</u> do anything to help me!"

Slowly, she replaced the birth certificate in the envelope, her cheeks burning with shame as she realized the full implications of what she had just read. She knew that Mother was right. "I can never try to find Mama and Papa. I'm an illegitimate child. By this time, Mama may be married and have other children, and having me show up would only be an embarrassment to her. And Papa—there's absolutely no way I could ever contact him either. It could destroy his marriage too!" As she closed the envelope and handed it back to Mother, she knew that she was closing much more than an envelope.  She was also closing forever a whole chapter of her life—never to be reopened!

That night, as she lay in bed, tears streamed down her cheeks as she talked to her Heavenly Father.  "Thank You for helping me find out the truth about Mama and Papa.  And since I will never be able to tell them about You, <u>please</u> send someone else into their lives to tell them.  Help them to come to know Jesus as their Savior!"  Several hours later, with this longing still crying out from her heart, she finally fell asleep.

# Chapter 4—Decisions

The rest of Beth's senior year sped by in a blur of activity. On a balmy night in June, Beth marched down the aisle and received her high school diploma, plus several honors for high academic achievement, as Dad, Mother, Dot, and Bake watched proudly from the audience.

The following evening, as Beth was washing the supper dishes, Dad walked into the kitchen. He smiled down at her. "Beth, I want you to know that your mother and I were mighty proud of you last night. Not everyone has a daughter who has earned the right to be a member of the National Honor Society. Your hard work in school really paid off."

Beth smiled happily. "Thank you, Dad."

"What are you planning to do, now that you have graduated?"

Beth's mouth dropped open in surprise, and her hands stopped working, right in the middle of scrubbing an especially dirty dish. She searched his face to see if he were teasing her, as he often did, but she could see that the look in his eyes was completely serious.

"Why, Dad! You <u>know</u> what I want to do! You know that all of my life I've wanted to go to art school and become an artist!"

A look of sadness crossed Dad's face. "Yes, Beth. I do know what you <u>want</u> to do, and ordinarily I would agree with you. You have great artistic talent, and I believe you could become an exceptionally good artist. But these are not ordinary times. In case you've forgotten, there's a depression going on. When so many folks are struggling just to get the money to put a roof over their heads and to buy enough food to keep body and soul together, I don't think that there is going to be much work for a young artist fresh out of art school, no matter how talented she is!"

"But Dad--," Beth began, then stopped. She felt like protesting, but she knew that her dad was right. "What do you think I should do then?" she asked in confusion.

"Well, in a time like this, you need to have a practical skill in order to get a job. I would like to suggest that you go to business school, learn typing and shorthand, and prepare for secretarial work. Your mother and I have talked it over, and we will pay for you to go to business school for a year. Then perhaps later, when conditions improve in this country, you can still fulfill your dream of attending art school."

"I suppose you're right, Dad," Beth agreed reluctantly. She dreaded the thought of going to boring business classes instead of to the fascinating art classes that she had looked forward to for so many years.

Dad came over and gave her a hug. "That's my sensible girl. It's a big relief to me to know that you are going to get training that will always enable you to support yourself, Beth."


The following year dragged by, as Beth dutifully attended classes at the local business college. The only bright spot was that Betty was also taking the secretarial course. She was in most of Beth's classes, so they saw each other every day. One day, just before class started, Betty glanced over at Beth's open shorthand pad and began to laugh. "What's so funny, Betty?" Beth asked curiously.

"You haven't changed a bit since I first met you, Beth Conrad!" Betty teased. "That's a lovely picture of Miss Stanford, the shorthand teacher, there on your pad!"

It was true. Everywhere she went, Beth's mind was still on art. Even when she and Betty were riding the bus to school and back, she kept an open pad on her lap, a pencil in her hand, and her eyes open for interesting people to sketch. She would steal furtive glances at them and quickly draw what she saw. She was able to produce remarkable likenesses in a very short period of time, all the while trying to hide what she was doing from her unsuspecting models. For a while, she was successful in concealing what she was doing, but one day, just as she was putting the finishing touches on a picture of the lady sitting across the aisle from her, the bus stopped. The woman rose to get off the bus, and as she did, she glanced in Beth's direction, noticed the pad on her lap, and stopped in her tracks. "What do you think you're doing, young lady?" she asked indignantly. "Let me see that!"

Reluctantly, Beth handed her the pad. The lady took it, studied the portrait of herself, and broke into a pleased smile. "Why this is good! Would you mind if I take it home and show it to my husband?"

"Go right ahead, ma'am," Beth agreed, relieved that the woman was not offended.

Others on the bus, overhearing the conversation, crowded around to see the picture, and after that, Beth was besieged each day with requests to "Draw me," which she gladly fulfilled.

Finally, the long year of secretarial training came to an end. Beth received her diploma, and immediately began looking for a job. Day after day, she diligently searched the "help wanted" ads, visited prospective employers, and filled out applications. Every night, she prayed and asked the Lord to guide her to the right job. Still she found nothing.

One evening at the supper table, she expressed her growing frustration to Dad. "Everywhere I go, it's the same story, Dad. Everyone wants experienced people, but if I can't find a job, how can I ever get any experience?"

Dad sat for a moment in deep thought. "You've got a good point, Beth, and I think that I just might have a solution to your problem—one that would help both of us at the same time!"

"Really, Dad? What is it?"

"Well, I need someone to work in my office as receptionist, secretary, and dental assistant. Mrs. Simmons' health has gotten so poor that she isn't going to be able to continue working for me. Why don't you work for me for a while? That will give you the experience that you need, and later on, if you want to, you can look for another job."

"That's a great idea, Dad! I'd love to do that!" Beth had always enjoyed working with her dad, and she was sure that in his dental office, there would be enough variety so that her work wouldn't be boring. She breathed a silent prayer of thanks to her Heavenly Father for answering her prayers.

Beth's days soon settled into a comfortable and predictable pattern. Her days were spent helping Dad in his dental office, and most of her evenings were spent quietly at home with Dad and Mother. Since she had few expenses, she was able to save most of her paycheck, and the money that she was putting aside to fulfill her dream of attending art school grew steadily. However, she realized that it would still take several years of working and saving before she would be able to realize that dream.

One evening, as she was lying in bed, it suddenly occurred to her that even though it would be some time before her dream of going to art school could come true, there was no reason to wait any longer to fulfill another dream that she had had since early childhood—that of learning to play the cello. Now that she was working, she would be able to pay for cello lessons from her earnings, and she certainly had plenty of time to practice. "But how can I find the right person to give me cello lessons?" she puzzled. As she did with everything that concerned her, she talked with her Heavenly Father about it, and asked for His guidance. As she was praying, a name popped into her mind. "Why, of course," she said out loud, "Mr. Barnett, my band teacher from high school, would know where I can get cello lessons. I'll run over there on my lunch hour tomorrow and ask him."

As Beth walked into the band room the following day, Mr. Barnett looked up with a pleased smile. "Beth Conrad! It's so good to see you again. You know, I really miss having you in my French horn section! I haven't found another French horn player as talented as you are since you graduated! What can I do for you?"

"Well, Mr. Barnett, I'd like to ask your advice about something."

"I'd be glad to help you in any way that I can. What kind of advice do you need?"

"Well, even though I thoroughly enjoyed playing the cornet and the French horn in the band, I've always longed to learn to play the cello," Beth confided. "Now that I'm working, I have enough money to take cello lessons, but I don't know of a good teacher. I thought that you might be able to recommend one to me."

Mr. Barnett smiled. "Yes, I certainly can. Go to Johann Aebahn. He is a fine cellist and a wonderful teacher. He has a shop in downtown Hackensack where he sells stringed instruments, and he also gives music lessons there. He is a most interesting man—an immigrant from Germany. You'll like him, Beth."

The following Saturday morning, Beth boarded a bus bound for Hackensack, and soon reached the address that Mr. Barnett had given her. "Aebahn's Music Store—Instruments for Sale, and Music Lessons," read the sign in the window.

As Beth opened the door and entered the store, a bell jingled, and a short, slender, balding man, wearing wire-rimmed glasses, hurried out of the back room. "May I be of help to you?" he inquired cheerfully.

"Yes, sir. I am looking for Mr. Aebahn."

"Vell, you haf found him," he smiled, his English colored with a decided German accent.

"I'm interested in learning to play the cello. I've dreamed of playing the cello ever since I was a small child."

"Ah, the cello! I too think that it is the most beautiful of instruments, and though I play also the violin and viola, the cello my favorite is. Ven would you like to begin learning?"

"As soon as possible!" Beth's eyes shone with eagerness.

So it was that the next Thursday afternoon after work found Beth sitting in Mr. Aebahn's practice studio receiving her very first cello lesson. While Beth watched in fascination, he opened the cello case, removed the instrument, and sat down, placing the instrument between his legs. "You hold the cello between your legs—so."

A moment later, Beth was sitting in the chair, with the cello positioned between her legs, holding onto the fingerboard with one hand and the bow with the other. Looking down at her, Mr. Aebahn gave an amused chuckle.

Beth's cheeks flamed crimson with embarrassment. "Am—am I holding it incorrectly, Mr. Aebahn?"

Mr. Aebahn's chuckle turned into a hearty laugh, as he shook his head. "Ach, nein, Fraulein Conrad," he lapsed for a moment into his native German. "You are holding it perfectly. I was just thinking of how much easier it now is to teach young ladies the correct way of holding the cello. Thirty years ago, ven I first began to give cello lessons, that was a most difficult thing to teach!"

Interest replaced the embarrassment in Beth's face. "Why was that, Mr. Aebahn?" she asked curiously. "And please—call me Beth," she added.

A far-away look came into Mr. Aebahn's eyes, as his mind went back to the time when he had given his first cello lesson. "Vell, Beth, thirty years ago, in the Old Country, it was considered most improper for a gentleman to ever speak of a lady's legs. I still remember the first time that I tried to tell a young lady how to hold the cello. As I was in the middle of instructing her how to hold it, I suddenly realized that I could not say 'Put it between your legs'!"

"What did you do, Mr. Aebahn?"

"I said, 'Put it between your—between your—between your feet!'" he laughed, "and then I just showed her how to hold it."

Beth laughed with him. She liked the kindly old man already, and knew instinctively that he would be more than just a teacher to her. He would be a valued friend.

As the weeks passed, Beth showed an unusual ability for learning to play the cello. She could hardly wait until her work was done each evening, so that she would be free to practice, and the highlight of her week was her lesson with Mr. Aebahn. One day, as she finished playing her latest assignment for him, he commented, "Ach, Beth, I haf had many students in my life, but few haf made such rapid progress as you. Your musical ability is a rare gift of Gott!"

"Thank you, Mr. Aebahn." Beth's cheeks turned rosy with pleasure at the compliment. "And you're right. Any abilities that I have are gifts from God, and I'm so grateful to Him for them!"

One sunshiny May afternoon, shortly after her twentieth birthday, Beth hopped off the bus and walked briskly to Mr. Aebahn's store for her weekly cello lesson. As she walked, she reflected on how much she had learned from him during the past year. "Thank you so much, dear Heavenly Father, for making it possible for me to learn to play the cello," breathed Beth in gratitude.

As the cheerful jingle of the bell over the door announced her arrival, Mr. Aebahn rushed out from behind the counter to meet Beth, a joyful smile on his face. "Ah, there you are, Beth. I haf some goot news for you!"

"Good news?" Beth asked curiously. "What is it?"

"Vell, the Newark Symphony Orchestra, in vich I play, has need of another cellist, and they haf asked me to recommend one. And who else should I recommend but Beth Conrad, my star pupil?"

Mr. Aebahn beamed as he looked into Beth's shining eyes. For a moment she was speechless with joy, and then she exclaimed, "Oh, Mr. Aebahn, I've always dreamed of playing in a symphony orchestra! How can I ever think you for recommending me?"

"No thanks are necessary," he smiled. "I simply gave them the name of the most talented young cellist that I know."

So it was that the following Saturday found Beth hurrying breathlessly into the large hall where the Newark Symphony Orchestra practiced. Suddenly, she came to an unexpected stop, as she collided with a young man coming from the opposite direction. He was carrying a violin case in one hand and a folder of music in the other. The folder flew out of his hand, scattering music across the floor.

Quickly, Beth laid down her cello, and helped him retrieve his music, her face flaming with embarrassment. "I—I'm so sorry," she stammered, as she looked shyly up into the bluest eyes she had ever seen. "I should have looked where I was going."

"Oh, no," the tall young man replied. "It was entirely my fault. I should have looked where I was going. You are so tiny that you couldn't possibly have seen me coming from behind that big cello that you're lugging! By the way, I'm Dave Monroe. And you're---?"

"Beth Conrad."

"Well, I'm glad to meet you, Miss Conrad. How long have you been playing in the orchestra?"

"This is my first rehearsal. I'm really looking forward to it. How long have you been with the orchestra?"

"What a coincidence! This is my first rehearsal too. Well, I guess we should be getting to our places. Good luck!" And with a friendly wave, he strode off toward the violin section.

The next hours were pure joy for Beth, as she received her music and began practicing the classical music she so dearly loved. She thrilled to the glorious sounds of all the instruments blending so harmoniously together. "How amazing that I'm actually a part of all this!" she mused in wonder.

The next morning, Beth was sitting next to Betty in her usual place at church, when her friend nudged her with her elbow. Beth turned and looked questioningly at Betty. "Look—across the aisle," Betty whispered. "Who's that? I've never seen him at church before, and he sure is handsome!"

Beth turned her head slightly to the left to sneak a glance, and barely stifled a gasp of astonishment. It was Dave Monroe! Out of the corner of her eyes, she studied him. He had dark wavy hair and well-formed features, and she knew even without looking that he had the bluest eyes she had ever seen. "I'd like to draw him sometime," she thought.

When the service was over, Beth and Dave stepped into the aisle at exactly the same moment, and to her tremendous embarrassment, her arm brushed against his. Dave turned and looked at her. "Well, I didn't realize that I would be bumping into you again so soon," he teased, "but I'm glad to see you, Miss Conrad."

"Please call me Beth, Mr. Monroe," Beth blushed.

"And please call me Dave."

Several weeks later, as Beth was carrying her cello up the steps to the rehearsal hall, she noticed Dave standing at the top of the stairs watching her. "Well, well, here comes Cello, with little Beth," he laughed. "It must be really hard for you to haul such a big instrument around."

"Oh, I don't mind," Beth replied self-consciously. "I enjoy playing it so much that I hardly think about it."

Later that evening, when rehearsal was over and Beth was putting her cello back into its case, she looked up to see Dave smiling down at her. "Practicing for all these hours has sure made me hungry," he announced. "I think I'll go get some pie and coffee. Would you like to come with me?"

Beth was astonished and speechless. It was the first time in her twenty years that a young man had ever asked her for a date. Although Dave had been friendly to her, both at church and at orchestra practice, she had never expected him to ask her to go out with him. She had figured that it was only a matter of time before he would ask her friend Betty for a date, as most young men who met Betty did. At last, she recovered enough from her amazement to reply softly, "Yes, thank you. I'd like that!"

With most young men, Beth would have been tongue-tied with shyness. However, with Dave, she found that their mutual love of music gave them plenty to talk about. As they lingered over blueberry pie a la mode and sipped their coffee, they compared notes on their favorite music and composers.

Then Dave began to tell her a little about himself. "I just moved here from Pennsylvania. I couldn't find work in my hometown, because all the employers want experienced workers. I figured that if I came to a bigger city, I would have a better chance of finding work. After a lot of pounding the pavement, I finally found a job as a waiter. It's not much, but I thank the Lord for it. It's better than nothing, and it's enough for me to live on, if I'm careful."

"I know what you mean about having trouble finding work. I'm working for my dad in his dental office right now, because I faced the same problem. I'm so thankful that the Lord provided that way for me to get some work experience!"

"I'm really enjoying attending your little church. It reminds me of my church back in Pennsylvania. I was afraid that all of the churches in the city would be big and unfriendly, but the people at your church have made me so welcome that I already feel right at home."

Dave's remark gave Beth the courage to ask him the question that had been uppermost in her mind ever since she had met him. "Dave," she inquired shyly, "You're a Christian then?"

"Yes. I've been saved for about three years now. A boy in my high school class invited me to go to church with him, and I heard the Gospel and received Christ there. How about you, Beth? When did you find the Lord?"

Joyfully, Beth told him of her lifelong desire to know God, and how she had found Christ on the Easter morning of her senior year of high school. As she concluded her story, she happened to glimpse the clock on the wall. She gasped as she realized that they had been talking for more than two hours. It had seemed like only a few minutes! "Oh, I must get home!" she cried. "Mother and Dad will be wondering what has happened to me!"

"Please let me take you home."

"All right."

As they parted at Beth's front door, Dave smiled down at her. "I've really enjoyed our evening together, Beth. Let's do this again—often!"

"Yes, that sounds like fun, Dave!"

The following Saturday, Dave again invited Beth to go out for dessert after rehearsal was over, and she happily accepted. As another enjoyable evening of conversation drew to an end, Dave remarked, "This has been so much fun that I think we should make it a tradition. Why don't we just plan to go out for a snack together every Saturday evening after orchestra practice? Would that be all right with you?"

"Yes, I'd love that!" Beth replied, her hazel eyes shining.

Later that night, as she lay in bed, Beth suddenly sat bolt upright, startled by an unexpected thought. Then she began to giggle. "How funny!" she murmured to herself. "If I go out with Dave every week, that means he's my steady boyfriend, and I didn't even think about that when he asked me!"

As they were standing on Beth's porch saying goodnight several weeks later, Dave said, "I hear there's a new Shirley Temple movie playing at the Ritz now. How about going with me to see it next Friday night?"

"That would be great! I love to watch Shirley Temple. She's such a cute little thing!"

The following Friday night, as the theater darkened, Beth's heart skipped a beat as she felt Dave reach out and gently enfold her small hand in his large one. Just before the feature film, they laughed together at the antics of a lively cartoon character named Mickey Mouse, and then they settled back to enjoy watching Shirley Temple in "Dimples".

The next Sunday morning, as Beth sat in her usual place at church, she looked up as she heard a familiar voice. "Mind if I sit here?" Dave asked.

"Of course not," Beth replied, sliding over to make room.

After the service, as Dave and Beth stood at the back of the church talking, he remarked, "You know, I've been thinking. Since you play the cello and I play the violin, why don't we try playing some duets together? I think it would be a lot of fun! Would you like to do that?"

"That's a great idea, Dave!"

Before either of them could say another word, Pastor Browning, who had been standing nearby talking with Betty's parents, turned to face them. "I couldn't help overhearing what you just said, Dave, and I have a wonderful idea. Why don't you and Beth play some special numbers for us here at church? The Lord has given unusual talents to both of you, and we would be so grateful if you would share them with us."

"We'd love to!" Dave and Beth chorused in unison.

Beth was thrilled. She had longed to use her musical talent for her beloved Lord, but she had never before had the opportunity to do so.

"When do you think would be the best time for us to get together to practice, Beth?" Dave asked.

"How about Sunday afternoons?"

"Sounds great to me. How about starting today?"

"Fine. Why don't you come over to my house and practice?" She paused for a moment, as a new thought struck her. "Why don't you come over for dinner, and then we can practice afterward?"

"I would sure like that!" Dave agreed heartily. "It would be great to get a home-cooked meal. I'm getting awfully tired of my own cooking!"

Later that afternoon, as Dave sat beside Beth at the Conrads' dining room table, Dad remarked, "I've heard a lot about you, young fellow! It's great to get to know you a little better."

Beth blushed pink in embarrassment, but Dave replied, "I'm glad to get the chance to know you better too, Dr. Conrad. And you too, Mrs. Conrad."

After that Sunday afternoon, Dave was a regular guest at the Conrad home. Dave and Beth found that their instruments blended beautifully together, and soon their string duets were a regular feature at their little church. They both rejoiced in being able to serve the Lord with their musical abilities.

One afternoon, as Beth was tuning her cello, in preparation for their weekly practice, Dave suggested, "Why don't we take some time to read the Bible and pray together before we start practicing?"

"That's a wonderful idea, Dave," Beth replied, her face aglow. The following few minutes of sharing prayer needs and reading God's Word seemed to create a bond between them as nothing else had done, and Beth found herself looking forward eagerly to this special time together each week.

The following months flew by for Beth in a delightful flurry of activity—work, cello lessons, orchestra rehearsals and performances, church activities, and best of all, the increasing amount of time that she spent with Dave. Each time they said goodnight, she could hardly wait until the next time she would see him. "Is this what it is like to be in love?" she wondered, as she lay in bed one evening, after attending a movie with him.

When Christmas came, Dave joined the Conrad family for the festivities, since he was too far away from home to make the trip to spend the holidays with his own family. As he handed Beth her present, he said softly, "I wanted to get something special for my girl. I hope you like it!"

Beth eagerly tore open the wrappings and found a dainty necklace. It was a golden heart, suspended on a delicate chain.

"Oh, thank you, Dave," she murmured, smiling up into his eyes. "It's lovely!"

One cold January night after orchestra practice, as Dave and Beth sipped their usual cups of coffee and savored a delectable apple pie, Dave turned to Beth with a somber look on his face. "I had some bad news yesterday, Beth," he sighed. "My boss told me that he can't afford to keep me on the job after this coming week, so next Friday will be my last day."

"Oh, how awful!" Beth sympathized. "I'll be praying for you to find another job soon."

However, weeks passed, and in spite of Dave's diligent efforts, he was still unable to find a job. One Sunday afternoon, after a delicious dinner at Beth's house, Dave said gently, "I'm afraid that I have some bad news, Beth."

Beth gasped. "What is it, Dave?"

"Well, you know that I haven't been able to find a job around here, and I've been praying about what the Lord wants me to do." He paused, reluctant to go on.

"Yes?" Beth encouraged, with a strange sinking feeling in her heart.

"I got a letter yesterday from my brother Tom. As you know, he's been living in Ohio and working in a factory. Anyway, he says that there are some jobs available at the plant where he works, and that I am welcome to come and live with him. I can't afford to keep living in this area without a job, so I think the only thing I can do is to move out there. I hate to do it, but it seems to be the only choice I have. The worst thing will be leaving you, Beth! You will write to me, won't you?"

"Of course," Beth assured him, looking away to hide the tears that were beginning to fill her eyes. "I'll really miss you, Dave."

"And I'm going to miss you!  But I'll be back to visit.  Please don't forget me, Beth!"

"I'll never forget you, Dave," Beth promised.

The following Sunday, Dave came over for one last visit, and on Monday, he boarded a bus for Ohio.  Beth had gone with him to the bus station, and she stood watching for as long as she could see him leaning out of the bus window and waving goodbye.  Then she turned and trudged slowly home.  How dreary the winter weather seemed now.  Beth shivered and pulled her coat more closely around her.  The drab gray sky and the chilly air seemed a fitting reflection of the sadness that filled her heart.  Dave's parting words to her echoed in her ears, "I'll write to you, and I'll be back, Beth.  Wait for me!  Please don't forget me!"

"Oh, Dave," her heart cried.  "How could I ever forget you?  I love you!"  It was the first time that she had admitted that fact, even to herself.  Already, she could hardly wait for his first letter.

Every day for the next week, Beth was at the mailbox as soon as the mailman had departed, and finally, the following Tuesday, the long awaited letter arrived.  She hurried up the stairs to her room, shut the door, and eagerly tore it open.  "Dear Beth," she read, "How I miss you!"  She stopped for a moment and hugged the letter to herself, as she savored that short sentence, and then continued reading, "The Lord has answered prayer, and I have found a job at the same factory where my brother works.  It doesn't pay much, but it is enough for me to live on."  The letter continued, as Dave described the area he was living in, and then closed with, "Write back soon, Beth.  I am longing to hear from you.  Love, Dave."

Immediately, she sat down at her desk, and began writing a long letter to Dave, telling him about all the things that had happened since she had seen him, and relating to him the news about their mutual friends at church and in the orchestra.

At least once a week, for the next several months, the letters sped back and forth between Ohio and New Jersey. Beth enjoyed Dave's descriptions of his life in Ohio, his job, and the people he was meeting. She rejoiced to hear that he had found a good church and was making new friends there. And she reveled in the endearing words that let her know that he was continually thinking of her and longing to be with her. Although she missed him terribly, his letters helped to soothe the aching loneliness.

Then, as summer approached, Dave's letters stopped coming so frequently. In May, he sent her a beautiful card for her twenty-first birthday, but his next letter didn't arrive until almost three weeks later. For a while, Beth continued to write him faithfully every week, but then decided that she should wait until she had received a letter from him before she wrote to him again.

When the entire month of June and most of July had passed with no word at all from Dave, Beth began to become concerned about him. "Has something happened to him? Could he be sick?" she worried. He had never let so much time go by without writing before.

Finally, on the last day of July, Beth found a letter in the mailbox bearing his familiar handwriting. Quickly, she ran up to her room, shut the door behind her, sat down on her bed, and tore open the letter, her hands trembling. A strange and unexplainable sense of foreboding filled her heart.

"Dear Beth," she read, "I'm sorry that it has been so long since I have written to you. I guess I have been putting it off because this is the hardest letter that I have ever had to write. When you and I were together, I felt sure that I was in love with you, and that you were the girl who would someday be my wife. However, a couple of months ago, I met someone else. Her name is Mary..." The words swam before Beth's eyes, as tears began to stream down her cheeks. After several moments of quiet weeping, she forced herself to continue. "While I will always consider you one of my very dearest and best friends, my feelings for you have changed, and I thought that it was only fair to write and let you know what has happened. Your friend always, Dave."

Heartbroken, Beth collapsed into a heap on her bed, great silent sobs shaking her slender body. "I <u>love</u> you, Dave! I <u>love</u> you!" her heart cried out. "How could you do this to me?"

Then she turned to her Heavenly Father and poured out her grief to Him. "Father, I don't understand why this has happened. Dave seemed like the perfect one for me—the answer to my prayers. But I know that <u>Your</u> plan is best. Help me to accept this, and please, Father, help it not to hurt so much!" Then, after several hours of agonized praying and weeping, Beth finally fell into an exhausted and troubled sleep.

The next few days passed in a blur of unreality. It was so hard to believe that her relationship with Dave was over! The bright warm sunshine, the cheerful songs of the birds in the oak tree outside her window, and the smiling faces of the purple and yellow pansies in Mother's flowerbed seemed to mock her grief. She wondered how it could be summer in the world outside when it felt like winter in her heart.

Beth briefly related the contents of Dave's letter to her parents, Dot, and Betty, but she kept her grief locked inside her heart, and shared it with no one except her Heavenly Father. Each night, in the privacy of her bedroom, she poured out her anguish to God, praying and sobbing herself to sleep. Gradually, a new prayer was added to her pleas for comfort. "What do you have for me now, Father?" she asked one night. "I really thought that Dave was the one that You had planned for me to marry. Please show me Your will!"

After a few moments of quiet reflection, an idea began to take shape in her mind. Perhaps now was the time to fulfill her dream of getting the training she needed to become an artist! She had been working in Dad's office for several years and had carefully saved her money. Surely by now she would have enough to pay for her art school education! As she continued to consider the idea, she felt the familiar peace that she had come to recognize as God's confirmation that she had accurately interpreted His leading.

The very next day, Beth wrote a letter to the Newark School of Fine Art, requesting information and an application. For the first time since Dave's last letter had come, she eagerly checked the mailbox daily. About a week later, she received a reply. She tore open the envelope and quickly sorted through the papers until she found the financial information. Glancing at the list of expenses, she gasped in astonishment. The total was exactly the same as the amount of money that she had in her savings account! "Thank You, Father, for Your perfect timing!" she breathed in gratitude.

Within the next few days, she joyfully shared the good news with Dad, Mother, Dot, Bake, and her best friend Betty. However, as Beth began thinking through all that was involved in attending art school, she realized that if she decided to go, she would be beginning a whole new chapter in her life. "Newark is too far away for me to commute every day," she thought. "If I go to school there, I'll have to move away from home and live on my own!" Although she was twenty-one years old, the thought of leaving home and living among strangers terrified Beth. Also, she realized that, although she had enough money to pay for her schooling, she would have to find a job to pay for her living expenses.

"Father, I believe it is Your will for me to go to school in Newark," she prayed one night, "but if it is, You will have to provide a place to live and a job for me there."

The following Sunday, as Beth approached the church building, Betty was waiting impatiently for her on the steps. "You'll never guess what's happened, Beth! Dad has gotten a new job, and we'll be moving to Newark!"

"That's wonderful, Betty! I'm so glad that you'll be living in Newark. I won't be nearly so lonely going to art school if you are nearby."

"Oh, you haven't heard the best part of the news yet. I told Mother that you're going to go to art school in Newark this fall, and that you will need a place to live, and I asked her if we would have room for you to stay with us, and she said 'Yes'!"

# Chapter 5—On Her Own

The remainder of the summer passed in a whirlwind of activity, as Beth prepared for her move to Newark. September found Beth living with the Roth family in Newark, attending art school, and working evenings and weekends as a waitress in a little diner just down the street from the Roths' home, to earn money for her living expenses. One evening as she walked home from work, she lifted her heart in thankfulness to God. "Thank You for making it possible for me to go to art school, Father. Only You could have provided so perfectly for everything I needed."

Art school was all that Beth had dreamed it would be. She reveled in being in a school where the whole curriculum consisted of art classes—drawing with pencils, pastels, and ink, lettering, oil painting, and Beth's favorite—painting with watercolors! Her technique improved daily, and her teachers noticed her unusual talent. One day, the watercolor painting teacher, Miss Cooper, was watching Beth put the finishing touches on her portrait of a model who was posing for the art class. Looking over Beth's shoulder, she commented, "The object of art is to portray the subject realistically, and you are doing an excellent job, Miss Conrad."

Beth flushed with pleasure. "Thank you, Miss Cooper. That's always been my goal for my artwork."

One of the most difficult things that Beth had to face because of her move to Newark was the fact that she had to leave her former church family behind, and find a new church home. "Father," she whispered, as she lay in bed that first Saturday night in her new home, "You know how much I miss my friends at Calvary Baptist. Please guide me to the church that you want me to be involved in here in Newark."

A moment later, a thought came to her mind. She suddenly remembered that she had passed a little Baptist church as she had walked home from the bus stop after school the previous day. It was only two blocks from the Roths' house! "Thank You, Father," she breathed. "I'll try that church tomorrow." Then she turned over and fell into a peaceful sleep.

The following morning at breakfast, Beth told the Roth family of her decision to visit the nearby church. "That's a good idea, Beth," Mr. Roth remarked. "Now that you mention it, I remember noticing that church too. We'd like to go with you."

"That would be great!" Beth replied enthusiastically. She had been dreading attending a new church alone, but it wouldn't be nearly as hard to do so in the company of her friends.

Later that morning, Beth and the Roth family entered the little Mount Pleasant Baptist Church together and found a seat in a back pew. How thankful Beth was to join in the familiar hymns, and to listen to a helpful and practical sermon from God's Word! Although the pastor was just a young man, he seemed unusually able to explain God's Word in a way that made it plain and understandable. She felt sure already that she had found a new church home.

However, as the congregation rose to sing the last hymn, Beth's knees began to shake. Although she had enjoyed the service tremendously, she shivered as she realized that soon she would have to face the ordeal of meeting a whole church full of strangers! Beth's shy soul shrunk from this, and she was tempted to flee out the door and down the street as soon as the pastor said the final "Amen." Only the presence of Betty by her side kept her from acting upon her impulse.

As she turned to go into the aisle, she found herself face-to-face with a friendly-looking young woman who was holding a tiny baby in her arms. "You're new here, aren't you?" she smiled. "I'm Louise Mierop, the pastor's wife. We're so glad that you came to worship with us this morning."

Beth was amazed that the pastor's wife was so young. "She doesn't look much older than I am," she thought in astonishment. "Pleased to meet you, Mrs. Mierop. I'm Beth Conrad. "

"Glad to meet you, Miss Conrad," the pastor's wife responded. "But please call me Louise."

"And please call me Beth."

"Do you folks have any plans for lunch?" Louise's welcoming glance extended not only to Beth, but also to the whole Roth family. "If you don't, Frank and I would love to have you come to our house. We live right next to the church."

Before Beth could say a word, Mrs. Roth spoke up. "That would be lovely."

Before the afternoon was over, Beth was beginning to feel at ease with Frank and Louise Mierop. Drawn out by their interested questions, she found herself telling them of how she had come to Christ, of her concern for her unsaved family, and of her coming to Newark to attend art school.

As the months went by, Beth gradually made other friends in the church, and began to feel that once again she had a church family.  One Sunday, shortly before the beginning of Beth's second year of art school, Pastor Mierop announced, "We have a great need for a new Sunday School teacher for the junior Sunday School class.  Miss Bennett, who has taught that class for many years, will no longer be able to do so, because of her poor health.  If any of you feel that the Lord is leading you to take this class, please let me know."

As Beth sat in her customary place at the back of the church, she felt the gentle nudge in her heart which she had learned to recognize as the voice of her Heavenly Father.  Instantly, she protested inwardly, "<u>Me</u>, Lord?  You want <u>me</u> to teach that class?  You know how shy I am!  I've never had any teaching experience, and You know how terrified I am to get up in front of people!"

However, the inner conviction persisted, and by the end of the service, Beth had yielded, although with fear and trembling, to the will of her Savior.  As she greeted Pastor Mierop at the door, she said timidly, "The Lord spoke to me this morning about taking that Sunday School class, Pastor Mierop, and I'm willing to do it if you want me to."

"That's great, Beth!  I'm sure that you will do a wonderful job, and it will be good for the children to have a younger person as a teacher.  Wait just a moment, and I will get you the lesson materials.  You can start next Sunday."

Beth spent many hours during the next week in earnest prayer and preparation, but when she walked into the Sunday School classroom the following Sunday, she still felt as if she were walking into a den of lions!  "Help me, Father," she breathed a quick prayer as she stepped through the door

As she continued toward the front of the room, she heard a loud whisper behind her, "Look, we've got a new teacher!"

"Naw," came the reply. "She's not a teacher. She's just a big girl."

Beth's cheeks flushed pink with embarrassment, and her heart sank at the overheard comments. It was true. Her height of barely five feet, two inches, and her slender figure of only one hundred ten pounds did make her look much more like a girl of sixteen than a young lady of twenty-two. How could she ever hope to teach a group of kids who thought of her as just a bigger kid?

However, as she reached the front of the room, she turned and faced her class with a warm smile. "Good morning, boys and girls," she said cheerfully, with just a slight tremor in her voice. "I'm Miss Conrad, your new teacher. Today I'm going to tell you the story of how a little boy gave his lunch to Jesus, and Jesus used it to feed thousands of hungry people!"

Immediately, a boy with an unruly shock of red hair and a face liberally sprinkled with freckles called out, "Aw, we've heard that story before!"

"Yeah," agreed a chubby blond boy in the back row. "I'm tired of hearing those same old stories over and over again."

Somehow, Beth got through the next hour and taught the Bible lesson, in spite of the bored looks on the faces of her class and their continual squirming in their chairs. As she was closing in prayer, she felt a slight breeze, as something sailed by her head, and when she opened her eyes and turned to look, she saw that a Sunday School paper airplane had landed on the floor just behind her.

That afternoon, alone in her room, a discouraged Beth poured out her heart to God, tears of frustration rolling down her cheeks. "Father, I just can't do it! Those kids were so bored today! How can I ever hope to hold their attention and teach them anything about Your Word?"

In the quietness that followed, a gentle suggestion worked its way into Beth's troubled mind. "Of course," she exclaimed. "That's the answer! This is just another way that I can use the artistic talent that You've given me, Father."

The following Sunday found Beth standing in front of an easel with a large pad of paper on it, using pastels to illustrate the story of Jesus calming the storm. After that day, her class never failed to sit on the edge of their seats in fascination as they watched their "Miss Beth" make the familiar Bible stories come alive with her artwork.

The next two years rushed by in a joyful flurry of activity, as Beth continued with art school, cello lessons, orchestra rehearsals, and teaching Sunday School. One winter Sunday morning, during her last year of art school, as she looked out over the eager faces of her young pupils, her heart was saddened as she thought of Dot's kids, Stu and Nancy, who had never had a chance to hear of the wonderful love of Jesus. "I know what I'll do," she thought. "I'll ask Dot if I can take them to Sunday School. I'm glad that they live within walking distance of Mount Pleasant."

The following week, Beth stopped by Dot's house for a visit after school. "I'm sorry that I haven't gotten over to visit you more often, Dot," she apologized. "It's just that I stay so busy all the time."

"And you love every minute of it!" Dot smiled. "I'm really glad that you have finally gotten to fulfill your dream of going to art school. Bake and I are really looking forward to attending your graduation in a few months!"

Beth shook her head in amazement. "I can't believe that I'll be graduating this spring. It seems like only a few months since I started art school."

Just then, Bake walked into the room. "Well, if it isn't my long-lost sister-in-law," he teased. "I was beginning to think that we would never see you again."

Beth blushed in embarrassment.

"Let her alone, Bake!" Dot reproved laughingly.

"Well, now that you're here," Dot continued, turning to Beth, "I'd like to have a nice long visit. Can you stay for supper, or do you have something else you have to do?"

"I'd love to stay, Dot."

As Dot, Bake, and Beth lingered over their cherry pie after supper, Beth sent a quick prayer heavenward and then introduced the subject that was the main reason for her visit.

"Dot," she said hesitantly, "I've started teaching Sunday School at the little church I've been attending, and I'd love to have Stu and Nancy in my class. Would it be all right with you and Bake if I stopped by each week and took them to Sunday School?"

Instantly, Beth could feel the atmosphere at the supper table change and become just as icy as the wintry day outside. "Beth, I'm sure that you remember the discussion that you and Bake and I had several years ago about religion. As you know, we really don't feel that religion is necessary, either for ourselves or for our children. However, since you're their aunt, I will let them go with you one time—but only once, mind you!"

Beth's heart sank in discouragement. She had prayed much before this visit, and she had gone to Dot's house with such high hopes. As soon as she could, she thanked Dot and Bake for dinner and trudged home through the chilly twilight.

The following Sunday after church, she shared her disappointment with Pastor Mierop. "So she said that they could only come to Sunday School with me one time!" she concluded miserably.

However, to her surprise, Pastor Mierop didn't seem to share her dejection. "Well, praise the Lord for once, Beth!" he exclaimed with a big smile.

Later that day, alone in her room, the pastor's words echoed in Beth's ears. "He's right," she thought. "Instead of giving up in despair, I need to use the opportunity that the Lord has given me."

Easter came early that year, and Beth decided that that would be the perfect time to use her one chance to take her niece and nephew to Sunday School. She called her sister on the phone the week before Easter, and even Dot seemed to agree that that Sunday would be a good time for her children to have their one visit to Sunday School with their Aunt Beth.

As the early spring sunshine streamed through the church windows that Easter Sunday morning, Stu and Nancy sat in Beth's Sunday School class and listened and watched in fascination as she poured her heart and all of her artistic ability into telling them the glorious story of Jesus' death on the cross for their sins and of His resurrection from the grave.

Later, as they walked slowly home, each child holding one of Beth's hands, Nancy spoke up. "Aunt Beth, I want to ask Jesus to forgive me, like you were talking about today in Sunday School. Can I do it right now?"

Beth's heart leaped for joy. "Yes, you certainly can!" She turned to give her niece a big hug.

So the three stopped right in the middle of the sidewalk, and Nancy bowed her head and prayed a simple, but heartfelt prayer. "Dear Jesus, I know I've done lots of bad things, and I'm really sorry. I believe that You were punished for all the bad things I've done, just like Aunt Beth said today. Please forgive me, so that I can come and live in Heaven with You someday. Amen."

As they opened their eyes, Beth looked at Stuart. "Would you like to do that too, Stu?"

"Yes, if you want me to, Aunt Beth." He immediately bowed his head and said a prayer very similar to Nancy's. However, Beth had an uneasy feeling that he might have just done it to please her, rather than out of a genuine desire to receive Christ.

"Stu, I hope you understand that you shouldn't ask Jesus to forgive you just because I asked you to. You must be really sorry for your sins and truly believe in your heart that Jesus died for you."

"Sure, I understand, Aunt Beth."

However, Beth still felt a nagging uncertainty about his decision. About Nancy's, though, she had no such doubts. Her heart was filled with a song of praise to God for her niece's salvation.

As they approached the Baker house, Beth's heart began to pound as she thought of how Dot and Bake would react to the announcement that she knew Nancy would soon make. Just as she had expected, Nancy bounced into the house, filled with excitement. "Guess what, Mommy! Aunt Beth told me all about how Jesus died for me and came alive again, and I asked Him to forgive me, and someday I'm going to go live with Him up in Heaven!"

Instantly, Beth saw the welcoming smile in Dot's gray eyes change to stormy anger. She looked at Beth icily. "Well, it seems that I was wrong. Even <u>once</u> was too much!" However, not even Dot's anger could dim Beth's joy as she walked home in the warm spring sunlight!

The last few weeks of the school year sped by, and on the balmy spring night of May 20, 1940, shortly after her twenty-fourth birthday, Beth walked down the aisle to receive her diploma from the Newark Public School of Fine and Industrial Art. In the audience were Dad, Mother, Dot, Bake, Stu, and Nancy, come to share in Beth's accomplishment.

"I knew that my girl could do it!" Dad beamed after the ceremony.

"Congratulations, Beth!" Mother smiled.

"Yes," Dot chimed in. "Bake and I are really happy for you. I always knew that you had unusual talent, and I'm so glad that you've gotten a chance to develop it!"

Beth's eyes shone with happiness. "Thank you, all of you!"

Later that night, in her room, her heart overflowed in thankfulness to God. "Thank You so very much, Father, for making it possible for me to attend art school. And please show me what Your plan is for me now."


On a warm evening in June, several weeks after Beth's graduation from art school, the phone rang at the Roth house. Mr. Roth answered it and turned to Beth, who was standing nearby. "It's for you, Beth." He handed her the receiver.

"Hello," Beth said, and was stunned to hear her sister's heartbroken sobs on the other end of the line.

"Dot, what is it? What's the matter? Has something happened to Mother or Dad?"

"No, it's Nancy," Dot sobbed. "She's—she's <u>dead</u>!"

Beth almost dropped the phone in her shock. "Dead! What happened?"

"It happened so fast. She had polio. She was only sick for three days, and now she's gone!"

"Oh, Dot, I'm so sorry," Beth wept into the phone. "Is there anything I can do to help?"

There was a slight pause, and then Dot said slowly, "Yes, I think there is one thing you can do. As you know, Bake and I have no connection with any church, but it does seem fitting to us that we should have a pastor perform Nancy's funeral. Do you think you could ask your pastor if he would be willing to do it?"

"Yes, I'd be glad to, Dot, and I'll be praying for you too."

"Thank you, Beth."

After she had hung up the phone, Beth bowed her head in prayer. With tears still streaming down her cheeks, she thanked God that for Nancy, as for herself, hearing the good news of salvation just once had been enough!

As Beth had expected, Pastor Mierop was glad to perform Nancy's funeral. On the day of the funeral, Beth was surprised to find joy even in the midst of her sorrow, in knowing that Nancy was alive in Heaven, and that her other loved ones were having another chance to hear the Gospel through the pastor's message.

As Pastor Mierop stood beside the little coffin, he looked out with compassion at the grieving loved ones. "I only had the privilege of meeting Nancy once, but I know that if she could be here with us and speak to us today, she would hold up her little hand and tell us that there are five very important things that she wanted us to know." He held up his own hand and counted them off on his fingers. "First, she would tell us that God loves each of us. Second, she would tell us that all of us have sinned. Third, she would tell us that Jesus Christ, God's Son, paid for our sins when He died on the cross. Fourth, she would tell us that He arose from the grave and is alive in Heaven. And last, she would tell us that each of us must receive Him as our own personal Savior. Because she believed this, she is at this moment safe in the Arms of Jesus. My prayer is that each of you will find the peace that only comes from receiving Christ, and the comfort that only God can give at such a difficult time as this."

As he closed in prayer, Beth prayed earnestly that God would use this time of sorrow and this simple message to touch the hearts of Dot, Bake, Mother, and Dad, and to draw them to Himself.

Later that afternoon, after Nancy's little body had been committed to the grave, Dot held Beth in a long hug. As she felt her sister's tears mingling with her own, she heard Dot whisper, "Thank you, Beth." Then Dot turned away and walked with Bake to their waiting car.

The remainder of the summer passed in a blur of job interviews, as Beth sought employment as an artist at various publishing houses and greeting card companies in Newark and New York City. However, although they were impressed by Beth's talent, it seemed that none of them needed any additional artists on their staffs at that time.

One Saturday night, following another fruitless week of job-hunting, Beth lay in bed reviewing her latest job interview—at Norcross Greeting Card Company. After looking over her portfolio, Miss Sloane, the art director, had sighed and shook her head. "Miss Conrad, I'm truly impressed with the fine quality of your work, and I would love to hire you, but unfortunately, we just don't have any openings at the moment. However, I will certainly give you a call if something opens up." This had been a big disappointment to Beth, not only because she would have loved to use her creative talents in designing greeting cards, but also

because Norcross had been the last on her list of potential
employers.

As Beth pondered what she should do next, she lifted her heart
to God. "Father, I know that you led me to go to art school, but
I'm not sure what Your plans are for me now. You know that I'd
really like to have an art job, but if that isn't Your will for me at
this time, then that's okay. Please show me what you want me to
do."

The following morning, as Beth sat in church, Pastor Mierop
announced that they would be having some special speakers that
evening—a missionary couple who had recently returned from
Africa. "Rev. and Mrs. Wentworth will not be going back to the
mission field. Instead, they will be heading up the Newark
Evangelistic Committee. They would like to tell our church about
the plans they have for reaching our community with the good
news of salvation. I would encourage all of you to come back
tonight to hear their message."

That evening, Beth found herself amused at the contrast
between Rev. and Mrs. Wentworth. Rev. Wentworth was a
slender, short, soft-spoken man with thinning dark hair. However,
his wife was a large imposing woman with snow-white hair, and
was several inches taller than her husband. She spoke with a loud,
authoritative voice and did most of the talking. "Well," Beth
thought to herself, "I suppose the old saying that 'opposites attract'
is really true."

However, Beth soon found herself forgetting their differences in
appearance and personality, as she began listening carefully to
their message. They both spoke of the great need to reach the
metropolitan area of Newark with the Gospel, and they revealed
several strategies for doing so. "We would like to have weekly
open-air meetings in the park, with all of the evangelical churches
in the area participating," Mrs. Wentworth explained. "And we
would also like to invite the well-known evangelist Charles E.

Fuller of 'The Old Fashioned Revival Hour' to come to Newark for a city-wide revival meeting."

"Pray with us about these plans," Rev. Wentworth added, "and also pray concerning the needs of the evangelistic committee itself. One crucial need that we have at present is for a secretary to work in our office. We can't afford to pay much, so the person accepting the job must be able to live on a small salary, and be willing to do their work as unto the Lord."

Beth hardly heard the rest of their presentation. "Why, I could do that job!" she realized. "I don't have many expenses. I've never wanted to be a secretary, but if my secretarial training could be used for the Lord, I wouldn't mind being one at all!" As she considered the idea, her thoughts turned into a prayer for guidance. "Father, is this Your answer to the prayer that I prayed last night?" The quiet assurance that filled Beth's soul confirmed to her that indeed it was.

At the close of the service, Beth shyly approached Rev. and Mrs. Wentworth, "I'm a business school graduate, and I'd be glad to work as your secretary if you want me to."

"Praise the Lord!" Mrs. Wentworth exclaimed enthusiastically. "The Lord has already answered one of our prayers!" So it was settled that Beth would begin work the very next day.

The following year flew by. Beth loved her job with the evangelistic committee. She soon found that there were many opportunities for her to use her musical and artistic abilities as well as her secretarial training. The highlight of her week was the Saturday evening open-air service in the park. Each week, Beth would bring her cello and join in providing music for the service, and many times she would also do a chalk talk, presenting the way of salvation and illustrating it with her artwork.

One evening, as she was drawing a dramatic picture of the great gulf separating sinners from God, which could only be spanned by the cross of Christ, she heard a mocking voice from the back of the crowd. "Aw, there ain't no God, and there ain't no heaven nor hell neither," yelled a tall young man with an unruly shock of red hair. "Don't listen to these people, folks. All they want to do is to scare you into their churches so that they can get your money!" With a quick, silent prayer for courage and calmness, Beth continued her drawing, ignoring the heckler, and several people remained after the service to inquire more about the way of salvation.

The following week, Beth's heart sank when she saw the same young man standing at the back of the crowd, along with several snickering friends. This time, however, as soon as he began his cynical comments, he was interrupted by Rev. Wentworth's gentle voice. "God loves you, young man, and He wants you to know Him, but He will not allow you to mock Him and discourage others from following Him. You are hearing the truth, but you are rejecting it and making fun of it. You are on very dangerous ground, son, because God's Word says, 'He that being often reproved hardeneth his neck shall suddenly be cut off, and that without remedy.'"

The young fellow's face reddened with anger. "Aw, go to ____, old man! Let's get out of here, guys!" Then he and his friends turned and stalked off, talking and laughing loudly.

The following Monday morning, as Beth was typing a letter in the office of the evangelistic committee, the door was suddenly yanked open, and several young men burst in. Beth recognized them as the friends of the red-haired young man who had caused such disruption at the open-air meeting.

"Miss, could we see the Reverend? We need to talk to him right away!"

"Certainly." Beth rose from her desk and hurried into Rev. Wentworth's office. She was burning with curiosity about the purpose of this unexpected visit.

When she returned a moment later with Rev. Wentworth, one of the boys cried out, "Please, can you tell us how to be saved? We're scared that we're going to die and go to hell!"

"Gladly!" Rev. Wentworth smiled. "But I must admit that I'm wondering what has caused your sudden change of heart. You didn't seem to have much interest in salvation last Saturday night. And where's your friend who had so much to say?"

At the mention of their friend, all of the boys turned pale. "You mean Red? He's <u>dead</u>! That's why we're here!" explained a short young fellow with wavy brown hair and a face covered with pimples. "After we left your meeting, we went to a bar and drank a few beers. When we came out of the bar, Red started to cross the street, and he walked right in front of a car. It hit him, and he was killed instantly! Just like you told him, he was 'suddenly cut off'. And we're here because we're afraid that the same thing might happen to us!" Beth watched and rejoiced as Rev. Wentworth led the frightened young men to Christ.

Several weeks later, at the close of the Sunday morning service, Pastor Mierop announced, "I would appreciate it if our members could remain for a few minutes after the benediction. Louise and I have some important news that we need to share with them."

When the visitors had gone home and the members had gathered together, the pastor said, "After much prayer, Louise and I believe that it is the Lord's timing for us to move on to another field of service. We have truly enjoyed our ministry here at Mount Pleasant, and we will really miss all of you dear folks. On the last Sunday of this month, I will be giving my final message as your pastor. We'll be praying that the Lord will bring the man of His choosing to lead His flock here."

During the weeks after Pastor Mierop and his wife left, the pulpit at Mount Pleasant Baptist was filled by a steady stream of special speakers and candidates for the position of pastor. One

Sunday morning in early fall, the speaker was Rev. Marson, a pastor from a small town in northern Illinois. Beth was impressed with the clear and challenging message that he gave from God's Word. Several weeks later, at a congregational meeting, the members of Mount Pleasant voted unanimously to call him to be their new pastor.

During the following weeks, the entire congregation waited eagerly for Pastor Marson's reply, and finally it arrived. The next Sunday morning, Mr. White, the chairman of the board, requested all of the church members to stay after the service to hear Pastor Marson's decision. "Dear Friends at Mount Pleasant," Mr. White read, "We are pleased to inform you that we have accepted your call to be your pastor. The Lord showed us His will concerning this decision in a most unusual way! When we received your letter, we noticed that it was charred around the edges. There was a handwritten note scrawled on the outside of the envelope which said, 'This is the only letter which was rescued from a burning mail plane!' Because of the unusual circumstances, we felt that the Lord had indicated His will in such a definite way that there was no doubt about what our decision should be. The first Sunday of November will be my first Sunday as your pastor. We are looking forward to seeing you then!"

On a cold Sunday afternoon in early December, about a month after the Marsons had come to Mount Pleasant, Beth and the Roth family were relaxing in the living room, listening to the weekly symphony concert that they always enjoyed after their Sunday dinner. Suddenly the music was interrupted by the somber voice of a news announcer. "We interrupt our regular programming to bring you a special news bulletin. At 7:55 a. m., Hawaii time, the Pacific Fleet of the United States Navy at Pearl Harbor was attacked and bombed by the Japanese Air Force. According to early reports, at least eighteen ships have been sunk, and several thousand people, both servicemen and civilians, have been either killed or wounded. For comments from the President about this reprehensible act, we now go to our White House correspondent."

Beth and the Roths listened in stunned silence to President Roosevelt's impassioned speech, in which he called December 7, 1941 "a day that will live in infamy," and asked for an immediate declaration of war against Japan by the United States Congress. For Beth, as for all her countrymen, the world had changed in an instant. The United States was at war!

# Chapter 6—Clifford

It was a cold, snowy day in January. Beth was sick with a bad cough, and had been forced to stay home from work. As she lay drowsily in her bed, watching the giant snowflakes drifting lazily down outside her window, she heard the phone ring downstairs. A moment later, she heard footsteps ascending the stairs, and there was a light tap on her door. "Beth," Mrs. Roth called, "You have a phone call. It's a Miss Sloane from Norcross Greeting Card Company."

Beth jumped out of bed, threw on her robe, and hurried downstairs, her heart pounding with excitement. Miss Sloane had promised to call her if a job opened up at Norcross, but Beth hadn't really expected to ever hear from her again. Could it be possible that she was finally going to get a job as an artist?

"Hello," she said breathlessly, as she picked up the receiver.

"Miss Conrad," Miss Sloane said, "You may remember that I promised to contact you when we needed another artist on our staff, and I'm pleased to tell you that we now have a job for you, if you still want it."

"Yes, Miss Sloane," Beth responded excitedly. "I certainly do want the job, but I'll need to give my present employer two weeks' notice."

"Of course. We'll be looking forward to seeing you two weeks from Monday, then."

So it was that Beth's career as a greeting card artist began. She loved every minute of it. At last her childhood dream had been fulfilled. She had a job as an artist! It was hard for her to believe that she was actually getting paid for doing something that was so much fun! She enjoyed using her creativity and artistic ability to produce unique cards for every occasion, and her supervisors soon noticed her unusual talent and rewarded it with a promotion.

Winter gave way to spring, and the spring and summer flew by in a happy flurry of busyness. Weekdays found Beth happily designing greeting cards, and evenings and weekends found her helping with secretarial work for the evangelistic committee, participating in open-air meetings, and teaching her Sunday School class.

One evening in late July, Beth sat in her room wrapping a bridal shower present for Millie Thomas, a friend from church who was soon to be married. As her fingers skillfully fashioned a lovely bow of pink ribbon, she began to wonder if she would ever be the guest of honor at such a joyful occasion. "It seems that almost everyone my age is either engaged or already married," she thought wistfully. "I'm twenty-six now. Before long, people are going to start calling me an old maid!" For just a moment, thoughts of Dave, and of what might have been, filled her heart, and a tear traced its lonely path down her cheek, but she resolutely brushed it away and murmured, "Forgive me, Father! I know that You know what is best for me. And thank You for all the wonderful blessings that You've given me!"

The morning of the wedding shower, Beth awoke feeling nauseated, and so dizzy that she could hardly stand up. "I'll never be able to go to the shower tonight," she thought. "I wonder how I can get my present there." Then she remembered that Pastor and Mrs. Marson had offered to give her a ride to the shower. "I'll just call them and ask if they could stop by and pick up my present," she decided.

By evening, Beth was feeling a little better, although she still had a decidedly queasy feeling in her stomach. When she heard Pastor Marson's knock, she grabbed the present and hurried to open the door.

"I'm so sorry that you're not going to be able to go with us tonight," Pastor Marson remarked. "There's someone out in the car that I wanted you to meet—a friend from the church that I pastored back in Illinois. He's a young man who really loves the Lord!"

Unexplainably, Beth felt her heart sink in disappointment. "My, I sure would like to meet that young man!" she thought to herself. She had an impulsive desire to announce that she was feeling much better, and that she would be able to go after all. Her cheeks flushed in embarrassment as she realized what such a sudden change in plans would imply.

If Beth could have heard the conversation that took place in the Marsons' car during the next few minutes, she would have been even more embarrassed, however. "Clifford," Mrs. Marson said to their young visitor, "I'm so sorry that Beth was sick tonight. We wanted you to meet her. She really loves the Lord, and she serves Him so faithfully that we call her 'Faithful Beth'. She's a real jewel of a girl, but there's just one thing that she needs, and that's a man!"

By Sunday morning, Beth was well enough to attend church. As she sat in the front row, she was surprised to see a stranger sitting on the platform with Pastor Marson. He was a dark-haired, ruddy-faced young man dressed in a military uniform. "We are privileged to have a special speaker this morning," Pastor Marson announced. "He is Clifford Frazier, a dear friend of ours from our former church in Illinois. Clifford is now in the Army Air Force at Fort Dix, and he will be leaving soon to go overseas."

The young man rose and began giving a powerful message, warning sinners to repent and turn to God and cry to Him for mercy and salvation. Many times during the message, Beth had the distinct feeling that the intense eyes of the young preacher were fixed directly on her.

As Beth walked past Pastor Marson and Mr. Frazier on her way out of church, Pastor Marson stopped her. "Beth," he said, "this is the young man that I was telling you about the other night. I'd like you to meet Mr. Clifford Frazier." Then, turning to Clifford, he added, "And this is Miss Beth Conrad."

"Pleased to meet you, Miss Conrad," Mr. Frazier beamed, his warm hazel eyes glowing. "The Marsons have been telling me that you work with the evangelistic committee here in Newark. Do you think that you could possibly send me some tracts and some Gospels of John after I go overseas? I'm sure that I'll have many opportunities to witness over there, and I'll really need some literature."

"Certainly. I'd be glad to, Mr. Frazier."

"And could you write to me too?" he continued eagerly. "I'd love to hear from you."

"Why, of course, if you want me to," Beth replied in surprise. "I wonder why he asked <u>me</u> to write to him," she wondered to herself. "There are a lot of girls in this church who are prettier than I am. Well, he's probably just a lonely soldier who wants to make sure that he'll get some mail."

Later that afternoon, as Beth was sitting in the living room with the Roths and listening to the weekly symphony concert, the phone rang. Mr. Roth went to answer it, and soon returned to the room with a broad smile on his face. "It's for you, Beth—a young man!"

Beth hurried to the phone, wondering who could possibly be calling her. "Hello," she whispered hesitantly.

"Miss Conrad, this is Clifford Frazier. I enjoyed meeting you this morning, and I was wondering if we could get a little better acquainted before I have to leave. The Marsons have invited us both to dinner next Saturday night. Would you be able to come?"

"Yes, I'd love to," Beth whispered, her heart beating so loudly that she was afraid that Clifford could hear it over the phone. It wasn't until after she had hung up that she realized that, for the first time in more than five years, she had a date!

The following week passed in a blur, with Beth's emotions swinging wildly back and forth from excitement to fear. She was looking forward to her date, but her shyness filled her with apprehension. "It was easy for me to talk to Dave," she thought, "because we had our music in common, but what will I talk about with Clifford? Well, at least I can ask him how he found the Lord. That's a start anyway."

Saturday dawned bright and sunny. As Beth looked through her closet trying to decide what to wear, she found that she couldn't make up her mind. She pushed the hangers back and forth in frustration. "I think I'll go shopping after my cello lesson this afternoon and buy a new dress," she mused. "It's been a long time since I've had one anyway. My lesson is over at three, and I don't have to be at Marsons until four-thirty, so that should give me plenty of time."

When the lesson was over, Beth walked to a nearby clothing store and looked through the dresses, but she couldn't find anything attractive that was within her price range. Leaving there, she hurried to another shop, where she encountered the same problem. As she walked out the door to leave, a large sign in a window across the street caught her eye. "Going Out of Business Sale!" the sign proclaimed. "50% Off! Everything Must Go!"

Quickly, Beth crossed the street. "Praise the Lord!" she thought. "This is exactly what I need!" However, when she entered the establishment and began looking through the merchandise, she found herself in a different dilemma. There were so many attractive dresses at reasonable prices that she couldn't decide which one to choose! After trying on at least a dozen different dresses, she narrowed her choice down to two—a pale lavender dress and a rose pink one.

As she stood there holding the dresses and trying to make up her mind, a clerk approached her. "Excuse me, miss. Did you wish to make a purchase? Our store will be closing in five minutes."

In sudden panic, Beth glanced at her watch. It was almost five-thirty! She was already an hour late for her date with Clifford, and she was on the opposite side of town from the Marsons' house! It would take her another hour of riding the bus to get there. "How could I have let the time slip away like that?" she berated herself. Quickly, she chose the rose pink dress, paid for it, and asked permission to use the dressing room to change into it

.

Stuffing her old dress into the shopping bag, she rushed out the door and ran down the street toward the nearest bus stop. As she passed a pay phone, a sudden thought halted her in her tracks. "I should at least call and let them know that I'm going to be late," she thought.

Hurriedly, she stuck a coin in the slot, and asked the operator to ring the Marsons' number. "Hello," she heard Mrs. Marson's familiar voice answer on the other end of the line.

"Mrs. Marson, this is Beth," she replied, her cheeks burning with embarrassment
.

"Beth, where are you? We expected you an hour ago. We were afraid that something had happened to you!"

"No, Mrs. Marson, I'm fine. After my cello lesson, I went shopping, and I just lost track of the time," Beth explained sheepishly. "I'll be there just as soon as I can. I'm sorry that I'm so late. And please give Mr. Frazier my apologies too."

As Beth sat on the bus on the way to the Marsons, she was filled with consternation at the thought of facing them, but most of all she dreaded seeing Clifford. "What in the world will he think of me?" she wondered in humiliation. "By the time I get there, I'll be two hours late for our date! I'm sure that this will be our first, last, and only date!"

However, when she reached the Marsons' house, no one even mentioned her extreme tardiness. After Mrs. Marson had heated up the food, which had gotten cold, they all sat down at the table together, and Pastor Marson asked Clifford to give thanks for their meal.

After they had all enjoyed Mrs. Marson's delicious dinner of roast beef, mashed potatoes, green beans, and salad, topped off with a dessert of apple pie a la mode, Pastor Marson said, "Why don't you young folks go sit in the parlor and get better acquainted? I'll help Mrs. Marson with these dishes."

With trepidation, Beth walked into the living room and found a seat on the Marsons' sofa. Clifford followed and took a seat beside her. "So tell me, Miss Conrad," he smiled down at her, "How did you find the Lord?"

Beth looked up at him shyly. "Please call me Beth."

"And please call me Clifford."

For the next few minutes, Beth shared her testimony with Clifford. She was unaware of what a pretty picture she made as she sat there on the sofa. Her dark brown hair curled gently around her face, the rose pink of her dress accentuated the rosy color in her cheeks, and her hazel eyes sparkled as she spoke enthusiastically of the Lord Whom she loved so much, and of all that He had done for her. "So that's my story," she concluded. "But I'd like to hear about you, Clifford. How did you find Christ as your Savior?"

"I never heard the Gospel while I was growing up. I guess you could say that I come from a pretty bad background. The only time that I ever heard the Name of God or Jesus or Christ spoken in my home was when it was used as a curse word. My father worked for the railroad, and he made good money, but every weekend, he drank up most of what he made, so our family was really poor. With ten kids, there was hardly enough food to go around, and if you didn't get there on time for meals, you just got left out. As my father always used to say, 'We'll wait for you just like one dog waits for another.'"

"Anyway," he continued with his story, "I dropped out of school when I was in tenth grade to try to find work. For the next couple of years, I worked at different jobs, and I lived a pretty rough life. Then one Sunday night, a couple of weeks after my seventeenth birthday, one of my buddies invited me to go to Pastor Marson's church with him. I went, I heard the Gospel for the first time, and I was saved that very night! And ever since then, my whole life has been transformed. I still remember that the next morning when I woke up, the whole world seemed to have changed. The sun seemed to shine brighter, the sky looked bluer, and everything seemed more beautiful than it ever had before, but of course what had happened was that I was a new person!"

Beth rejoiced with Clifford over the marvelous change that Christ had made in his life. As he continued talking and sharing how the Lord had used him as a witness to his family and to many other people, she soon found that her fears of not knowing what to say to Clifford were unfounded. She soon discovered that he would do most of the talking himself, and that all she had to do was to be an interested listener!

The evening flew by, and Beth was amazed when the clock struck ten. "Oh! I had no idea that it was getting so late! I must get home!"

"Let me take you home, Beth. Pastor Marson has been kind enough to let me have the use of his car."

A few minutes later, as Beth and Clifford stood on the porch of the Roths' home, Clifford said, "I don't know when I've enjoyed an evening this much. I wish that we could do this again, but unfortunately, my unit is leaving for Europe in two days, so I won't be able to see you again before I leave. Please write to me! I'll be looking forward to getting your letters!"

"I will," Beth promised, her eyes shining. "And I'll be praying for you too."

Beth fully intended to write Clifford soon, but she decided to wait and send her letter at the same time that she mailed the tracts and Gospels of John that she had promised him. It took some time for her to obtain the needed literature, and when it finally arrived, she was dismayed to realize that almost a month had passed. After packaging the booklets, she finally sat down to write a letter. She wrote, and discarded, several different letters, before she was finally satisfied with what she had written. At last she addressed the package to the address in England that he had given her, and sent it on its way.

Several months passed with no reply from Clifford. Beth anxiously hurried to the mailbox each day, only to be disappointed.

"Is he all right?" she worried. "I wonder if my letter ever reached him! Oh, how I wish that I had written him sooner, and not waited until I could send him the literature!"

Finally, on a gray day in November, as big snowflakes drifted down and covered the dingy landscape with their fresh whiteness, the long awaited letter arrived. Eagerly, Beth tore it open, and scanned the tiny writing that filled every available space on both sides of the thin sheet of paper.

"November 10, 1942
North Africa

Dear Beth,

Thank you so much for your wonderful letter, and for the tracts and Gospels of John. It was great to hear from you, and I have already had many opportunities to give the literature to other soldiers. I'm having a marvelous time witnessing, and I've seen a lot of men get saved! It's amazing to see how open men are to the Gospel when they realize that each day might be their last!

Unfortunately, your package took a long time to reach me, because after a brief stay in England, we were sent here to North Africa, so it had to be forwarded to me here. But I sure am thankful that I finally got it all right!" Beth heaved a sigh of relief and went on to read the rest of the letter, which described conditions in North Africa and then mentioned several prayer requests.

After that first letter, their letters flew back and forth across the Atlantic regularly. Beth eagerly awaited each letter from Clifford, and whenever she received one, that night would find her sitting at her desk writing a reply. Soon she felt that she knew him well, and felt free to confide in him about anything that was on her heart, and from his letters, she could tell that the feeling was mutual.

One night in the spring of 1943, Beth sat on her bed rereading a particularly interesting portion of the letter that had come that day. "You asked me to tell you more about my family. As I told you, I come from a family of ten children. When my mother married my father, she was only sixteen years old, and he was twenty-three. She had led a very sheltered life, and she had no idea that my father was already a drunkard. In fact, for the first few months of their married life, when my father was recovering from a weekend of drinking, she believed him when he told her that he was sick, and she nursed him tenderly. That all ended one day when her brother paid them a visit, saw what was happening, and exclaimed in disgust, 'He's not sick, Docie! He's just plain stinkin' drunk!' I imagine that must have been when my mother and father started fighting with each other. All throughout my childhood, they seemed to be in one continual fight!

Anyway, I am the fifth child in the family. I have four older brothers, three younger brothers, and two younger sisters, but two of my brothers died in infancy. I was born when my mother was twenty-three years old, on the day before my brother Roy's first birthday. Since I was the fifth boy in a row, and I was born so close to my next older brother, I never felt that my mother really wanted me. In fact, when I was born, she must have run out of ideas for boys' names, because she just named me after the doctor who delivered me. His name was Clifford U. Collins, so she named me Clifford U. Frazier, and to this day, I don't know what the 'U' stands for! During all the time I was growing up, she always told me that I was no good, and that I would never amount to anything, and my father, brothers, and sisters all agreed with her opinion of me.

When I found Christ, it was so wonderful to know that Someone loved me, and I began to realize that one reason my family had been so miserable was that they didn't know Him. I tried to tell them about Him, but when I began talking about Jesus, my father got furiously angry, started cursing at me, and threw me out of the house. A kind Christian couple from my church, Ida and George Wohner, took me in, and became like a second mother and father to me. They don't have any children of their own, and Mother Wohner says that I am the son that she always longed for, but never had. I'm so thankful that the Lord brought them into my life!

I've been praying for my family and trying to witness to them for the last twelve years, but the only one who has found Christ is my mother. Last July, shortly before I met you, I was able to visit my mother when she was in the hospital to have a gall bladder operation, and I was able to once again tell her about the way of salvation, and she accepted the Lord! She begged me to forgive her for the way she had treated me when I was growing up, and then begged my brothers and sisters to receive Christ too, but none of them were interested. How thankful I am that she received Christ, because right after her operation, a blood clot took her life, and she went Home to be with the Lord! I still miss her so terribly! How I wish that she could have lived and been a witness to the rest of our family!"

Beth laid aside the letter, tears streaming down her cheeks in compassion for this young man who had had such a hard life. "How thankful I am that he has found You, Lord," she murmured. "Please help me to be a good friend to him and to encourage him in any way that I can!"

On an early summer afternoon in 1943, Beth sat in the Roths' living room, reading Clifford's latest letter, when suddenly she began to giggle. "What's so funny, Beth?" asked Mrs. Roth, who was sitting nearby and reading a magazine.

"Listen to what happened to Clifford." She began reading the letter aloud. "Recently, I made friends with Tom Freese, a missionary who works with the tribes in this area of North Africa. He invited me to join him when he visited a camp of sheepherders. They asked us to come into their tent, and after visiting for a while, they invited us to eat with them. The food was delicious. However, I was shocked when immediately after the meal, Tom began belching loudly!  He poked me in the ribs and whispered, 'Belch, Clifford, belch!'  I followed his instructions, and was amazed to see our host's face break into a broad smile.  He said something to Tom in the tribal language, and Tom turned to me and interpreted, 'He says that he is glad that we enjoyed the meal so much.'  Then Tom explained, 'You see, Clifford, in this tribe, you show your appreciation of a meal by belching.  If you don't belch afterwards, they will think that you didn't enjoy your food!'

Our host then said something else, and once again, Tom interpreted.  'He would like to give you some eggs as a present. Eggs are very valuable here, and the fact that he wants to give you some eggs shows that he really likes you.'

I accepted the eggs and asked Tom to give my thanks to the host, but I was at a loss to know how to carry them.  Finally, I stuck them in my pants' pocket.  A few minutes later, Tom asked, 'Clifford, how would you like to try riding an Arabian horse?'

'That would be great!' I exclaimed excitedly.  I climbed onto the horse that our host brought to me, and it galloped off, its black mane streaming in the wind.  I was having a wonderful time, but suddenly I became aware of something wet and sticky running down my right leg.  It was the eggs!  I had been so excited about riding the horse that I had totally forgotten them, and I had sat on them!"

Mrs. Roth joined Beth in laughing at the amusing incident, and then Beth finished reading the rest of the letter to herself.  She was thrilled to read of all the preaching opportunities that Clifford was having there in North Africa.  "It's amazing how he is able to find so many opportunities to witness for the Lord—even in the middle of a war!" she thought to herself.

As she finished the letter, she noticed a Bible verse reference written at the bottom of the page, so she hurried to get her Bible and look it up.  Beth loved the way that Clifford closed his letters with a Bible verse reference, and also the fact that he always wrote "Jesus Saves Man's Soul From Sin" on the outside of the envelope, in order to be a witness to anyone who might handle the letter on its journey.

Quickly, she opened her Bible, found the reference and read it to herself. It was Psalm 107:23-24, "They that go down to the sea in ships, that do business in great waters; these see the works of the Lord and His wonders in the deep." She closed her Bible, her brow furrowed in puzzlement. "That's a strange verse for Clifford to send me," she thought. "Usually, he sends me some encouraging promise. I wonder why he sent me that verse."

The mystery was solved when she received Clifford's next letter, which was dated July 15, 1943, and was sent from Sicily, an island located near the southwestern coast of Italy. The Bible verse had been Clifford's way of trying to communicate to her something that the army wouldn't allow him to tell her directly— that their unit was soon going to leave North Africa and go to Sicily, because the invasion of Italy by the Allies was about to begin.

"Praise the Lord with me for His protection, Beth!" he wrote. "As we flew toward Sicily, our ground forces mistook our planes for the enemy, and some of our planes were shot down by 'friendly fire'! Except for the grace of God, I could have been on one of those planes!"

Several weeks later, Beth received a letter on which was written the same verse reference that Clifford had sent her just before he left North Africa, so Beth was not at all surprised when his next letter was written from Naples, Italy. "Thank you so much for your faithful prayers, Beth," he wrote. "Just last night, the Lord once again spared my life in a miraculous way! Around two in the morning, we were awakened by air-raid sirens, and we could hear the roar of German planes passing overhead. We rushed to the air-raid shelter and crouched down inside. As we huddled together, we could hear the impact of something hitting the ground close to the shelter, and we braced ourselves for an explosion, but nothing happened! Several minutes later, we felt another thud, but still nothing happened. Finally, the 'all-clear' signal sounded, and we were free to leave the shelter and return to our barracks. The next morning we found that two bombs had landed right outside the air-raid shelter, but both of them were duds! Immediately I thought of the verses in Psalm 91 that say, 'Thou shalt not be afraid for the terror by night; nor for the arrow that flieth by day; nor for the pestilence that walketh in darkness; nor for the destruction that wasteth at noonday. A thousand shall fall at thy side, and ten thousand at thy right hand; but it shall not come nigh thee. Only with thine eyes shalt thou behold and see the reward of the wicked. Because thou hast made the Lord, which is my Refuge, even the Most High, thy Habitation; there shall no evil befall thee, neither shall any plague come nigh thy dwelling. For He shall give His angels charge over thee, to keep thee in all thy ways. They shall bear thee up in their hands, lest thou dash thy foot against a stone.' Praise the Lord for His protection!"

Beth had been standing in the middle of her bedroom reading this letter. Now she sank down on her bed, her knees weak, but her heart overflowing with gratitude. Bowing her head, she cried out, "Thank You, dear Lord! Oh, thank You for sparing Clifford's life!"

One thing that Beth had been thankful for, during this long and terrible war, was that Clifford's work as a medic, and later as a cook, and then as a chaplain's assistant, had not required him to be involved in the actual fighting. In spite of this, though, she had always been aware that his life was still in danger, and she had prayed many times daily for his safety. However, this letter once again brought home to her, with a deadly seriousness, what tremendous peril he was in each day.

Clifford's next several letters were full of the many opportunities that he had to help the Italian people in Naples and to tell them about Christ. "The Italian tracts and Gospels of John that you sent me are such a tremendous help, Beth," he wrote. "The

Italian people are starving—both for food, and for the Bread of Life!  Every day I go out into the streets and distribute the food that is left over after our meals in the mess hall, and at the same time, I give out Gospel literature to the people.  I've met several missionaries recently, and now I'm preaching through an interpreter several times a week in their churches."  As Beth read Clifford's enthusiastic accounts of his ministry, she thanked God for how He was using Clifford as a witness for Himself, even in the midst of war, and prayed for God's continued protection for him

On a cold winter day in late February 1944, Beth sat on the edge of her bed, her eyes wide, her mouth hanging open in disbelief, as she reread the letter that she had just received from Clifford.  By this time, he was stationed on the island of Sardinia near the west coast of Italy.  "February 14, 1944, the Island of Sardinia," she read.  "Dearest Beth, How I wish you could be here with me tonight!  There is a beautiful full moon shining, and I wish that you could walk with me on the beach this Valentine's Day night under that moon, so that I could tell you all that is in my heart!

Since that's not possible, I will just have to try to tell you about it in this letter.  Beth, we've been writing to each other for a year and a half now, and even though we haven't had much time together, I feel that I know you well.  I've been praying much about this, and I believe that you are the one whom the Lord has chosen to be my wife.  Beth, I love you!  Will you marry me?"

Beth clasped the letter to her heart.  Throughout the course of their correspondence, she had come to feel very close to Clifford too, and although she had never before admitted it to herself, she realized now that she had come to love him too!  "We've hardly spent any time together, yet I feel that I know him so well through his letters," she mused, and then murmured a prayer.  "Father, is this Your plan for me?  Please, Lord, show me what Your perfect will is!"

After several weeks of earnest prayer about the matter, Beth sensed a gentle confirmation from God that Clifford was indeed the one whom He had chosen to be her husband, and she joyfully wrote him back, accepting his proposal.

Clifford's next letter was exultant. "Praise the Lord!" he wrote. "The Bible says that 'he who findeth a wife findeth a good thing, and obtaineth favor from the Lord', and I am so thankful for you, my dearest Beth, the precious wife that He is giving to me! Now I finally feel free to tell you what the Lord said to me the very first time that I saw you. As I stood at the pulpit in your church and looked down and saw you sitting in the first row, the Lord spoke to my heart and said, 'Clifford, there's your wife!' And from that moment on, I've never doubted that you are the one whom the Lord has chosen to be my life companion."

The year of 1944 sped by in a joyful flurry of activity. Beth poured her heart into her artwork at Norcross Greeting Cards, and on weekends, she continued taking cello lessons, participating in open-air meetings, and teaching Sunday School. And each day, she looked forward to the next letter she would receive from Clifford.

One day in early December, as Beth sat at her drawing board, Miss Sloane, the art director, walked up behind her and said with a smile, "Beth, I have a special assignment for you and Rae." Rae was a good friend of Beth's, who sat next to her in the art studio, and who had also recently become engaged.

"Yes, Miss Sloane," Beth responded.

Miss Sloane's eyes twinkled. "Something gives me the feeling that you girls might be in the mood for designing Valentine's Day cards, so I want you two to work on our line of greeting cards for Valentine's Day, 1945."

"We'd love to, Miss Sloane!" Beth and Rae chorused in unison, and they spent the next month on the delightful task of trying to design and illustrate the most flowery, romantic cards that they could imagine.

On a cold, snowy day in early January 1945, Beth hurried up the icy walk and into the Roths' house. "Any mail for me?" she inquired eagerly of Mrs. Roth, who was just coming down the stairs.

A shadow crossed Mrs. Roth's face. "No, Beth," she answered sympathetically. "Nothing today."

Beth had been asking that same question and getting the same answer for the past few weeks, and now an icy hand of fear clutched at her heart. Right after Christmas, Clifford's letters had abruptly stopped coming. He had always written her so faithfully. "Is he all right?" she wondered in dread. "Perhaps he's been wounded, or—or even killed!" Without saying a word, she rushed up the stairs to her room, threw herself to the floor beside her bed, and sobbed out her burden to the Lord.

A week later, as Beth and the Roth family were sitting at the dinner table, the phone rang. Mr. Roth went to answer it. "It's for you, Beth," he said, as he handed her the receiver. "It's a man."

"Hello," Beth answered, filled with curiosity about who could be calling her.

The voice she heard on the other end of the line caused her heart to leap with joy. "Beth darling, this is Clifford!"

"Clifford! Where in the world are you?"

"I'm in Boston, darling! I managed to get a month's furlough, and I came home so that we could be married! How soon can you be ready for the wedding?"

Beth's breath was taken away with the joy and suddenness of it all. She had never expected to get married until after the war was over, and Clifford was safely home. She had had no idea that he was on his way back to the States and that he was expecting her to be ready to get married as soon as he arrived! After she had collected her wits, she replied, "I'll need a couple of weeks to get everything ready."

"Great! That will give us a couple of weeks for a honeymoon before I have to go back overseas. I'll see you soon!"

The next two weeks were a happy whirlwind of activity. Clifford arrived and presented Beth with a beautiful diamond engagement ring. Beth sent out invitations, chose her wedding gown and veil, and asked her sister Dot to be her matron of honor. Since none of Clifford's family was able to come, he asked Dot's husband Bake to be his best man. The wedding date was set for Sunday, January 28, 1945, immediately following the evening service, at Mount Pleasant Baptist Church.

"That will be a perfect time to have our wedding, Clifford," Beth exclaimed excitedly. "My parents and Dot and Bake and Stu will have to attend the evening service, in order to be there on time for the wedding, and that will give them another chance to hear the Gospel."

"Yes, Beth. I'm so glad that the Lord gave us the wonderful idea of having it right after the evening service. I want even our wedding to be a testimony for Him!"

"So do I!" Beth's hazel eyes shone with happiness.

At last the joyous day arrived! That Sunday evening, as soon as the last notes of the invitation hymn, "Just As I Am", had died away, and Pastor Marson had closed the service in prayer, the majestic chords of "The Wedding March" filled the air. Beth, radiant behind her veil, walked down the aisle in her white satin and lace wedding dress, to meet Clifford, who stood beaming at her from the front of the church.

Clifford and Beth stood together and listened intently as Pastor Marson gave a brief message about the responsibilities of Christian husbands and wives and about how God intended marriage to be an earthly illustration of the beautiful relationship between Christ and His bride, the Church.

Then, as if in a wonderful dream, Beth heard Clifford's voice saying, "I, Clifford, take thee, Beth, to be my wedded wife, to have and to hold, from this day forward, for better, for worse, for richer, for poorer, in sickness and in health, to love and to cherish, till death do us part!"

And then, like a beautiful echo, Beth heard her own voice responding, "I, Beth, take thee, Clifford, to be my wedded husband, to have and to hold, from this day forward, for better, for worse, for richer, for poorer, in sickness and in health, to love and to cherish, till death do us part!"

The next few minutes passed in a blur of excitement for Beth, as she and Clifford exchanged rings, and then she heard Pastor Marson's voice solemnly proclaim, "I now pronounce that you are husband and wife. Those whom God hath joined together, let not man put asunder." Then turning to Clifford with a smile, he announced, "You may now kiss your bride!"

As Clifford lifted her veil, and their lips met in their first kiss—the first kiss that Beth had ever received from a man—Beth felt filled to overflowing with a great joy! The only time in her life when she had experienced a greater joy had been on the day that she had received Christ. She felt that all of her dreams had come true, and she lifted her heart in a prayer of thankfulness to God for bringing Clifford and her together in marriage.

# Chapter 7—"All Artists Are Crazy!"

The following Wednesday morning, Beth sat nervously beside Clifford on a train speeding toward Kankakee, Illinois. She was filled with apprehension at the thought of meeting all of Clifford's family and friends. "What will they think of me? What will I say to them?" she wondered. "I hope they'll like me!" She could feel her shyness washing over her like a huge tidal wave, threatening to engulf her in terror.

In the seat next to her sat Clifford, oblivious to her fear, talking excitedly. "I can hardly wait for you to meet Mother Wohner, and for her to meet you, Beth! You'll just love her, and I know that she will love you too!"

"I hope so."

Several hours later, the train pulled into the station. As Beth looked out the window, she noticed a tall, angular woman, with her graying hair pulled back severely into a bun. She was scanning the disembarking passengers eagerly, obviously waiting for a loved one to arrive. Behind her stood a short, slender, balding man. Clifford pointed to the couple. "There they are! It's Mother and Father Wohner! They're waiting for us! Come on, Beth!" He grabbed her hand and hurried her off the train.

As they approached the Wohners, and Mrs. Wohner saw Clifford, her face lit up with a joyful smile, and she ran to meet him with open arms. "My dear boy! It's so good to see you again! Thank God that you are home safe from that dreadful war!" Beth felt almost forgotten as they embraced each other. Finally Mrs. Wohner released Clifford and seemed to notice Beth for the first time.

"Mother Wohner, I'd like you to meet my wife, Beth!" Clifford announced proudly, drawing her forward, his arm around her shoulders.

Beth was stunned at the sudden and unexpected transformation that came over Mrs. Wohner's face as the older woman turned to look at her. The joy abruptly vanished, just as if a light had been turned off. Her gray eyes appraised Beth coldly, and her eyebrows drew together in a frown of disapproval. Beth read an intense dislike for her in their steely gaze. She flushed uncomfortably and wished that there were someplace where she could hide from that withering gaze.

"Clifford," Mrs. Wohner said sternly, "I certainly wish that you had consulted me before you took the drastic step of marrying her! All artists are crazy, you know! I would have warned you about that. I'm afraid that you've made a big mistake, and that you'll soon regret it."

Beth stood frozen to the spot in horror, her face flaming crimson, and for once, even Clifford was speechless. Finally, Clifford recovered enough from his shock to protest, "But, Mother Wohner, you've just barely met Beth! When you get to know her, I'm sure you'll love her just like I do!"

"Well, what's done is done, I suppose," Mrs. Wohner conceded reluctantly, "but let me give you both a piece of good advice. Even though you have gotten married, from now on you should pledge to live together in undefiled love as a brother and sister. George and I have found that as we have grown closer to Christ, we no longer feel the need to gratify the base desires of our fleshly natures. Isn't that right, George?"

Beth turned an even deeper shade of crimson and fixed her embarrassed gaze on the pavement at her feet. Behind her, she heard Mr. Wohner mumble an unintelligible reply. Even in the midst of her astonishment at this bizarre conversation, she couldn't help wondering if Mr. Wohner actually agreed with his wife's strange definition of marriage.

Having ended her admonition, Mrs. Wohner proceeded to take Clifford by the arm and propel him to their waiting car, totally ignoring Beth and leaving her and Mr. Wohner to follow along behind. As they drove through the streets toward the Wohners' house, the conversation consisted of Mrs. Wohner's eagerly questioning Clifford about his experiences overseas, and of Clifford recounting many of the interesting events that he had related to Beth in his letters. Normally, Beth would have enjoyed just listening to them talk and would have felt relieved that she didn't have to participate in the conversation. However, after what had happened at the train station, she felt a terrible sense of being deliberately ignored and excluded from the conversation.

Later that night, as Beth lay in the shelter of Clifford's arms, he whispered, "Don't let what Mother Wohner said today bother you, dear! I know that it must have seemed strange to you, and I'll have to admit that it even shocked me. But you just have to get used to her. She's a very blunt person—the kind that speaks her mind about everything. She still hasn't gotten over her shock that we got married so quickly. I'm sure that when she gets to know you, she'll come to see how wrong she was, and that she'll learn to love you. She's got a truly good heart, you know. Like I told you, she's been like a second mother to me ever since my family kicked me out of the house when I got saved."

"All right, Clifford." Beth vowed to try to be understanding of the woman who had been such a blessing to her husband. Then she lifted her heart in a silent prayer to her Heavenly Father, asking that He would give her the grace to forgive this woman who had so offended and misjudged her. A few moments later, after Clifford had kissed her goodnight, she fell into a peaceful sleep.

The next morning, as Clifford and Beth came to the breakfast table, Beth summoned a smile to her trembling lips and greeted Mrs. Wohner. "Good morning, Mother Wohner," she said cheerfully, using the name that Clifford used for her hostess. "I hope you slept well."

"I got the best sleep that I've had since Clifford left," she replied curtly. Then turning to Clifford, she motioned him to the seat next to her. "It's so good to have you home, Son," she beamed. "Come sit here by me and tell me more about what's happened to you while you've been away!"

All throughout breakfast, Mrs. Wohner continued to monopolize Clifford's attention and ignore Beth. Several times, Clifford tuned to Beth and attempted to include her in the conversation. Each time he did, Mrs. Wohner's lips compressed into a tight line, her face flushed, and her gray eyes smoldered with anger. Observing her reaction, Beth suddenly came to a startling realization. "Why, she's jealous of me!" she thought in astonishment. "She wants Clifford all to herself, and she resents anyone who might take him away from her!"

Fortunately for Beth, there were many other people whom Clifford wanted her to meet during their brief honeymoon, so she was spared having to spend much time with the Wohners. Even though it was an ordeal for her to meet so many new people in such a short time, she was thankful that it took her away from Mrs. Wohner's jealous resentment of her relationship with Clifford.

That Friday evening, a wedding supper and shower was planned for the newlyweds by the people of Clifford's home church. In contrast to the icy reception that she had received from Mrs. Wohner, the other ladies of the church welcomed Beth as a new friend, even as they rejoiced to see Clifford once again. As they ate the delicious dinner, and the conversation swelled around her, Beth was once again thankful for Clifford's ability to do most of the talking. She relaxed and enjoyed listening to him sharing with these friends his opportunities to witness and his experiences of the Lord's protection from danger.

After Beth and Clifford had cut the wedding cake and opened their presents, various members of the congregation came up to them to offer their congratulations. A jovial, rather rotund man slapped Clifford on the back heartily. "Well, Clifford, the Bible says that 'he who finds a wife finds a good thing', and as far as I can tell by looking, you've definitely found yourself a good one!" He winked at Clifford.

As Clifford turned to reply, Beth found herself facing a short, pudgy old lady wearing a white blouse with pink polka dots, and a purple skirt with yellow stripes. Stifling her artistic amusement at such an odd mismatch of colors, Beth greeted her with a friendly smile. However, instead of introducing herself, the woman merely looked Beth up and down with a pair of sharp black eyes, scrutinizing her from head to toe. Beth's cheeks flushed with embarrassment at this unnerving examination, and her mind groped unsuccessfully for something appropriate to say. However, before she could come up with a suitable remark, the woman completed her inspection, drew herself up to her full height of five feet, and snapped, "<u>Well</u>, when I read in the paper that Clifford had married 'a New York designer', I thought you would be '<u>confisticated</u>', but you're not! You're just like all the rest of us!"

Then, having delivered this pronouncement, she stalked off, without waiting for a reply, leaving Beth weak-kneed, but giggling inwardly. "Why, it's no wonder she looked at me so strangely," she thought. "She must have thought I was a <u>clothing</u> designer instead of a designer of greeting cards! Of course she would have expected me to be fashionable and sophisticated." And then she went off into another gale of inward mirth, as she thought of the old woman's mangling of the word "sophisticated".

The following day, Clifford announced, "Well, I think it's about time that my family met my wife!" Borrowing the Wohners' car, they drove across town to an area where the houses looked rather dilapidated. They stopped in front of a small frame house, which had once been white, but was now in dire need of a coat of paint. One of the porch steps was broken and there was a sizeable tear in the screen of the front door. A broken-down car was parked in the yard. There were more weeds in the yard than grass, and even the half-hearted attempt at a flower bed seemed strangely out of place in its surroundings.

Jumping out of the car and taking Beth by the hand, Clifford ran across the yard, up the steps, and into the house, letting the screen door bang noisily behind them. "Hey, everybody, I'm home!" he yelled, in what seemed to Beth an unnaturally loud voice. However, as Beth listened to the din of voices in the small living room, it soon became apparent to her that this was the normal volume of conversation for those in the Frazier clan. The room was filled with several clusters of young men and women, all gesturing and shouting at each other, and continually interrupting each other. Beth got the uncomfortable impression that they were all in the midst of an angry argument, but glancing at Clifford out of the corner of one eye, she could see that he considered it nothing unusual. In one corner of the room, a thin old man, whose dark hair and skin revealed his Cherokee Indian heritage, sat in a rocking chair. In another corner, several small children squabbled noisily over a toy car.

"Hey, I said, 'I'm home'!" Clifford yelled. "Do you want to meet my wife or not?" At this, the babble of voices quieted down, and at least a dozen pairs of curious eyes fixed on Beth. Her head swam as Clifford made the introductions. "This is my father." He gestured to the old man in the rocking chair. The old man nodded at her, and tried to speak, but Beth was unable to understand his words.  Looking at him more closely, she could see that the left side of his body was paralyzed by the stroke which had also robbed him of his ability to speak clearly.

Then in rapid-fire succession, Clifford began pointing out his brothers and sisters and their spouses.  "Beth, this is Earl and Mildred, LaVerne and Marge, Roy and Mary, Murray and Othella, Ione and Frank, Urban and Betty, and Betty and Walter, and these are their kids.  Everybody, I'd like you to meet Beth, my wife!"  Beth's head spun as she strove vainly to connect all of the names with the correct faces.

Once again the babble began, as the group converged around Beth and greeted her excitedly.  A handsome young man in the uniform of an army officer slapped Clifford on the back.  "Well, big brother," he laughed, "You've finally gone and gotten yourself 'hitched'!  I was beginning to think that you were going to be a bachelor for the rest of your life."

"Yep, Murray, I finally did it!" replied Clifford with a proud grin.

The following week sped by in a blur of dinner parties at the homes of various friends.  Each night, Clifford shared the tremendous needs of the people in war-ravaged Italy and collected donations of money, food, and clothing for them.  Clifford seemed to be enjoying himself immensely, but Beth's stomach rebelled at the enormous amount and variety of food which was set before her, and her head reeled with the continuous demands of trying to carry on conversations with so many strangers.  How she longed for some quiet time when she and Clifford could just be alone and enjoy each other's company!

However, it was not to be, for Clifford's furlough was rapidly coming to an end.  She and Clifford hurried back to the East Coast, where he had to embark on a ship for Italy, and Beth had to return to her job at Norcross. Their honeymoon was over!

The following day, as she and Clifford lingered in a final goodbye kiss, her heart cried out, "Oh, Clifford, how long will it be before I see you again?" That night she lay in bed alone, with tears streaming down her cheeks. Once again, she committed Clifford's future safety to the One Who had so miraculously spared his life in the past. "Please, Father, take care of him, and bring him safely home to me," she whispered. Then her heavy burden lifted, and she fell asleep.

The next several months dragged along like a parade of snails, their monotony broken only by Clifford's newsy and affectionate letters. Then on Beth's twenty-ninth birthday, May 8, 1945, she received what she considered to be the very best birthday present of her entire life! Hitler's forces surrendered to the Allies, ending the war in Europe, and that joyful day was forever recorded in history as V-E Day!

Beth hoped that Clifford would soon be coming home, but his next letter bore the disappointing news that he would have to stay on in Italy for some time, as a member of the Allied occupation forces. "How I long to be with you, my dearest sweetheart!" he wrote on May 15th. "But only the Lord knows how long it will be before I can get back to the States!"

For the next month, Clifford's letters came regularly, but toward the end of June, they abruptly stopped. For several long weeks, Beth heard nothing from him. Then one hot night in July, she heard a knock at the door. When Beth went to answer it, she was astonished to see Clifford standing there beaming at her! "Clifford! You're <u>home</u>!" she exclaimed rapturously. "Why didn't you tell me you were coming?"

"I wanted to surprise you!" He grinned mischievously. "Did I succeed?"

Beth fell into his outstretched arms. "You certainly did!"

Later that night, they lay in each other's arms, with Beth's head resting on Clifford's shoulder. She ran her fingers through his hair. "It's so wonderful to have you home, my dearest! I'm so thankful to the Lord that He brought you safely through the war, and that we're together again at last!" For several minutes, Clifford lay there quietly and didn't say a word. His uncharacteristic silence made Beth feel uneasy, and suddenly a cold hand of foreboding clutched at her heart. "Clifford, something's wrong, isn't it?" she cried in alarm. "Tell me what it is!"

"Well, Beth, you were so happy to see me that I didn't want to tell you until I had to. I'm only home for a month's furlough, and the only way I could get to come home now was to agree to go and fight in the war in the Pacific after my furlough is over."

"Oh, Clifford," Beth moaned, "I can't bear the thought of you having to go into a war zone again! I would rather have waited longer to have you home, if only you could have been home for good!"

"I suppose it was a foolish decision," Clifford agreed reluctantly, "but I got so lonesome for you over there that I was desperate! When they gave me the chance to come home, I jumped at it, without even considering the cost!"

"Well, it's done now," Beth comforted him. "Let's enjoy our time together as much as we can. We'll just have to trust the Lord to keep you safe in the war in the Pacific like He did in the war in Europe."

The next several weeks flew by all too quickly. Beth was able to get a week's vacation from her job, and she and Clifford spent it at her parents' cottage at Green Pond, enjoying a real honeymoon at last! To her delight, she found out that Clifford loved the water as much as she did. He was an excellent swimmer, and they spent

many delightful hours swimming and canoeing together.
However, Beth's bliss at being with Clifford was continually
tempered by the sobering knowledge of what he would have to
face when he left her.

One evening in mid-August, shortly before Clifford was to
leave for the Pacific, they decided to attend a symphony concert in
New York City. They boarded the subway and managed to find
seats in a crowded car that was filled with many other young men
in uniform, most accompanied by their wives or girlfriends. As the
car rushed along on its underground track, Beth nestled in the
shelter of Clifford's protecting arm.

Suddenly, the loudspeaker system crackled to life. The voice of
the engineer exclaimed excitedly, "Ladies and gentlemen, I have
wonderful news! Japan has unconditionally surrendered to the
Allies! The war is over!"

The car erupted into joyful cheers. Total strangers began
hugging each other and slapping each other on the back. When
Clifford and Beth emerged from the subway at their stop, the scene
was repeated on a much larger scale. Car horns were blaring and
church bells were ringing. People were running down the street,
delirious with happiness, shouting, and embracing anyone who
happened to be nearby. So it was that August 14, 1945 was
celebrated as V-J Day—the day that brought the long nightmare of
World War II to an end at last!

Although Beth thought that the music played at the concert that
night was some of the most beautiful that she had ever heard, it
couldn't compare with the song of praise that filled her heart. How
she thanked the Lord that Clifford was safely home with her at
last!

The next day, when Beth returned from work, she was surprised
to see a shiny new black Lincoln Continental car parked by the
curb in front of the Roths' house. "I wonder who could be visiting
the Roths," she thought. "It certainly must be someone rich and

important to own a car like that." She ran quickly up the steps and into the house, burning with curiosity to find out who the mysterious guest might be.

As soon as she entered the living room, Clifford jumped up from the sofa where he had been sitting, swooped her up in his arms and spun her around. "Well, Beth, what do you think of our new car? Isn't it beautiful?"

Beth was momentarily speechless with amazement. When she found her voice again, she cried, "Our new car? I thought that it belonged to someone visiting the Roths! Oh, Clifford, it's a lovely car, but isn't it terribly expensive? How can we afford a car like that?"

"Don't you worry about that, Beth. That's my business," Clifford reassured her. "I'll get a job and make the payments, of course. Besides, we're going to need a big car, because we're moving!"

"Moving!" Beth exclaimed in stunned surprise. "What in the world are you talking about, Clifford?"

"I got some great news today, Beth. I made a few phone calls, and I found out that since the war is over, I can get discharged from the service immediately—just as soon as the paperwork is done!"

"Praise the Lord! I'm so glad that you're finally home to stay!"

"And that's only half the good news, dear! As soon as I found out for certain that I could get out of the army, I called Mother Wohner, and she invited us to come and live with her and Father Wohner! So then I went out and bought the car, and as soon as you can give your notice at Norcross and get packed, we're going to hit the road for good ol' Illinois!"

At this most unwelcome news, Beth stood frozen in shocked silence. She felt as if her heart had fallen from its normal place in her chest and was now competing for space in the toe of one of her shoes. "But, Clifford, I had hoped that we could get a little place of our own—just the two of us," Beth protested timidly. "Besides, you know the old saying, 'No house is big enough for two families'."

"Oh, that doesn't apply in this case. We're all part of the same family," Clifford countered. "I can understand that you may feel a little hesitant to move out there, because you and Mother Wohner got off to such a bad start. But this is just what you both need to get to know each other better. It will work out wonderfully. You'll see!"

As Clifford continued to chatter excitedly about his plans for their future, Beth listened in a quiet daze. Her head spun with the rapidity with which he had made his decisions. She felt as if her whole life had been suddenly turned upside down. For the first time, she began to wonder how well she really knew this exuberant, impulsive young man whom she had married!

The following two weeks flashed by in a blur of packing and good-byes, and soon Beth and Clifford were on their way. As they sped down the Pennsylvania Turnpike, Beth was filled with dread of what lay ahead. As she thought of the new home awaiting them in Illinois, she thought wryly that she had never before noticed the two words that seemed to be contained in the name of that state— "ill" and "annoy". From the queasy feeling in the bottom of her stomach, she admitted to herself that those words accurately summed up the present state of her feelings. However, despite her tempestuous emotions, she resolutely turned her burden over to her Heavenly Father. "Father," she breathed in silent prayer, "You've promised that You'll be with me wherever I go, and I know that that even includes Illinois!"

With that settled, she looked out the window and tried to enjoy the passing scenery, which seemed to be zipping by at an unusually rapid rate. She furtively sneaked a glance at the car's speedometer, and was alarmed to see the needle inching up toward ninety miles per hour. "Cliff, dear," she said gently, "don't you think that we're going a little bit too fast?"

"I don't need you to tell me how to drive!" Clifford yelled angrily at her. "And another thing—don't <u>ever</u> call me 'Cliff'! My name is 'Clifford'! I <u>hate</u> nicknames!"

"I'm sorry, dear." Beth was shocked at his unexpected harshness. She had never imagined that her Clifford could lose his temper so easily. Once again, she questioned how well she really knew this man with whom she had promised to spend the rest of her life!

The next two months were a nightmare for Beth. Shortly after they moved in with the Wohners, Clifford found a job as a clerk in a department store in Kankakee. This left Beth alone each day with Mrs. Wohner, who was no friendlier to Beth than when she had first met her. Although Beth cheerfully helped with the work around the house, Mrs. Wohner continually found fault with whatever she did. No matter how hard Beth tried, nothing seemed to be good enough to please Mrs. Wohner.

One day, as Beth was washing the lunch dishes and Mrs. Wohner was drying them, Mrs. Wohner remarked critically, "You simply <u>must</u> try to keep your mind on what you're doing, Beth. You've missed a spot on almost every dish. And this morning after you vacuumed the living room, I found several places that looked like they hadn't even been cleaned. It's the same when you mop the floor or dust the furniture. There's always something left undone. If I have to come along and do the job after you, I'd prefer that you don't even try to help me. I'd rather just do it myself!"

"I'm sorry, Mother Wohner. I'll try to be more careful." Beth fixed her eyes on the pan she was scrubbing, her cheeks burning with embarrassment. She suddenly felt as if she were a little girl at home again, with her mother scolding her for not properly doing her share of the weekly housecleaning.

"Well, I told Clifford that if he married an artist, he wouldn't get much of a housekeeper," Mrs. Wohner continued gloomily. "You artists are all alike. You always have your heads in the clouds. Why, I've noticed that whenever you have any spare time, you spend it either drawing a picture or else playing music on that cello of yours. You could be doing something useful, you know, like sewing or knitting or crocheting!"

It was true. Whenever Beth had a spare moment, she would either retire to her room and pour out her soul in her music, or else she would walk to the little park nearby, sketch pad in hand, and sit on a bench drawing pictures of interesting-looking passersby. It was the only escape that she had from the depressing environment in which she was forced to live.

That night, as Beth lay in Clifford's arms, she sobbed, "Oh, Clifford, I don't know what else to do. I've tried my best to please Mother Wohner, but nothing I do is ever good enough!"

"Don't let it worry you, dear," Clifford comforted her. "It is just taking a while for her to get to know you. I'm sure that she'll soon learn to appreciate the special talents the Lord has given you."

"That's the worst part of it," Beth confided. "She thinks that art and music are just a waste of time, and that the only worthwhile use of time is to do something that she considers useful, like sewing or knitting."

"Well, let's turn this problem over to the Lord," Clifford counseled. After they had both poured out their hearts to their Savior, Beth drifted off into a peaceful sleep. Her last conscious thought was a prayer of thanksgiving to God for giving her a Christian husband with whom she could pray about things.

However, as the weeks passed, Beth began to notice a change in Clifford's attitude toward her. He seemed to be absorbing Mrs. Wohner's critical disposition. One night as they sat together in their room, he looked around at the assorted piles of their belongings, which occupied almost every available inch of space, and remarked irritably, "I don't understand why you can't keep our room neat. Mother Wohner keeps this whole house spic and span, but you can't even keep this one room clean."

"I'm sorry, dear. I'll try to do better." She looked around at the confused jumble of all their earthly possessions, which were crammed into one small bedroom. Despairingly, she thought, "Mother's housekeeping motto was always 'A place for everything, and everything in its place'. But what do you do when you don't have 'a place for everything'?"

The following Sunday, Clifford sat impatiently out by the curb in the Lincoln and honked the horn, as Beth hurried down the steps. "You're late again!" he yelled angrily, as she slid into the seat beside him. "I'm sick and tired of always being fifteen minutes late for church! It's embarrassing! I was never late before I married you!"

Once again, Beth found herself murmuring an apology, and this time she knew that Clifford's reprimand was deserved. Ever since she had been a little girl, being late had been one of her worst faults, and it seemed that no matter how many good resolutions she made, she could never seem to overcome it.

Several times during the next week, Beth came into the living room to find Clifford and Mrs. Wohner talking together in low tones, engaged in an earnest discussion. Each time she entered, however, the conversation abruptly ended, so she could only conclude that she had been its subject.

The Sunday before Thanksgiving, Beth felt unusually tired. After dinner, she went up to the bedroom to rest and soon dozed off. Several hours later, she awoke, feeling refreshed, and went downstairs and walked quietly into the living room. As she entered the room, she heard Mrs. Wohner say emphatically, "I told you it was a big mistake!" Beth cleared her throat nervously, and Clifford looked up at her in guilty embarrassment.

"Sit down, Beth." Mrs. Wohner had a cruel gleam in her icy gray eyes. "Clifford and I have something important to talk to you about."

Clifford fidgeted uneasily in his chair. Beth thought that she had never seen him look so uncomfortable. "Beth," he said nervously, "Mother Wohner and I have been doing a lot of talking during this past week, and I've finally come to the conclusion that she is right about you and me. We didn't really know each other when we got married, and I'm afraid that our marriage was a terrible mistake. She has suggested that we should just admit that we made a mistake and end our marriage and go our separate ways. I'll give you the money to go back to New Jersey. You can be home in time to spend Thanksgiving with your folks."

"Yes, Beth." Mrs. Wohner's thin lips twisted upward in a smile of triumph. "You must put this unfortunate episode in your life behind you. Go back to New Jersey, and be all that Beth Conrad ever was!"

Instantly, Beth was overwhelmed with a greater grief than she had ever known. Almost faint with the shock of it, she was totally at a loss to know how to reply to this unexpected announcement. "But, Clifford," she finally protested when she had found her voice, "we promised God that we would stay together 'till death do us part'! Surely we can work through our differences!"

"No, Beth, the decision has been made," Clifford replied firmly. "There is nothing else that we need to talk about."

Several days before Thanksgiving, as the train pulled into the Newark station, with a heartbroken Beth on board, Mrs. Wohner's cruel words echoed and re-echoed in her mind, "Go back to New Jersey, and be all that Beth Conrad ever was!"

In reply, her heart cried out, "But I <u>can't</u> 'be all that Beth Conrad ever was'! I'm not Beth Conrad anymore! I'm Beth Conrad <u>Frazier</u>!"

During the endless ride from Illinois to New Jersey, Beth had come to one firm decision, however. She would not go home immediately. She needed some time to be alone—to think and pray—to pour out her heart to her Heavenly Father and to seek His guidance.

After disembarking from the train, she called a cab and directed the driver to take her to the YWCA. Later that night, in her tiny rented room, she lay sobbing on the bed. "Oh, Father," she cried out in despair, "How can I go home and tell Mother and Dad and Dot and Bake that our marriage has failed? They don't even know You, and yet <u>they</u> have <u>happy</u> marriages. What a terrible testimony this will be to them! Oh, Lord Jesus, what should I do?"

As she lay on the bed, weeping inconsolably, she gradually felt an unexplainable and supernatural peace begin to quiet her troubled soul. She also felt an unmistakable conviction that she did not need to immediately tell her family all the facts of her situation. After all, it was Thanksgiving time, and for the next several days, they would just think that she had come home to visit for the holiday. She felt a quiet assurance that when the time came for her to speak, the Lord would give her the right words to say.

With this decision made, she rose from the bed, went to the washroom, and splashed cold water on her face to try to erase the evidence of her tears. Then she went downstairs, found a phone, and called her parents' number. The phone rang several times, and at last she heard her mother's voice on the other end saying, "Hello?"

"Mother, it's Beth," she tried to say brightly. "Guess what! I'm coming home for Thanksgiving!"

"What a wonderful surprise! Is Clifford coming with you?"

"No, he wasn't able to get away from his job," Beth answered truthfully.

Beth tried to keep her voice light and cheerful during the rest of the brief conversation, but she was relieved when it was finished, and she could once again escape to the privacy of her room.

The day before Thanksgiving, Beth sat at the breakfast table with Dad and Mother, eating Mother's delicious blueberry pancakes and trying to make cheerful conversation. Suddenly and unexpectedly, a wave of nausea engulfed her. She rose abruptly from the table and fled hurriedly into the bathroom, where she promptly lost her breakfast. As the day went on, Beth's stomach gradually recovered from its queasiness, and by suppertime, she felt normal once more and enjoyed a hearty meal.

On Thanksgiving morning, Beth and Mother and Dad sat leisurely chatting at the breakfast table, joined by Dot, Bake, and Stu, who had come for the day. Even as Beth's nose inhaled the delicious smell of the ham and eggs on her plate, she could also smell the delectable aroma of turkey and pumpkin pies wafting in from the kitchen. The odd blend of odors overpowered her, and her stomach once again began to churn. Quickly excusing herself and covering her mouth with her hand, she again rushed to the bathroom, arriving there just in time to prevent a disastrous accident.

When she returned to the table, she was surprised to see broad smiles on the faces of both her mother and her sister. "We know what's the matter with you!" they chorused knowingly in unison, and then burst out laughing.

Beth stared back at them in speechless surprise. "How did they find out about what has happened to my marriage, and why are they <u>laughing</u> about it?" she wondered in horrified amazement.

However, before she could say a word, Dot continued, "Well, I can see that I'm going to be 'Aunt Dot' in just a few more months! I can hardly wait!"

"And I'm going to be a grandpa again!" Dad beamed.

Suddenly, the wonderful truth of what they were talking about dawned upon Beth, like the sunrise of a beautiful new day. She had been so upset during the previous weeks that she hadn't noticed that the event which had taken place like clockwork each month since she was thirteen years old had not occurred this month. "When was the last time it happened?" she silently questioned herself. After a moment of thought, she concluded, "I think it was around the first part of October." That, put together with her unusual tiredness and her unpredictable nausea, confirmed in Beth's mind that her family's diagnosis of her problem was correct. She was going to be a mother! Her cheeks glowed with a rosy blush and her eyes shone with joy, as she raised them to meet those of her delighted family.

As her family chattered excitedly together about the new baby, Beth came to a quiet, but firm, decision. She would never tell her family the real reason she had come back to New Jersey. She would return to Clifford and make their marriage work. She <u>must</u> do so for the sake of the new little life that she was carrying within her! That dear little one, whom she loved already with a mother's love, needed both a mother <u>and</u> a father!

The following day, Beth walked determinedly down the street to the nearest payphone, and asked the operator to ring the Wohners' number. Her hands trembled as she held the receiver and waited as the phone rang. She breathed a quick prayer for strength and wisdom. "Hello?" she heard Mrs. Wohner answer on the other end of the line.

"Mrs. Wohner, this is Beth," Beth said through quivering lips. "I need to speak to Clifford, please. Is he there?"

"Yes, he's here, but he wouldn't want to speak to you! Like he told you, your marriage is over!"

"But Mrs. Wohner, I must speak to him!" Beth pleaded. "This is an emergency!"

"Oh, very well," Mrs. Wohner conceded reluctantly
.

A moment later, Clifford came onto the line. "What is it, Beth?" he asked abruptly.

"Clifford," Beth said, gently, but firmly, "I'm coming back to Illinois. I will not let our marriage end! This doesn't involve just the two of us anymore!"

"What on earth are you talking about, Beth?"

"You're going to be a father, Clifford! I'm expecting a baby!"

Dead silence greeted this announcement, but a moment later, Beth heard Clifford's shout of joy. "Praise the Lord! That's wonderful news!" he shouted into the phone. Then he continued more calmly. "You're absolutely right, Beth. This changes everything! We need to stay together. Let me know when you're coming home, and I'll be there to meet the train!"

# Chapter 8—New Life!

When the train pulled into the Kankakee station, Beth was relieved to see that Clifford was there alone. He swept her into his embrace. "I don't know what I was thinking when I sent you away! I really <u>do</u> love you, Beth! I know now that the devil was trying to use Mrs. Wohner to destroy our marriage. Can you ever forgive me?"

"Of course, Clifford!" Beth turned her face upward to receive his tender kiss.

As they drove through the streets toward the Wohners' house, Clifford announced, "Ever since you called me, I've been thinking and praying about what we should do next. I can see now that you were right when you said, 'No house is big enough for two families'. Anyway, I've decided that, after everything that has happened, we need to get a place of our own. I'm planning to go back to school at Moody Bible Institute in January, so we might as well just move to Chicago and get settled there right now."

"That's a wonderful idea, Clifford!" Beth's eyes shone. Inwardly she breathed a heartfelt prayer of thanksgiving to her Heavenly Father for such a marvelous answer to prayer.

Clifford and Beth soon found a little apartment that was within walking distance of Moody Bible Institute, and also of Henrotin Hospital, the place where they planned for their baby to be born. Though the apartment was tiny, consisting of only one room, which served as living room, bedroom, and kitchen, plus a small bathroom, Beth felt that she could not have been happier if it were a palace! At last, she and Clifford had a place of their very own, where they could be by themselves and no longer experience Mrs. Wohner's jealous interference. The first night in their little dwelling, as Beth lay in the circle of Clifford's embrace, she murmured, "I feel like we're home at last!"

As the months went by, Beth was agreeably surprised to find that her pregnancy was not nearly as uncomfortable as her mother and Dot had warned her that it would be. By the time that Clifford started school at Moody in mid-January, her morning sickness had already become a thing of the past, and the only evidence that she had of her pregnancy was her steadily expanding waistline.

However, on Valentine's Day evening, as she and Clifford were lying in bed talking, she received a very special reminder that there was indeed a new little person growing inside of her. Suddenly, she felt, for the very first time, the gentle movement of her child. "Clifford," she cried joyfully, "I just felt our baby kick!"

"That's wonderful, Beth! By the way, I've been thinking a lot lately about what we should name our little son."

"What do you mean—our son?" Beth questioned in amazement. "What makes you so sure that we're going to have a boy? We have just as much chance of having a little girl, you know!"

"Naw." Clifford replied confidently. "I'm absolutely certain that this baby is a boy. Boys run in my family, you know. Why, my mother had <u>seven</u> boys before she ever had one girl. You just wait and see; we're going to have a son!"

Beth was quiet for a moment, wondering how Clifford would respond if the baby did turn out to be a girl. Then she asked curiously, "Well, have you thought of a name that you like?"

"Yes, I've thought of the perfect name! I have decided that whether our child is a boy or a girl, it will be named Eberly Wohner Frazier. You see, I want to honor both of my mothers— my physical mother, and also my spiritual mother. Like I've told you, my mother's maiden name was Eberly, and she had one brother and two sisters. Since she and her sisters all got married, and her brother never had any children, the Eberly name is in danger of being lost and forgotten. So I'd like our child to carry on my mother's family name. And I want to honor Mother Wohner too. In spite of everything, she has done a lot for me, and I appreciate it."

Beth lay for a moment in stunned silence, groaning inwardly as she thought of her baby being burdened for life with such a strange name. "Are you sure that you really want to give our baby such an unusual name?" she questioned doubtfully. "The poor child will have to spend his entire life explaining what his name is, and then telling people how to spell it!"

"Of course I'm sure! It will be a great name for our son—one that he can be proud of!" With this important matter settled, Clifford promptly turned over and went to sleep.

As Beth lay awake in the stillness, which was punctuated by Clifford's snores, she realized that it would be fruitless to argue with him about the matter. Already, in their short married life, she had learned that he usually made his decisions without consulting her, and then expected her to accept them without question. "How I wish that Clifford and I could talk things over calmly and reach a decision <u>together</u>, like Mother and Dad do, and like Dot and Bake do, in their marriages," she thought wistfully. "There's <u>one</u> thing that he can't control, though," she thought with a repressed giggle. "If this baby is a girl, there's not a thing that he can do about it! The Lord has already made that decision!"

The next several months dragged by, as Beth waited with eager anticipation for the birth of her child. July in Chicago was hot and muggy, and the baby's due date of July 16<sup>th</sup> came and went without incident. As Beth's abdomen swelled to a gigantic size, and the little person inhabiting her womb performed his daily gymnastics workouts, she began to feel as if she had been pregnant forever.

On the evening of July 29<sup>th</sup>, the phone rang, and Clifford picked it up. He listened for a bit and then replied, "I'm sorry to hear that, Mother Wohner! Yes, I'll be right over."

Turning to Beth, he announced, "Father Wohner is having chest pains, and Mother Wohner is afraid that he might have a heart attack. She wants me to stay there with them tonight. She really needs me, Beth! You'll be all right until tomorrow, won't you?"

"I suppose so," Beth agreed reluctantly. "But, Clifford, what if the baby comes tonight?"

"Oh, I don't think it will," he assured her. "But, if it does, call me and I'll come right home!"

Beth went to bed early that night, and tossed and turned in a fitful sleep filled with outlandish dreams. At two o'clock the next morning, July 30, 1946, she awoke with a start, gripped with a strong painful pressure in her lower abdomen. She lay motionless, breathing deeply until the pain subsided. "Is this it?" she questioned herself. For the next half-hour, she timed the contractions, which came regularly every ten minutes. Then she rose from her bed, went to the phone, and asked the operator to ring the Wohners' number.

"Hello?" she heard Mrs. Wohner's sleepy voice answer.

"Mrs. Wohner," Beth gasped as another contraction seized her, "Tell Clifford that it's time! Tell him I'm having our baby!"

The next moment, Clifford was on the line. "I'll be there as soon as I can, Beth. Just wait till I get home, and I'll take you right to the hospital."

"I don't know if I can wait that long, Clifford!" Beth panted into the phone, but he had already hung up. Looking at the clock, Beth saw that it had only been eight minutes since the last contraction. "I've got to get to the hospital right away," she thought.

Quickly, she packed a small suitcase with the things she would need, and hurried out the door, down the stairs, and out into the hot summer night. "The hospital is only three blocks away," she thought. "I'm sure that I can walk that far."

She started down the street carrying her suitcase, but before she had taken ten steps, another contraction held her in its grasp. "Lord Jesus, help me!" she pleaded. She laid the suitcase down and sat on it, breathing hard, until the pain had passed.

So began a recurring sequence of events. Beth would walk as far as she could go between contractions. Then, when a contraction began, she would sit on her suitcase, crying out to the Lord for strength, as she endured the pain.

At last, she reached the hospital and went inside. Just as she approached the nurse's station, she doubled over with the most excruciating pain she had yet experienced. The nurse rushed to support her and helped her into a wheelchair. "Where's your husband?" she demanded.

"He's out of town," Beth gasped. "I walked here."

"You <u>walked</u> here!" the nurse exclaimed in astonishment. "How on earth did you manage to do that?"

"The Lord helped me," Beth responded wearily.

For the next several hours, Beth's contractions increased greatly, both in frequency and in intensity. By six o'clock in the morning, she felt that she was living in a world where the only reality was continual, agonizing pain. She tossed and moaned on her bed, but she set her lips firmly and would not allow herself to cry out.

As the hours passed, she felt an increasing weariness begin to deaden her awareness. She felt as if she could not endure even one more contraction. "Father, I'm <u>so</u> tired!" she groaned. "Please give me strength!"

Through the relentless waves of pain, Beth became dimly aware that a doctor was examining her. Turning to the nurse at his side, the doctor announced abruptly, "This woman can't have this baby naturally. She is too small to deliver it. If this keeps up, both she and the child will die! We've got to get her to the operating room fast!"

Through a haze of anguish, Beth struggled to focus on the papers that the nurse brought for her to sign. Her father had always told her that she must never sign anything without reading it carefully first. However, as the letters on the page danced and swam before her eyes, she knew that in this instance it would be impossible to follow his advice. Grasping the pen in her shaking hand, she signed the consent form for her own emergency Caesarian operation.

Moments later, in the operating room, the anesthesiologist instructed Beth, "Now, take a deep breath." She inhaled deeply and immediately sank, exhausted, into a blessed oblivion.

From far away, Beth could hear a voice faintly calling her name. She stirred slightly in her sleep. She did not want to wake up. It was such a blessed relief to be free of pain at last, that she felt she wanted to sleep forever. But the insistent voice would not be stilled. It continued calling her—summoning her back to consciousness. The voice seemed vaguely familiar, but in her drugged state, her mind refused to identify it. Hours later, as the voice continued pulling her back from the brink of eternity, she drowsily opened her eyes and saw Clifford's worried face bending over her. "Oh course," she thought sleepily. "It was Clifford who has been calling me all of this time."

"Oh, Beth, I thought I had lost you!" Clifford cried in relief. "The doctors said that they didn't know if you would ever wake up or not, because you were so exhausted from all the labor that you went through before they gave you the anesthesia. They said that the only hope was if someone that you knew well stayed here by your bedside and called your name. I've been calling you for hours! Praise the Lord! You're going to be all right now!" Beth tried to reply, but her weary lips refused to respond to her brain's commands, and she soon drifted off into a restful sleep.

That evening, Beth finally regained full consciousness of her surroundings. "Well, Mrs. Frazier," a nurse smiled down at her, "We're so happy that you are still with us. I'm happy to tell you that you're the mother of a healthy eight-pound, six-ounce baby girl! Would you like to see her?"

Beth's mouth fell open in amazement. Their baby was a girl! She wondered how Clifford had taken this unexpected news. "A girl?" she questioned weakly. "But my husband had his heart set on having a son! How did he take the news?"

The nurse chuckled in amusement, remembering the scene that had taken place that morning. "Well, when I said to him, 'Mr. Frazier, you have a healthy baby girl', he was totally speechless. His mouth just dropped open in astonishment, and he didn't say a word. Finally I asked him, 'Well, do you want her, or shall we take her back?' By that time, he had recovered enough from his shock to say, 'Oh, yes, we'll keep her! We'll keep her!'"

"Let me go get her for you," the nurse continued, bustling out of the room. A few moments later, she returned with a tiny bundle enveloped in a pink blanket. She placed the baby in Beth's arms, and for the first time, Beth gazed into the face of her newborn daughter.

Looking down, she saw a rosy face, surrounded by thick dark hair, which had been shaped into a curl on the top of Eberly's head. Sleepy baby eyes blinked up at Beth, a little mouth opened in a yawn, and a tiny baby fist escaped the confinement of the blanket and waved back and forth in the air. "Why, she's beautiful!" Beth breathed in rapture. "I always thought that newborn babies were ugly, red, wrinkled little things, but she's beautiful!"

"Yes, she is!" exclaimed Clifford, who had quietly followed the nurse into the room, and was now standing at Beth's bedside, beaming down at his wife and his new daughter. He bent and kissed Beth's cheek gently. "Thank you, my dearest, for giving me such a precious gift!"

Beth leaned back on her pillow with a contented sigh, cradling Eberly in her arms. As she looked from the peaceful face of her now-sleeping infant to the joyful face of her husband, her heart felt almost ready to burst with happiness. She closed her eyes and breathed a prayer of thanksgiving, which rose from a spirit overflowing with gratitude. Words failed her, and all she could utter was, "Thank You, Father! Oh, thank You so much!"

The following months flew by in a rosy haze of joy and busyness, as Beth adjusted to her new role of mother. She reveled in watching Eberly's growth, and rejoiced in each new milestone in the development of her tiny daughter. She and Clifford didn't have much time together, since school and work kept him extremely busy. However, when he was at home, he joined Beth in marveling at the miracle of the new life that was unfolding before their eyes.

One night, as they were entertaining friends in their tiny apartment, one of them commented on Eberly's amazing resemblance to Clifford. "Look at that face!" she exclaimed. "She looks just like her father. You should have named her Clifforeen!" Clifford beamed with pride at this remark, and Beth could tell that he had completely gotten over his disappointment that Eberly was not a boy.

The school year sped by, and soon it was spring. One balmy night in early April, as Clifford and Beth were eating supper, the telephone rang insistently. Clifford answered it and listened for a moment, his face suddenly turning pale with shock and sorrow. "That's terrible, Mother Wohner! I'm so sorry! Yes, I'll be there as soon as I can!"

Hanging up the phone, he turned to Beth. "Father Wohner died this afternoon. He just suddenly dropped dead on the sidewalk. It must have been a heart attack. I've got to go to be with Mother Wohner. She needs me!" Without even finishing supper, he grabbed his hat and car keys and hurried out the door.

The night after Mr. Wohner's funeral, Clifford and Beth lay in bed talking. "Poor Mother Wohner is heartbroken!" Clifford said sadly. "She told me this afternoon that she just can't face living alone in that big empty house. She asked us to come and live with her, and I told her that we would be there as soon as we can get packed."

Beth's heart sank. She had been so thankful when they had moved to Chicago, and the thought of once again living with the woman who hated her so much seemed like more than she could bear. "But, Clifford," she protested, "what about your schooling? You've been doing so well at Moody! Don't you think that you should stay here and finish your training? After all, you prayed about it, and you felt sure that the Lord led us here."

"I've already thought about that. I'll just transfer to Olivet Nazarene College in Kankakee."

Beth knew her husband well enough by now to realize that further discussion of the matter was pointless. However, long after Clifford had fallen asleep, Beth lay wide awake, tears streaming down her cheeks. Silently, she poured out her broken heart to God and begged Him for strength to respond in a Christ-like way to this terrible trial.

For Beth, living with Mrs. Wohner proved to be like the recurrence of a terrible nightmare. Once again, Clifford was gone most of the time, leaving her and Eberly alone with Mrs. Wohner. Beth soon found that grief had not improved either Mrs. Wohner's disposition or her acceptance of Beth's place as Clifford's wife. Clifford spent most of each evening reading the Bible and praying with Mrs. Wohner, and attempting to console her in her bereavement. Meanwhile, Beth sat upstairs with Eberly, trying to keep her quiet, so that she wouldn't bother Mrs. Wohner. Whenever Eberly started to cry, Beth would immediately hear angry footsteps on the stairs. A moment later there would be a sharp knock at the door, and a fretful voice would demand, "Can't you keep that child quiet? I've got a splitting headache!"

However, as the months passed, and Eberly began walking and saying her first words, Beth noticed a gradual change in Mrs. Wohner's attitude toward the child. One sunny day in early December, Beth took Eberly and some of her toys out onto the sun porch to get her out of Mrs. Wohner's way. "Look, Eberly!" Beth cranked the handle of a jack-in-the-box. "Look at the funny clown!" Eberly clapped her hands and giggled in delight as the jack-in-the-box popped up.

Just then, Mrs. Wohner walked out onto the porch and sat down in a rocking chair. Her face softened as she looked at Eberly's delighted smile. "She's so much like her father," she commented

"Yes, she is."

"Do you think I could hold her?" Mrs. Wohner asked hesitantly.

"Why, of course you could!" Beth replied pleasantly, scooping her baby up and handing her to Mrs. Wohner. Beth watched in wonder as the older woman cradled Eberly in her arms and rocked her gently back and forth, unconsciously humming a lullaby. "Perhaps this is how the Lord is going to answer my prayers," she thought hopefully, "Maybe He is going to use Eberly to heal the breach between Mrs. Wohner and me."

After supper that night, as Beth started up the stairs carrying Eberly, Mrs. Wohner called to her. "Why don't you and the baby stay down here with us tonight?"

"We'd be glad to!" Beth sat down beside Clifford on the sofa, as he opened his Bible to read aloud.

A few minutes later, Eberly began to fuss and squirm restlessly on Beth's lap. As Beth got up to leave the room, Mrs. Wohner rose from her chair. "Here, let me take her for a while." As she settled back down in her rocking chair, with Eberly on her lap, she murmured soothingly, "There, there! What's the matter with Grandma's dolly?" Beth watched in amazement as her little girl relaxed in the old woman's arms and soon drifted off into a peaceful sleep.

Much to Beth's disappointment, however, she soon found that Mrs. Wohner's acceptance of Eberly did not improve her own relationship with the old lady. Instead, it expanded Mrs. Wohner's jealousy of Beth to include envy of her closeness to Eberly. As Beth cared for her baby each day, she noticed in Mrs. Wohner's eyes the same smoldering anger that she had first observed when she and Clifford had been on their honeymoon.

Also, because she firmly believed that Beth was not only an incompetent housewife, but also an unfit mother, Mrs. Wohner now had a whole new arsenal from which to launch a barrage of critical remarks at Beth. At last, Beth was forced to conclude that Mrs. Wohner had included Eberly in her small circle of love and acceptance only because she was Clifford's daughter.

One snowy morning in January, Beth was struggling with the daily chore of combing the stubborn snarls out of Eberly's soft, fine hair after shampooing it. Hearing Eberly's unhappy wails, Mrs. Wohner marched up the stairs and entered the bathroom, without even bothering to knock. "What on earth are you doing to that child, Beth?" she demanded indignantly. "It sounds like you're killing her!" Then turning to Eberly, her voice softened. "What's that mean old mommy of yours doing to you, Sweetheart?" she cooed. "Is she hurting Grandma's dolly?"

Unable to think of a suitable answer to this rude interruption, Beth silently continued with her task, inwardly praying that the Lord would give her a patient and forgiving attitude toward Mrs. Wohner.

At lunchtime that same day, Beth sat at the table feeding strained carrots to Eberly, who promptly made known her dislike of this vegetable by spitting it out as quickly as Beth fed it to her. Mrs. Wohner frowned disapprovingly. "You really must be firmer with Eberly, Beth. If you don't make her obey you now, she will grow up to be a very rebellious girl! I declare, I can't imagine why the Lord saw fit to give you a child. You certainly have no idea how to care for one properly!"

With difficulty, Beth repressed the desire to angrily retort that since Mrs. Wohner had never had a child, she was certainly no expert on child rearing! Instead, she replied gently, "Well, I realize that I have a lot to learn, Mother Wohner, but I'm praying every day that the Lord will give me wisdom in raising Eberly, and He has promised to give wisdom to those who ask Him!"

That evening, after their regular Bible reading and prayer time together, Mrs. Wohner turned to Clifford. "I've been watching Beth taking care of Eberly, and I think that it's too much for her to do it all by herself. I'd be glad to care for Eberly part of the time. After all, I love her just as much as if she were my very own granddaughter."

"Why, that's really kind of you, Mother Wohner! Isn't it, Beth?" Clifford beamed, turning to Beth for her approval. And Beth had no choice but to agree.

So it was that each afternoon, Mrs. Wohner had Eberly all to herself. Beth enjoyed having some free time in which she could play music and do artwork, but she missed the company of her little daughter. Also, the selfish motives behind Mrs. Wohner's sudden burst of helpfulness grieved her heart, and she was deeply concerned about the effect that such an unbalanced person would have on her little girl.

As winter turned to spring, Beth noticed that a new word had been added to Eberly's growing vocabulary. In addition to "mama" and "dada", she was often heard to ask for "g'amma", much to Mrs. Wohner's delight. However, each time Beth heard her daughter referring to Mrs. Wohner by that endearing name, she cringed inwardly.

As the school year was coming to an end, Beth noticed that Clifford was growing more and more dissatisfied with the doctrine that he was being taught at Olivet Nazarene College. One night as they lay in bed, he remarked in frustration, "I just can't agree with my professors that it's possible for a person to lose his salvation if he sins. I believe that the Bible teaches that once we receive Christ, we are saved forever."

"So do I, Clifford! If you could lose your salvation, you wouldn't have eternal life, would you?" A moment later she suggested hesitantly, "Perhaps you should go back to Moody again. You really enjoyed the teaching of the professors there."

Clifford sighed. "I'd really like to, Beth, but I'm not sure if they would accept me again, since I dropped out during the middle of the semester when Mr. Wohner died."

"How about going to a different school, then?" Beth suggested. "Just the other day, I got a letter from my friend Mrs. Roth. She was telling me that Bill Mierop, the brother of my former pastor, is now the president of a Bible institute in Philadelphia. I'm sure that if he's the president, it's a good school!"

"That sounds interesting. Why don't you write and find out more about it for me?"

The next day, Beth wrote to Philadelphia Bible Institute to ask for information, and for the next several weeks she checked the mail eagerly every day. At last, the packet of literature came, and she could hardly wait for Clifford to come home so that she could show it to him.

After studying the school's catalog and praying about it together, Clifford and Beth both felt that the Lord was leading them to move to Philadelphia so that he could complete his schooling at Philadelphia Bible Institute.

Eberly's second birthday found Clifford, Beth, and Eberly settled in a small apartment in Philadelphia, within walking distance of the Bible school. How thankful Beth was to be living in a place of their own again, away from the critical eyes and caustic comments of Mrs. Wohner!

Soon, classes started, and Clifford was once again busy with the demanding schedule of attending school and working to support their family. Beth rejoiced as he shared with her what he was learning, and how much he enjoyed sitting under the teaching of the godly professors at the Bible institute. She was assured that Clifford had come to the right place for his training.

However, she was concerned about how hard he was working. "How I wish that I could help him in some way!" she sighed one day.

The following morning, as she was praying, a wonderful idea suddenly occurred to her, and caused her to exclaim excitedly, "Why, that's the answer! And it's something that I can do right here at home! Thank You, Father!"

That same afternoon, Beth put Eberly in her stroller and walked purposefully through the streets of downtown Philadelphia, carrying her portfolio of artwork. Stopping at several publishing houses, she managed to obtain interviews with their art directors and offered them her services as a free-lance artist.

Several of them informed her politely that they already had enough artists on their staffs and had no need of her help. However, at the last establishment that she visited, Mr. Browning, the art director, said, "I'm really impressed with the quality of your work, Mrs. Frazier. We've been looking for someone to illustrate a children's book that we will be publishing soon, and I think that you are just the person to do it." He handed her the manuscript of the book. "Could you have the drawings done in two weeks?"

"I certainly could!" Beth agreed joyfully.

Each afternoon for the next two weeks, while Eberly was taking her nap, Beth drew the pictures for a book about a little boy who had lost his pet cocker spaniel and about all the things that happened before his puppy was finally found. How she rejoiced that she was once again occupied with the work she loved, and that she was helping Clifford at the same time!

When she took the completed illustrations to Mr. Browning, he leafed through them and nodded approvingly. "You've really captured this story in pictures, Mrs. Frazier. Your style is perfect for this type of work. You can be assured that we will have many more assignments for you!"

# Chapter 9—"Spiritual Suicide!"

Only one thing marred Beth's joy during that happy fall of 1948. It was the weekly phone calls that Clifford received from Mrs. Wohner. Her plea was always the same. "Clifford," she would sob over the phone, "I just don't think that I can stand being all alone here any longer in this big old empty house. I miss you and Eberly so much! Won't you please, please, come back home again? I'm ready to die from loneliness!"

After several months of enduring Mrs. Wohner's sorrowful appeals, Beth could see that Clifford's resolve to remain in school was beginning to waver, and that he was beginning to doubt the wisdom of having moved so far away from Mrs. Wohner. "Beth," he said one night, as he hung up the phone after listening to another of Mrs. Wohner's tearful conversations, "Mother Wohner really does need us. She's all alone there in that huge house. Suppose she got sick or fell down and hurt herself! She'd have no one to help her. I'd never forgive myself if anything happened to her! I think that we should consider moving back to Kankakee again."

Beth's heart sank. "But, Clifford," she protested, "before we made this move, we prayed about it, and we <u>both</u> felt sure that it was the Lord's will. I'm sure that the Lord hasn't changed His Mind!"

"Well, perhaps we should pray about it again!" Clifford countered.

"All right," Beth agreed reluctantly.

Several days later, Clifford announced, "I've been praying a lot these last few days about whether we should stay here, or go and live with Mother Wohner again, and I believe that the Lord wants us to move back there. After all, the Bible says that we should care for our parents, and she's been just like a mother to me."

"I've been praying about it too, and I've felt strongly impressed that the Lord wants us to stay here. When I think of staying here, I feel God's peace, but whenever I think of moving back there, I feel a sense of dread, as if something terrible will happen to us if we do that. I can't understand how we can both pray about the same thing and get such opposite answers! Perhaps we are both too emotionally involved in this decision to be able to think clearly. Why don't we ask someone else for advice? The Bible says that 'in the multitude of counselors there is safety'."

Clifford considered her idea for a moment. "That sounds like a good idea. Who do you think we should talk to?"

"How about Dr. Mierop? He's a godly man, and I'm sure that he would give us wise counsel."

"All right. Let's go see him tomorrow."

The following day, Clifford and Beth sat together in Dr. Mierop's office. After they had told him the whole situation, Clifford concluded, "So you see, Dr. Mierop, we need an opinion from someone who isn't involved in this situation.  What do you think we should do?"

"Well, Clifford, you said that before you came here, you prayed about it together, and both you and Beth definitely felt that it was the Lord's will for you to come here to finish your Bible school training.  Is that correct?"

"That's right."

"Then, if God has led you here, He is not going to change His Mind now.  I think that you should stay here and finish your schooling."

"But Mrs. Wohner is just like a mother to me!" Clifford protested.  "I can't stand the thought of leaving her all alone over there!"

"Clifford," Dr. Mierop warned sternly, "I believe that if you choose to go back to Illinois after the Lord has so clearly led you here, you'll be committing spiritual suicide.  You are going to have to decide whether you are going to serve the Lord or Mrs. Wohner!"

"Thanks for the advice, Dr. Mierop," Clifford said curtly, rising abruptly from his chair.  "Let's go home, Beth."

Later that night, Clifford exclaimed, "Beth, I don't care what Dr. Mierop said.  I still think that we should go back and live with Mother Wohner again.  She needs us!"

"But I thought that we had agreed to let Dr. Mierop's opinion settle our disagreement about what we should do!" Beth cried.

"Well, Dr. Mierop isn't the head of this home!  I am, and I make the final decisions around here!" Clifford yelled angrily.  "We're going back to Kankakee, and that's final!  And the Bible says that wives are to submit to their husbands, so you have to do what I say!"

"Yes, dear," Beth replied reluctantly, her heart sinking. She knew that Clifford had made his choice, and that it was useless to discuss it further.

So it was that Christmas Day, 1948 found Beth, Clifford, and Eberly once again sitting with Mrs. Wohner at her dining room table. This time, however, they were not alone with the old lady. The meal was shared with her nephew, Walter Beecher, a newspaperman who had recently moved from Chicago to the Kankakee area.

For some unaccountable reason, Beth felt an instinctive distrust of this pudgy, balding young man. Although he seemed to be the epitome of friendliness, there was a crafty gleam in his eyes that made her feel uneasy. Beth reflected that his eyes resembled those of a fox appraising a chicken that was about to become its next meal. Then she instantly reprimanded herself for being so quick to judge a man whom she barely knew.

"Oh, Clifford, it's so good to have you home again!" Mrs. Wohner beamed affectionately. "And Eberly has grown so much! And she's talking so much more now!"

Mr. Beecher smiled. "Yes, it's really wonderful that you were able to come and visit Aunt Ida for the holidays. She's told me how much she misses you. How long do you plan on staying?"

"Why, we're planning on staying for as long as she needs us!" Clifford replied.

"But don't you have to get back to school again soon?" Mr. Beecher inquired in surprise.

"No, I've quit school. We just couldn't leave Mother Wohner all alone here. She needs our help."

For just a fraction of a second, Beth detected a flash of jealous hatred in Walter Beecher's eyes as he looked at Clifford. It mirrored the look that appeared in his aunt's eyes whenever she looked at Beth. However, it vanished as quickly as it came, his carefully guarded look returned, and she wondered if she were merely imagining things.

Walter said soothingly, "Why, that's really not necessary, Clifford. Now that I'm living here in Kankakee, I plan on looking in on Aunt Ida every day. If there's anything she needs, I'll be right here to take care of it. There's no need for you to sacrifice your education to stay here."

Beth agreed wholeheartedly with Walter's words. How she wished that Clifford would return to Bible school and leave the care of Mrs. Wohner to her nephew! However, she couldn't help mistrusting his motives for this sudden interest in his aunt. During all the time that she had known Mrs. Wohner, the old woman had never mentioned her nephew, and Walter had never before visited his aunt, even though Chicago was little more than an hour's drive away. Beth was aware that since Mrs. Wohner had no children, her money and property would pass to her nearest relative, who happened to be Walter, unless the old lady made other arrangements in her will. Suddenly she understood the reason for the angry glare that had appeared in Walter's eyes when he looked at Clifford! "Why, he's jealous of Clifford! He's afraid of losing his inheritance to Clifford, just like Mrs. Wohner is afraid of losing Clifford to me!" she mused.

"Oh, it's no sacrifice at all!" she heard Clifford state emphatically in response to Walter's offer. "We're glad to do it! Your aunt has been just like a mother to me, and the least we can do is to stay here with her now that she needs our help!"

True to his word, Walter immediately began checking on Mrs. Wohner every day. He faithfully stopped by each evening to chat

153

with her for a few minutes, and if he had to be out of town, he called on the phone each night to make certain that she was all right. And every Sunday, he came over for dinner. One day, as he was eloquently expressing his love and concern for his "favorite auntie", Beth thought wryly to herself, "I have a funny feeling that what he <u>really</u> cares about is the safety of his favorite <u>money</u>!"

At last the dreary winter came to an end, and sunny daffodils and bright tulips proclaimed the coming of spring, with its promise of new life. One warm April morning, as Beth was eating breakfast, she felt a sudden wave of nausea overwhelm her. She jumped up hurriedly from the table and rushed to the bathroom, where she promptly lost her breakfast. Several times during the following week this experience was repeated, and Beth rejoiced as she realized that once again a new little person was growing within her! She could hardly wait to share her wonderful secret with Clifford.

That Saturday night, as they lay in bed together, Beth murmured dreamily, "Clifford, do you remember how much you wanted a boy when I was expecting Eberly?"

"How could I ever forget that? I was sure disappointed when I found out that we had a girl, but now I'd <u>never</u> trade Eberly for a boy!"

Beth smiled. "Well, it looks like you're going to get another chance to have a son!"

Clifford sat bolt upright in bed. "Beth, what are you trying to tell me? Are you pregnant again?"

Beth beamed. "Yes, Clifford. We're going to have another baby!"

"Praise the Lord!" he exclaimed joyfully, gathering her into his arms.

The following day, as they lingered over dessert at the dinner table with Mrs. Wohner and Walter, Clifford announced excitedly, "Beth and I have some wonderful news to share with you, Mother Wohner! We're going to have another baby!"

However, instead of congratulating him, Mrs. Wohner reacted to his enthusiasm with a cold frown of disapproval. "Why on earth would you want another baby, Clifford?" she demanded angrily. "Isn't one child enough? Beth isn't even capable of caring for Eberly properly. How in the world is she going to manage when you have two children?"

Clifford's mouth dropped open in shocked disbelief. "But I thought you'd be happy for us, Mother Wohner! After all, the Bible says that 'children are a heritage of the Lord, and the fruit of the womb is His reward'!"

"Well, you just wait and see," Mrs. Wohner retorted sourly. "You'll find out that two children will be more than your wife can handle!"

By the time that the days grew warmer, and spring was replaced by summer, Beth's nausea had ended. She was very thankful that as her second pregnancy progressed, she had very little discomfort of any kind, and she felt just as well as she had during her first one.

One day toward the end of summer, as she sat in Dr. Bernstein's examining room following a prenatal exam, her doctor remarked, "Well, Mrs. Frazier, as I have told you, your baby is due around November 21$^{st}$, and your pregnancy seems to be going well. However, we don't want to take the chance of having you go into labor, because that would be life-threatening for both you and your baby, so we will schedule your Caesarian for two weeks before your due date. We'll do it on November 7$^{th}$." It seemed strange to Beth that she knew in advance what the birthday of her baby would be, but it was a great relief to know that she would not have to face the excruciating ordeal of labor again.

One night in early fall, as Beth and Clifford lay in bed, Clifford declared, "I'm just <u>sure</u> that we're going to have a boy this time, Beth! And I've got the perfect name picked out for him. I want to name him after my preacher friend Lowell Earnhart."

"I haven't met your friend Lowell yet, have I? Isn't he the one who is an airplane pilot?"

"Yep, that's the one. And he loves to play practical jokes too! Did I ever tell you about the time that Lowell bought me a big lunch, and then took me up in his plane afterwards and flew upside down? Boy, did I ever get sick!" He chuckled at the memory.

Beth joined in Clifford's amusement, and then inquired, "Have you thought of a middle name for our son yet?"

"Yes, I've thought of that too. Since he's my first son, I would like to give him my name for a middle name."

"Lowell Clifford Frazier." Beth tried out the name. "Why, that sounds like a wonderful name for our son, Clifford!"

On a chilly afternoon in late October, Beth was once again sitting in the doctor's office. She had just had her final prenatal examination, and all of the arrangements had been made for her to enter the hospital the following week for the Caesarian. Clifford had gone to do a few errands, and she was waiting for him to return to take her home.

Several hours dragged by, as Beth idly paged through the magazines in the waiting room. Suddenly she noticed that the hands of the clock on the wall were inching toward five o'clock. "Why, it's almost time for this office to close. Clifford should be here by now. Something must have happened to him!" she thought in concern. "Perhaps he had an accident! I sure hope that he's all right!"

Just then the phone on the receptionist's desk rang. The woman answered it, listened for a moment, and then replied, "Yes, she's right here." She turned to Beth. "It's for you, Mrs. Frazier. It's your husband."

Beth took the phone. "Clifford, where are you? Are you all right?"

"I'm in jail, Beth! I've been arrested and framed for something that I didn't do!"

"You're in jail?" Beth questioned in horrified amazement, almost dropping the receiver.

"Yes, and I need your help, because this is the only phone call that I'm allowed to make. Call someone at Moody Church and tell them what has happened to me. Ask them if they can find a Christian lawyer who can help me. I'm in the Cook County Jail."

The world spun crazily around Beth as she shakily handed the telephone back to the receptionist. Seeing Beth's pale face, the woman inquired in concern, "Are you all right, Mrs. Frazier? You look like you need to sit down for a moment."

Trembling all over, Beth sank into a chair and buried her face in her hands. Then she turned instinctively to her Heavenly Father for guidance. "Father, show me what to do," she whispered. A moment later, a name flashed into her mind. "Why, of course," she thought. "I'll call Don and Susan Stone. They were our best friends while Clifford was attending Moody. Don will know what to do."

Several hours later, Beth was sitting in the Stones' kitchen sipping a cup of hot tea. "I can't begin to tell you how much I appreciate your help, Don," she said to her host. "And I'm so thankful that you were able to find such a good Christian lawyer for Clifford!"

"I was glad to do it! And don't you worry about a thing. Clifford is going to be out in no time. Larry Burnside is an excellent lawyer, and he'll get to the bottom of this ridiculous mess." Don shook his head in disbelief. "I just can't believe that anyone would accuse Clifford of a crime. I wonder what in the world he's been charged with."

"Well, I guess we'll soon find out," Susan interjected. "I think I just saw Larry's car pull into our driveway."

A moment later, Clifford and Larry burst through the door. With a sob of relief, Beth fell into Clifford's outstretched arms. "Oh, Clifford, you're all right!" she wept. "I was so worried about you!"

"Tell us all about what happened," Don urged.

"Is it all straightened out now?" Susan inquired.

"Well, after I had done my errands, Beth, I still had a little time before I had to pick you up at the doctor's office, so I decided to go to the park and pass out some tracts," Clifford explained. "I walked over to give tracts to a couple of men who were sitting on a park bench, and suddenly one of them whipped out a badge and informed me that I was under arrest, and then the other one handcuffed me. I tried to ask them what I was being charged with, but they told me not to be a wise guy and said that I'd find that out down at the station. Then they roughed me up pretty good, pushed me into an unmarked car, took me to the police station and threw me in jail. That's when I called you." Beth let out a gasp of horror as she noticed a painful-looking bruise on Clifford's cheek and realized that it had been caused by his violent treatment at the hands of the plain-clothes policemen.

At this point, Larry took up the story. "After Don called me, I hurried right down to the police station and demanded to know what Clifford had been charged with. The officer on duty said that he had been charged with attempting to bribe a police officer, and that they suspected that he was a courier for the Mob here in Chicago." He paused, still unbelieving of the gravity of the charges. "Anyway, I was able to get Clifford out of jail on bail tonight, but he will have to appear at a hearing tomorrow to see if there are grounds for these charges and to determine whether or not he will have to go to trial."

Beth's heart sank. When she had seen Clifford, she had assumed that this nightmare was over, but now it seemed that it might have only begun! "What can we do, Larry?" she asked helplessly. "We all know that Clifford is innocent, but how can we prove it against the word of these men?"

"I'm sure that it must be just a case of mistaken identity, Beth," Larry reassured her. "Probably Clifford looks like someone that they suspect, and that's why they arrested him. Anyway, I've already contacted a number of people who are willing to appear at the hearing tomorrow as character witnesses for him. They should be able to convince the judge that this is all just a terrible mistake."

The following day, Beth sat in the courtroom and prayed, as Clifford stood before the judge. Appearing on his behalf were an assistant pastor of Moody Church, several of his former professors and classmates from Moody Bible Institute, and his music teacher, from whom he was currently taking voice lessons. They all spoke in glowing terms of Clifford's Christian testimony. "Why, I've known Clifford for more than ten years," declared the professor from Moody Bible Institute, "and he's a young man of undisputed Christian character. It's utterly preposterous to imagine that he could in any way be connected with the Mob or any other criminal activity!"

Oddly enough, the two detectives who had arrested Clifford failed to make an appearance, so the charges were dropped due to lack of evidence, and Clifford was released. However, before the court adjourned, the judge turned to the chief of police and gave him a severe reprimand. "There must be something seriously wrong with your department if an innocent man can be harassed and hauled off to jail on groundless charges like these," the judge said sternly. "I direct you to make a full investigation of this case and report back to me with your findings." Then he turned to Clifford. "You are free to go, Rev. Frazier, with this court's sincere apologies. Court adjourned." Upon hearing these welcome words, Beth sank back in her seat in relief, her heart overflowing with gratitude to her Heavenly Father for His protection throughout this whole nightmarish experience.

The following Monday, November 7, 1949, brought a wonderful event which completely eclipsed all thoughts of the bizarre happenings of the previous week. Beth rejoiced as she held her newborn son, Lowell Clifford Frazier. Although she was in pain from her surgery, she felt much stronger than she had felt following the long, excruciating ordeal of Eberly's birth.

As she looked from the sleepy infant that she cuddled in her arms to the beaming face of his proud father, her heart felt as if it would burst with joy, and a song of thanksgiving to God filled her soul. "Oh, thank You! Thank You, Lord, for this precious gift!" she breathed in awe, as she looked down into Lowell's deep blue eyes.

Then turning to Clifford, as she smoothed the fine blond fluff on Lowell's head, she remarked, "I wonder where Lowell got such light-colored hair. Eberly's hair has been dark since the day she was born."

"Oh, didn't I ever tell you that my brothers and I all had blond hair when we were little? Our hair got darker as we got older."

"And my real father had blond hair, too." A vivid picture of Papa's face flashed into Beth's mind. "Perhaps Lowell got it from him." Beth smiled tenderly as she watched Lowell insert a tiny thumb into his mouth, suck it vigorously, and then drift off into a contented sleep.

After a week in the hospital, Beth returned home with the new baby. Eberly was enchanted with her new baby brother. "Can I hold him, Mommy? Please! Please! I'll be real, real careful with him!"

"All right. Sit down in your little rocking chair, and I'll hand him to you. You must be very careful to support his head, though. He's still a very tiny baby."

Gently, Beth handed the baby to her small daughter. As Eberly sat carefully cradling Lowell in her arms, her face beamed with joy. "This is the happiest day of my life!"

However, Mrs. Wohner's reaction to the addition to the family was the exact opposite of Eberly's. She showed no interest in the new baby and no desire to even hold him, and she complained fretfully each time that Lowell cried. One morning at the breakfast table, she sighed pitifully. "I don't think I've had a wink of sleep since you brought that baby home from the hospital. I'm totally worn out. I don't see how I can endure this any longer. Why can't you keep him quiet, Beth?"

Beth suppressed a strong desire to retort angrily that all babies cry sometimes, and that, furthermore, she should be the one complaining of feeling exhausted, since she was up with Lowell every night, and that she would certainly appreciate some help in caring for him. Instead, she said quietly. "I'm sorry that we've been disturbing you, Mother Wohner. I'll try my best to keep Lowell quiet."

Several weeks later, Clifford failed to come home from work at his usual time. Suppertime came and went, and still Beth heard nothing from him. Mrs. Wohner paced the floor of the kitchen. "I wonder where Clifford could be. He's always home on time for supper!"

Just then, a soft knock sounded on the back door. Beth flung it open to find Rev. Collins, their pastor, standing there. An icy hand of fear clutched at her heart. "Something must have happened to Clifford!" she thought. "And Pastor Collins has come to tell us about it."

"Sit down, Beth," Pastor Collins said gently. He looked down into Beth's stricken face. "Clifford called me a few moments ago and asked me to come over and tell you what has happened. He would have called you, but he knew that you were still recovering from your surgery, and he didn't want to alarm you."

"Well, where is he? Is he all right?" Beth burst in, unable to wait any longer for news of her husband.

Pastor Collins hesitated for a moment. "He's in jail, Beth. As soon as he called me, I hurried down to the police station to find out what was going on. They said that he's been charged with attempting to bribe a police officer. The arresting officer said that he thinks that Clifford has some connections with the Mob in Chicago. Clifford said that he was passing out tracts on the street when it happened, and he told me that the very same thing had happened to him just last month in Chicago."

"Yes, it did!" Beth's tears spilled down her cheeks. She felt like she was trapped in a recurring nightmare. "Pastor Collins, would you please call our lawyer friend, Larry Burnside, in Chicago? He's the one who handled the false charges that were brought against Clifford there. He'll know what to do!"

"I've already called him, and he's on his way here right now. When Clifford called me, he gave me Mr. Burnside's name, and asked me to contact him."

"Oh, thank you, Pastor," Beth wept. "You've been a tremendous help!"

"Glad to do it, Beth!"

"Is there any chance that these charges could be true?" Mrs. Wohner interjected suspiciously. "After all, this is the second time that this has happened!" Beth turned to stare at her, open-mouthed in stunned unbelief.

"Of course not, Ida!" Pastor Collins' face mirrored Beth's shocked look. "How could you even think such a thing? Why, the very idea that Clifford could ever be guilty of anything like this is a laughingstock!"

Once again, a hearing was held—this time with character witnesses from the local church that Clifford and Beth so faithfully attended. And once again, the charges were dismissed. "Rev. Frazier," the judge said seriously, before they left the courtroom, "since this has happened to you twice within the past month, I would say that there is more involved here than a simple case of mistaken identity. I suspect that someone is 'out to get you' for some reason. I have ordered the police department here to make a full investigation of this case and to compare their findings with those of the Cook County Police Department in Chicago. When the report is in, we will contact you and let you know our conclusions."

Shortly before Christmas, Beth had to return to the doctor for a postoperative checkup. Since it was a long trip to Chicago, and Beth had not yet fully regained her strength, they decided to take both Eberly and Lowell with them, spend the night at the home of Don and Susan Stone, and return to Kankakee the next day.

The following day, as they stopped in front of Mrs. Wohner's house, Beth was shocked to see a huge stack of boxes and bags sitting on the sidewalk. Balanced precariously on the very top of the heap was her precious cello! "Clifford, what is going on?" she cried.

Upon hearing their car, Mrs. Wohner rushed out of the house, marched down the front walk and shouted angrily, "You're not welcome here anymore, Clifford! Walter has been trying to tell me for a long time that you're just a freeloader who is after my money, and I've finally decided that he's right. Besides, for all I know, you may be a criminal! So take your stuff and leave. I've cleaned it all out of my house." She gestured at the jumbled pile of their belongings, which was strewn haphazardly in the middle of the sidewalk. Without another word, she stalked back into the house and slammed the door.

In shocked disbelief, Clifford jumped from the car, rescued Beth's cello, placed it carefully in the back seat, and sped to Pastor Collins' house. For the next several days, Clifford, Beth, Eberly, and Lowell stayed with the kind pastor and his wife.

Finally, they were able to find a place of their own—a tiny one-bedroom apartment with very little storage space. After friends from church had helped them move in, Clifford surveyed the boxes piled in the living room and shook his head. "There's no way that we can fit all of our things in this place, Beth. We'll just have to put some of them in storage until we can find a larger place."

The next few days were spent sorting through their belongings and packing away anything that was not essential for daily life. Reluctantly, Beth packed away most of their clothes, her wedding dress, all of their wedding pictures except one, and the priceless gifts that had been presented to Clifford by grateful friends in Italy. At last, the boxes were carted away to be stored, and the small apartment began to take on a semblance of order.

On a cold, snowy day in January 1950, the phone rang. Beth picked it up, and heard the voice of Police Chief John Lane on the other end. "Mrs. Frazier, we've completed the investigation of your husband's case, and we've received the report from Chicago on the case that was brought against him there. We'd like you and Rev. Frazier to come down to headquarters so that we can share our findings with you."

Several hours later, Clifford and Beth were sitting in Chief Lane's office. He shuffled through some official-looking papers, and then looked up at Clifford. "Well, Rev. Frazier, we've found out that there was indeed a conspiracy to frame you for a crime that you didn't commit."

Beth gasped in shocked unbelief. "Why, whoever would do such an awful thing?"

"Both we and the police department in Chicago wanted an answer to that same question. The officers involved were questioned, and they admitted that, in both cases, they had been bribed by two individuals to falsely charge and arrest you, Rev. Frazier. Those two people are Mr. Walter Beecher and Mrs. Ida Wohner."

For a moment, both Clifford and Beth sat speechless. Then Clifford found his voice and cried in anguish, "I can easily believe that Walter could be capable of something like this, but why would Mrs. Wohner do such a terrible thing to me?"

"Well, as far as Mr. Beecher is concerned, we have determined that he is criminally insane and will do anything for the sake of money. And Mrs. Wohner seems to be a mentally unbalanced person too. Mr. Beecher managed to convince Mrs. Wohner that you didn't really love her, but were only interested in inheriting her money. Once he had persuaded her of this, she turned against you and was willing to join him in conspiring against you. Their plan was to send you to prison, Rev. Frazier, and then to charge that Mrs. Frazier was an unfit mother and to have the children removed from her custody. After they had accomplished that, Mrs. Wohner planned to adopt Eberly and place Lowell in an orphanage until a suitable adoptive family could be found for him."

At this overwhelming revelation, Beth felt suddenly faint, as she realized how very close these two evil people had come to destroying her entire family and robbing her of all who were dearest to her. "Thank You, Lord Jesus, for Your deliverance!" she whispered.

Later that night, as they sat together in their little apartment, Clifford shook his head in disbelief. "How could I have been so blind, Beth? Why couldn't I see what a wicked old woman Mrs. Wohner is? I should have realized it when she tried to break up our marriage, and when she treated you so terribly! I can't believe that I put you through so much misery!"

"I can understand exactly how it happened, Clifford," Beth soothed. "Your own mother never loved you, and when Mrs. Wohner offered to take you into her home, you were so hungry for love that you never noticed how she was manipulating and controlling you."

"Well, anyway, thank the Lord that my eyes were finally opened to the truth! There's one more thing that I regret, though. How I wish that we had never given 'Wohner' to Eberly for her middle name. For the rest of our lives, we'll be reminded of this horrible nightmare every time we say her name!"

Beth smiled gently. "I feel the same way, Clifford. I've been giving this problem some thought, and I think I've come up with a good solution. Why don't we change Eberly's middle name?"

"That's a great idea, Beth! Do you have any ideas about what we should change it to?"

"Yes. Let's name her 'Lillian', after your Aunt Lillian. That's a lovely name, and she's your favorite aunt, isn't she?"

"Eberly Lillian Frazier." He paused a moment as he considered Beth's suggestion. "I like the sound of it. Let's get her name changed as soon as possible."

The following week, a judge handed Beth an official document, which was to be kept with Eberly's birth certificate. It attested that from that day forward, Eberly Wohner Frazier was to be known as Eberly Lillian Frazier. Beth breathed a huge sigh of relief as she walked down the courthouse steps. She felt as if she had just awakened from a long nightmare to greet a sunny new day! Not only had her little daughter finally been rescued from carrying the burden of that depressing name, but she and Clifford were also free to begin a new chapter in their married life! They had been released from Mrs. Wohner's evil clutches, and they could be a real family at last! "Thank You, Lord Jesus, for setting us free!" her heart sang.

# Chapter 10—Little Schoolhouse in the Big Woods

One hot summer evening in 1950, as they were eating supper, Clifford announced, "I've been thinking and praying a lot lately, and I think that the Lord wants us to move to New Jersey."

Turning to Clifford in amazement, Beth almost dropped the spoonful of pureed peas that she was directing toward Lowell's open mouth. "New Jersey?" she exclaimed in shocked disbelief. "But Clifford, you've always said that it's too crowded back East, and that you like Illinois so much better."

"Well, that was before we had all of this trouble with Mrs. Wohner and Walter Beecher. Ever since that happened, everything in Kankakee reminds me of all the misery we've been through, and that makes me want to get as far away from here as possible. And besides, I'm just barely making enough to pay our bills here. I think that I'll be able to find a better-paying job on the East Coast."

It was true. Clifford's salary was hardly enough to cover the rent and utilities for their small apartment, and to buy food, because a large portion of his wages had to be used to pay their huge monthly car payment. How Beth wished that Clifford would be content with a less expensive car! However, before they had even finished paying for the Lincoln Continental, which Clifford had bought before they moved to Illinois, he had traded it in for a new Lincoln. Beth sighed as she remembered the day he had bought the new car and proudly driven it home—without even consulting her first! For the past two months, they hadn't even been able to pay their storage bill, and now she feared that they were in danger of losing their precious and irreplaceable belongings.

"What will we do about our things that are in storage?" Beth inquired. "I sure don't want to lose them!"

"As soon as I get a good job, we'll pay the storage company what we owe them, and have them ship our stuff to us in New Jersey."

Shortly after Eberly's fourth birthday, they moved to the little town of National Park, New Jersey, not far from the Pennsylvania border. Beth was overjoyed when they were able to rent a two-bedroom house with a small fenced yard, at a fairly reasonable price. It was so much more spacious than their tiny apartment had been, and she was thrilled that Eberly and Lowell would have a place to play outside. She was also happy that they were living closer to her family, so that she would be able to visit them more often.

True to his prediction, Clifford soon found a better-paying job, working in a department store. The following month, Beth was finally able to mail their long-overdue payment to the storage company and to request that their belongings be sent to them.

Several weeks later, an envelope bearing the return address of the storage company arrived in the mail. With a sudden foreboding, Beth ripped it open. Inside, she found the check that she had sent to them, along with a letter. "Dear Rev. and Mrs. Frazier:" she read, "We regret to inform you that the goods which you had stored with us were sold at a public auction last month, due to non-payment of your account. Therefore, we are returning your check to you…" The paper blurred before Beth's eyes, as hot tears fell onto it. "Our wedding pictures, my wedding gown, Eberly and Lowell's baby pictures, Clifford's mementos from Italy—all gone!" she sobbed. "We put some of our most precious possessions in storage, and now they're lost forever!"

That fall, Clifford once again began taking voice lessons. He soon made friends with one of his fellow students, Bart Conley, who began dropping by in the evenings to visit. One night, as Beth walked into the living room bringing coffee and cookies to the two men, she almost dropped the coffee cups in amazement, as she saw both Bart and Clifford puffing on cigarettes! "Why, Clifford," she exclaimed in astonishment, "I didn't know that you smoked!"

"Well, I haven't smoked for years, but I used to smoke—a long time ago. I just thought I'd have a smoke to be sociable—to keep Bart company, you know."

However, much to Beth's dismay, Clifford's "sociableness" soon developed into a full-blown smoking habit, as addiction to tobacco claimed him once again. She tried to tease him into quitting, but had no success. "You know, Clifford," she remarked laughingly one day, "Smoking picks your pockets and smells your clothes, and makes a smokestack out of your nose!"

"I know you're right, Beth." Clifford admitted ruefully. "I sure wish that I'd never started smoking again, but now that I have, I just can't seem to quit!"

Early one snowy winter morning, Beth was awakened from a sound sleep by Eberly's fretful cries. "Mommy, I itch all over!" she whined. Hurrying into the bedroom, Beth laid a hand on Eberly's forehead and found that she was burning up with fever. She was furiously scratching several small red spots on her face.

Later that morning, after the doctor had finished examining Eberly, he turned to Beth. "It's chicken pox, Mrs. Frazier. Give her some children's aspirin for the fever, and try to keep her from scratching herself, if possible. Calamine lotion should help with the itching. She'll be sick for a couple of weeks. Your son has probably also been exposed to it, so he may be getting sick soon too."

Just as the doctor predicted, Lowell soon developed chicken pox. The next several weeks were hectic for Beth, as she cared for her two sick children. One morning, just as Eberly and Lowell were beginning to recover from their illness, Beth suddenly noticed that the house had become unusually hot. Turning toward the oil-burning stove, she was alarmed to see that the stovepipe had turned a glowing red!

"Eberly, put your coat on quickly," she commanded, as she hurriedly scooped up Lowell and wrapped him in a blanket. Taking Eberly by the hand, she hurried outside, ran across the yard, and pounded on the front door of the Kellys, their next-door neighbors. Without even waiting for anyone to answer the door, Beth shouted, "Mrs. Kelly, something is terribly wrong with our stove. I'm afraid it might explode!"

Hearing Beth's cry, Mrs. Kelly flung the door open wide and welcomed Beth and her children in out of the cold. Hurrying to the phone, she called the fire department.

Soon, a clanging fire engine pulled up in front of Beth's house and several firemen hurried inside. Several minutes later, one of the firemen came to the Kellys' house to find Beth. "You were really lucky, Mrs. Frazier! We got here just in time to prevent your stove from blowing up and setting your house on fire!"

"It wasn't luck, sir." Beth responded quietly. "The Lord protected us!"

Later, at home, after she had put Eberly and Lowell back to bed, Beth sank weakly into a chair. "Why, we could have all been killed!" she thought in horror. "Thank You, Father, for sparing our lives!" she whispered gratefully.

Early in January 1951, Beth felt the familiar symptoms of tiredness and nausea, and she soon realized that she was pregnant again. She rejoiced at the thought of having another baby, and Clifford was also jubilant at the prospect. However, Beth felt overwhelmed when she realized that Lowell would not yet be two years old when her next child would be born!

"How am I ever going to manage, Father?" she questioned. "It seems like taking care of Eberly and Lowell are all that I can handle! But I know that You've promised that 'as our days shall be, so our strength will be'." And with that thought, she left her burden in the strong, capable Hands of her Heavenly Father.

Several weeks later, as Beth was walking through the house carrying Lowell to his crib for his afternoon nap, she suddenly felt as if something deep within her had pulled and torn loose. Immediately, she felt a gush of warm fluid leave her body and run down her legs. Looking down, she was shocked to see bright red blood pooling on the floor at her feet! She hurried to the bedroom, put Lowell in the crib, and then rushed to the phone and called Clifford at work. "Clifford," she cried into the receiver, "I need you to come home right away. I think I'm having a miscarriage!"

"I'll be right there, Beth!"

As Beth hung up the phone, the room swirled crazily around her, and then everything went black. Several hours later, Beth awoke in a bed at the local hospital. A man in a white coat was standing by her bedside taking her pulse. "Ah, Mrs. Frazier, you're awake at last."

"My baby?" she questioned fearfully, tears running down her cheeks.

"I'm sorry, Mrs. Frazier," he said gently. "There was nothing we could do. You've lost your baby, and the important thing now is for you to rest and get your strength back. You've lost a lot of blood, and it will take some time for you to recover."

For the next several weeks, Beth, Eberly, and Lowell stayed with Mrs. Moore, a middle-aged widow lady who attended the same church that they did. Since Beth had to have complete bed rest and was unable to care for her children, this kind woman took them into her home and tenderly cared for them, just as if Beth was her own daughter and Eberly and Lowell were her grandchildren. Though Beth deeply grieved the loss of her baby, she was extremely grateful for the help of this dear friend.

One day, as Mrs. Moore brought in Beth's lunch on a tray, Beth said, "You know, Mrs. Moore, even though I was only a couple of months pregnant, I miss my baby so much! I keep wondering what I did to cause my miscarriage, and trying to think if there was anything I could have done differently." She stopped, as a sob caught in her throat.

Mrs. Moore set down the tray on the bedside table, gathered Beth into her motherly arms, and let her weep out her grief. When Beth had quieted a bit, Mrs. Moore said soothingly, "Beth, I don't think that you caused this by anything you did or failed to do. Remember, our Lord is the One Who gives life, and 'our times are in His Hands'. Your baby is in His Arms now, and someday, when you see Him, you'll be able to hold your child in your arms!"

Wiping away the tears, Beth managed a wobbly smile. "I know you're right, Mrs. Moore, but sometimes it just hurts so bad!"

"I can understand what you're feeling, Beth." Mrs. Moore replied gently. "I lost two little ones myself."

Later, as she lay in bed, Beth pondered Mrs. Moore's words of comfort. Somehow, the assurance of knowing that her precious baby was "safe in the Arms of Jesus", and that she would see him in heaven soothed her wounded soul as nothing else could do. Beth was also encouraged as she realized that Mrs. Moore had experienced this same grief, and that the Lord had brought her through it. "And I know that You'll carry me through this too, Father," she whispered trustingly.

As spring passed, and summer began, Beth sensed a growing restlessness in Clifford. One evening, as they were lying in bed, he exclaimed in frustration, "Beth, I'm thirty-seven years old, and I want to do more with my life than what I'm doing right now! I've had some good Bible school training, and I want to use it. I want to go into the Lord's work full-time!"

"Why, that's a wonderful idea, Clifford!" Beth encouraged him. "What exactly do you think the Lord wants you to do?"

"Well, I've been praying about that, and I feel that the Lord is calling me to be a pastor, but I don't have any idea how to go about finding the church that He wants me in."

"Why don't you contact the Moody Bible Institute student placement service and let them know that you are interested in going into the pastorate? Churches write to Moody when they need a pastor, and the placement service recommends someone from their list of men who are seeking a church. Remember your friend Dan Stone from Moody? That's how he found his first pastorate."

"That's a great idea! I want you to write a letter to Moody tomorrow and let them know that I'm available to pastor a church."

"I'd be glad to!" Beth replied joyfully. However, in her heart, she felt an odd mixture of rejoicing and fear. She was thrilled that

Clifford was going to use his Bible training, and she looked forward with great anticipation to serving the Lord alongside him, but the mere thought of being a pastor's wife terrified her. Suddenly, all of her old feelings of shyness poured over her like a flood, threatening to overwhelm her with fright.

Long after Clifford's loud snores proclaimed that he was deep in slumber, Beth lay awake, battling her conflicting emotions. Then, at last, she murmured, "Father, You know how scared I am, but if You want me to be a pastor's wife, I'm willing. I know that You will give me the strength to do whatever You've called me to do!" Almost instantly, Beth felt her tense body relax. A gentle peace calmed her troubled soul, and soon she drifted off into a restful sleep.

Just as she had promised, Beth wrote to Moody the following day. Clifford spent the next few weeks impatiently waiting for a reply. Each night after work, he would burst through the door inquiring, "Have we heard anything from Moody yet, Beth?"

At last the night came when she was able to hand him a large envelope bearing the return address of Moody Bible Institute. Eagerly, he opened it and read the letter. "Look at this, Beth!" His face beamed with joy as he handed her the letter to read. "It's unbelievable! Only the Lord could work out something as perfect as this!"

Beth scanned the letter quickly. It announced that Boulden Church and Old Home Church, two country churches near the small town of Eddyville in southern Illinois, were seeking a pastor. The position was that of a "circuit-riding preacher", in which the minister would divide his time between the two churches. It sounded like an interesting opportunity, but Beth was mystified by Clifford's overwhelming excitement. She turned to him with a questioning look.

"Beth, don't you understand?" he cried. "I've been in that area and I already know the people in those churches! During the thirties, I worked at a Civilian Conservation Corps camp that was located just outside Eddyville. I attended those churches, and even preached for them some, while I was there! Pastoring those churches will be like going home!" He caught her up in his arms and spun her around the room.

At that, Beth joined in Clifford's rejoicing. Her heart sang with praise to the only One Who could have worked out all the details of such a perfect plan. The following day, Beth mailed Clifford's letter applying for the position, and two weeks later, a reply arrived from John Jackson, the chairman of the church board.

"Dear Brother Clifford," Mr. Jackson wrote. "Of course we all remember you! We were thrilled when we heard that you were interested in becoming our pastor. Since we already know you and have heard you preach, the congregation voted unanimously to call you as pastor. We will be providing a place for you and your family to live. We look forward to having you join us as soon as possible."

As their car turned off the rutted dirt road and stopped in front of a weather-beaten gray farmhouse, Beth felt as if she had stepped out of the present and into the previous century. "Well, here's our new home!" Clifford announced jubilantly. It was an old homestead that had recently been vacated by the death of its occupant, and which was now being utilized as a parsonage by the two churches that Clifford would be pastoring. Beth noted that there were no electric lines going to the house, and that there was a covered well in the front yard and a rickety-looking outhouse at the end of a path which wound through the back yard.

"Why, this house has no electricity, running water, or indoor plumbing!" Beth thought in shocked horror. "We'll be living just like the pioneers did a hundred years ago!" Stunned, she considered the ramifications of having none of the modern conveniences to which she was accustomed. Jumbled thoughts spun through her head like the dry autumn leaves that spiraled up

in a miniature whirlwind in the neglected front yard. She would
have to draw water from the well with a bucket attached to a rope
and then haul it into the house. A kerosene lamp would be their
only source of light, and a stove that was fueled by wood would
provide heat for their house. There would be no way to refrigerate
their food, and she would have to cook on a wood-burning
cookstove. All water for cooking, washing, or bathing would have
to be heated on the stove. She would have to wash clothes by
hand, on a metal washboard, in a round galvanized tub. That same
tub would have to serve as a bathtub for herself and her family.
She would have to iron clothes with heavy cast-iron flatirons,
which would need to be heated and reheated on the stove. And as
for toilet facilities, she and her family had the choice of either
using the outhouse, or a metal commode, which would be kept in
one of the bedrooms.

How different this place was from the comfortable home that
she had shared with Mother and Dad as she was growing up in
New Jersey! Beth realized that she faced a formidable challenge!
However, even as the disturbing thoughts surged through her mind,
an unexplainable peace quieted her soul. "You're right, Father,"
she murmured. "You have called us here, and You will enable me
to live here!"

It was a rainy Wednesday night—prayer meeting night. As
usual, Beth was running late. She still had to cook supper and iron
Clifford's white shirt, and it was less than an hour before the
service was scheduled to begin. After having tried unsuccessfully
several times to kindle a fire in the cookstove, she had finally
succeeded, and the stove was beginning to radiate a comfortable
warmth. She straightened up and wiped her brow, remarking to
herself, "I sure am glad that I learned how to build fires when I
was in the Girl Scouts!"

Quickly, she placed her cast-iron frying pan on the front of the
stove, and then reached out to check the temperature of the
flatirons that were heating up on the back of the range. "Good,"
she thought. "They're almost hot enough for me to begin ironing."

It was growing dark, so she hurriedly lit the kerosene lamp which sat on the kitchen table. She turned back to the stove and poured some scrambled eggs from a bowl into the frying pan. As the eggs were cooking, she took one of the flatirons from the stove and began ironing Clifford's shirt.

Suddenly, she smelled something burning. The pan had gotten too hot, and the eggs were beginning to burn. Quickly, she grabbed a pancake turner and removed the eggs from the pan, not noticing that she had left the flatiron sitting on top of Clifford's shirt! As she deposited the eggs on a plate and set it on the table, the smell of scorched cloth filled her nostrils. Whirling around, she saw smoke ascending from the ironing board. Seizing the flatiron, she replaced it on the stove, only to realize that she was too late. There was a distinct outline of an iron imprinted on Clifford's shirt. The shirt was ruined!

Turning back toward the table, she noticed that the oil lamp was behaving oddly. The flame seemed to be creeping down the wick toward the kerosene in the bowl of the lamp, instead of rising up and giving light through the lamp's chimney as it normally did. "I've got to get that lamp out of here right now!" Beth thought in alarm. "If the flame reaches that kerosene, it will explode!"

Instantly, she grasped the lamp in one hand and a box of baking soda in the other, and ran out into the back yard, leaving the screen door hanging open behind her. Setting the lamp on the ground, she removed the chimney and smothered the flame by dumping the baking soda onto it. With a sigh of relief, she turned and walked back into the house. She arrived in the kitchen just in time to see their dog Laddie, who had entered through the open door, devouring the eggs—the last eggs in the house! "Out, Laddie!" Beth yelled angrily, and then sank down onto the nearest chair, tears of frustration running down her cheeks.

Just then, Clifford walked into the kitchen. "Is supper ready yet, Beth?" he demanded. "And where's my shirt? We need to leave in ten minutes."

The next few minutes were a blur, but somehow Beth managed to iron another shirt for Clifford, and get Eberly and Lowell ready for church. As for supper, Beth realized that she had run out of time and that her family would not be able to have anything to eat until after prayer meeting was over.

At last, they were all seated in the car and ready to leave for the church. However, when Clifford attempted to pull out of the driveway, the wheels of the car began to spin in the mud and were soon trapped in deep ruts. Impatiently, Clifford pressed harder on the gas pedal, only to have the tires sink further into the mire. After several futile attempts to break free, Clifford left the car and hurried down the road to summon their neighbor, Elmer Clarity, to pull the car out with his tractor. Half an hour after the service had been scheduled to begin, the Frazier family finally arrived at Boulden Church!

Later that night, as Beth lay wearily in bed, she let her mind drift back over all the events of that nightmarish day. Now that it was over, her multitude of misfortunes seemed almost comical to her! She honestly couldn't think of even <u>one</u> more thing that could have gone wrong! For a moment, she shook with silent mirth, as she recalled the steady stream of small disasters that had filled her evening.

"Well, Father," she murmured, as she drifted off to sleep, "living here is certainly going to be a challenge! I'm really glad that 'Your grace is sufficient for me', even in this situation. Thanks for keeping the house from burning down tonight, and thanks for giving me a good sense of humor!"

By the following morning, the rain had stopped. As soon as breakfast was over, Eberly and Lowell raced out the door, eager to play outside again after having been cooped up in the house. Beth began mopping the kitchen floor, which was full of muddy footprints from the night before.

Just as she finished mopping, the door burst open, and Eberly and Lowell ran into the kitchen. Their feet were encased in a solid coating of dripping mud, all the way up to their ankles! "Children!" Beth exclaimed. "What on earth were you doing?"

"Oh, we were playing that we were cars getting stuck in the mud—just like our car got stuck last night!" Eberly announced with an excited grin. "It was fun, Mommy!"

With an exasperated look at the muddy tracks on her clean kitchen floor, Beth replied, "Well, let's get those dirty shoes and socks off and get you cleaned up. And don't you ever play that game again!"

A few minutes later, after outfitting her children in clean footwear, Beth allowed them to go outside again, having given them another stern warning to stay out of the mud. With a sigh, she returned to her mopping, wondering how she was ever going to keep the floor clean under such conditions.

As she mopped, she could hear Eberly and Lowell's excited cries, as they chased each other around the yard. Suddenly, she became aware of an ominous silence. "I'd better go see what those kids are doing," she remarked to herself, as she hurried out the door.

As she rounded the house and came into the front yard, she was horrified to see Eberly and Lowell standing ankle-deep in mud, making car noises and struggling to pull their feet out! "Eberly!" she yelled angrily. "I thought I told you never to play 'stuck in the mud' again!"

"Oh, we didn't mean to get stuck, Mommy!" Eberly looked up at Beth with an angelic smile. "We thought we'd see if we could just walk around on <u>top</u> of the mud, but all of a sudden we sank right down into it!"

"Well, this is a good picture of what happens when you choose to do something wrong, Eberly," Beth instructed her young daughter. "You may <u>think</u> that you can sin just a little bit, and that it won't hurt you, but you'll soon find out that you can't stop what you're doing. Before long, you'll be in a lot of trouble, just like you sank all the way down into that mud!" As she spoke, she walked over to a nearby apple tree and cut off a stout switch, which she promptly used on the bare legs of both of her wayward offspring.

As the weeks passed, Beth gradually became accustomed to keeping house in her primitive living conditions. Although the work was backbreaking, she loved living in the country, and she was especially delighted that there was a large apple orchard in the field behind the house.

One sunny day in October, Beth decided to make an apple pie. She instructed Eberly to watch Lowell, and then took a basket, and went outside to pick some apples. A few minutes later, as she walked into the house, she was dismayed to see Lowell happily playing in the middle of a mound of flour which had been dumped onto the floor. Eberly was watching him with a shocked look on her face. "Ooh, Mommy," she exclaimed, pointing at her little brother. "Look what Lowell did!"

The following day, when Beth went to pick apples to make applesauce, the identical scene was repeated, with a slight variation. This time, it was the sugar that was spilled onto the floor! "Well, I guess I just can't leave Lowell alone even for a moment," Beth thought. "He seems to be at the age when kids get into everything!"

Later that afternoon, as Beth was making applesauce, Eberly ran excitedly into the kitchen. "Mommy! Mommy! Come quick! Look what Lowell did!"

Following her daughter into the living room, Beth was appalled to see an open box of tacks and a half-empty bottle of glue lying on the floor. Most of the tacks were spilled onto the floor, and the glue had been dribbled over the tacks, making them a sticky mess. Lowell was standing wide-eyed in the middle of the room.

Beth glanced at Lowell's hands. They were totally clean! A sudden suspicion crossed Beth's mind, and she turned quickly to Eberly. "Eberly," she commanded sternly. "Let me see your hands!"

Instantly Eberly began squirming and trying to hide her hands behind her back. At last, reluctantly, she extended her telltale, sticky hands to her mother. "Eberly," Beth remarked in exasperation, "there's a verse in the Bible that says, 'Be sure your sin will find you out', and I think your sin just found you out, didn't it? You did all of the things that you've been blaming on Lowell, didn't you?"

"Yes, Mommy," Eberly confessed tearfully, her head down.

Beth reached for her switch. "Well, this should be a lesson to you. I hope that you'll never forget that you can't do wrong and get away with it!"

One wintry morning, as Beth sat playing the piano for the morning worship service, she let her mind drift back over the past few months. Being a pastor's wife had not proved to be as difficult as she had feared. Already she had learned to love the people who made up their congregation. She looked out over the now-familiar faces with a smile.

On the left side of the church, Beth could see their neighbor, Elmer Clarity, his red-haired wife Katie, and their thirteen children, several of whom had inherited Katie's brilliant red hair.

"How does Katie ever manage to care for thirteen children?" Beth wondered in astonishment. "I have my hands full with just two!"

Sitting on the right side, she saw tall John Jackson, the chairman of the church board, his stern-looking wife Wilma, and their pretty, dark-haired daughter Helen, who was several years older than Eberly. Toward the back was plump, cheery, white-haired Mrs. Lillie Rushing. "No—I mean 'Aunt Lillie'," Beth corrected herself in mid-thought. She had still not completely gotten used to the country people's custom of showing respect for elderly people by calling them "Uncle" or "Aunt", even if they were not actually related to them. Right next to Aunt Lillie was seated tiny, gray-haired Aunt Minta Boulden, for whose family Boulden Church had been named. Sharing the hymnbook with Aunt Minta was her bachelor son Ray, who was one of Clifford's best friends.

After she had finished playing the piano for the congregational singing, Beth joined Clifford at the pulpit and sang a duet with him, her soft alto voice blending perfectly with his tenor. Using her musical talents was one of the things that Beth enjoyed most about the ministry which the Lord had given them.

After the special music, she took her seat on the front row with Eberly and Lowell. In Clifford's sermon that day, he expounded on one of his favorite biblical themes, the judgment of God. "The Lord <u>loves</u> judgment!" he thundered, his face reddening, as he pounded the pulpit for emphasis.

"If Clifford gets much more excited, I'm afraid he's going to burst a blood vessel," she thought in concern. "I wish he wouldn't yell so loudly when he preaches."

After church that day, Aunt Lillie invited them to come to her house for dinner. As they drove along the rutted dirt road toward the Rushing farmhouse, Beth turned to Clifford. "Why doesn't Aunt Lillie's husband, Uncle Whit, ever come to church? He's a Christian too, isn't he?"

"Yes, he knows the Lord. In fact, during the time that I worked at the CCC camp, he preached quite often at Boulden Church. But one Sunday, he got mad about something that one of the other men said, and he left the church and has never come back since."

"How sad!" Beth was astonished that anyone could hold a grudge for so many years.

That Sunday afternoon was just the first of many happy days that Beth and her family spent at Aunt Lillie and Uncle Whit's home. The childless old couple acted as if Clifford and Beth were their own children and Eberly and Lowell were their grandchildren. Lowell and Eberly enjoyed playing outside under the big mulberry tree in the Rushings' backyard, and never tired of helping Aunt Lillie feed the chickens and hunt for eggs, or going to the barn to pet the horses and watch Uncle Whit milk the cows.

One rainy Sunday afternoon, Beth sat on Aunt Lillie's back porch, paintbrush in hand, trying to capture on paper the picturesque barnyard scene before her. After she had finished her painting, she walked back into the kitchen. As she came through the door, she could hear Aunt Lillie carrying on an animated conversation. "Someone must have come to visit Aunt Lillie while I was outside," she thought. "I wonder who it could be." However, much to her surprise, she found Aunt Lillie alone in the kitchen, stirring a pot of soup on the stove and enthusiastically carrying on both sides of the dialogue. Not wanting to embarrass the old lady, she stole quietly back outside.

Later, when she mentioned it to Clifford, he didn't seem in the least surprised at the news. "Yes, I've heard her doing that too. I imagine that she started doing it because she's really lonely. She and Uncle Whit live so far away from their neighbors that they don't have many visitors, and you know that Uncle Whit doesn't talk much."

Beth immediately decided that she would visit Aunt Lillie more often. When she carried out her resolution, she soon found that she was amply rewarded by Aunt Lillie's teaching her how to make homemade bread, to churn butter, and to can fruits and vegetables.

Several weeks later, as they all sat visiting around the Rushings' dining room table, after a delicious meal of Aunt Lillie's fried chicken, the phone rang. Since all of the phones on the community party line rang whenever anyone received a call, each family had their own particular combination of long and short rings, so that they would know when to answer their phone. Beth recognized the distinctive ring which announced that the call was for the Clarity family—two long rings and one short ring. Much to Beth's surprise, Aunt Lillie hurried over, picked up the phone and began listening in on the conversation. However, she was even more shocked a few minutes later, when the inquisitive old lady shouted into the phone, "Speak up, Wilma. I couldn't hear what you just told Katie!" After the call was over, Aunt Lillie walked back to the table and began serving the apple pie, just as if nothing unusual had happened.

"You know, Beth," Uncle Whit remarked a few minutes later, "I really appreciated that jar of wild grape juice that you canned and gave to me. There was just one thing wrong with it, though. There was a hole in the jar, and a lot of it leaked out."

"Why, that's terrible, Uncle Whit! I'll have to bring you another jar to replace it."

Uncle Whit walked out into the kitchen and returned, holding a half-empty jar of grape juice. He removed the lid and took a big swallow of grape juice. "See, Beth," he said, his eyes twinkling as he pointed to the open mouth of the jar, "there's the hole in the jar, and the juice keeps on leakin' out of it just like that!" For a moment, Beth's cheeks flushed with embarrassment, but soon she was laughing at herself for having been so thoroughly fooled by Uncle Whit's little joke.

As spring turned to summer, Beth was overjoyed to find that wild blackberries grew in abundance in the fields of southern Illinois. She and Eberly and Lowell spent many enjoyable afternoons picking blackberries, although the fruit of Lowell's labors usually ended up in his mouth. One of the best berry patches was in the field just across the road from the little log cabin where Aunt Minta Boulden and her son Ray lived. Whenever Aunt Minta noticed them there, she would walk out onto her porch and call, "Why don't you folks come on over for supper tonight?"

Beth and Clifford spent many pleasant evenings sitting on the front porch chatting with Aunt Minta and Ray, who quickly became known as "Uncle Ray" to Eberly and Lowell. As Clifford and Beth relaxed together on the porch swing, they could watch their children rolling around in the luxuriant grass or chasing elusive lightning bugs back and forth through the darkening twilight. "I'm so thankful that the Lord led us here," Beth thought happily to herself one evening. "It will be a wonderful place for our kids to grow up!"

On a warm July afternoon, shortly before Eberly's sixth birthday, Beth was busily kneading bread dough in the kitchen. Suddenly she heard Clifford come bounding up the steps of the old farmhouse where they lived. A moment later, she heard him shout excitedly, "Beth, where are you? Come in here! I've got some great news to tell you!"

She wiped the flour from her hands and hurried into the living room. Clifford was standing in the middle of the floor beaming at her, and the open door was swinging back and forth behind him. "Clifford U. Frazier," she playfully chided her husband, as she walked over and shut the door, "a person would think you were born in a barn, because you always leave the door open!" Then she turned to him expectantly. "Now, what's this wonderful news that you want to tell me?"

"I just bought us a place of our very own, Beth! Just wait till you see it! You're going to love it!"

Beth had thought that, after more than seven years of marriage, she had become accustomed to Clifford's whirlwind way of making decisions. However, once again, she found that her breath was taken away by the rapidity with which he could make choices that would radically change their lives, without even consulting her about it first. "Slow down, and tell me all about it," she encouraged him, after she had recovered a bit from her initial shock.

"Well, Ray and I went to an auction today, and there was some property up for sale, and I bought it for two hundred fifty dollars!"

"Where is it located?" Beth inquired curiously. "Does it have a house on it?"

"It's just a few miles from here, not far from Boulden Church. It's the old Boulden Schoolhouse. It's in the middle of the woods, on an acre of land, and it has a good well, a big cistern, and a real nice outhouse with two seats in it!"

"How many rooms does the schoolhouse have?" Beth asked, her heart sinking as she realized that, even in their new home, they would still be living in primitive conditions.

"Just one. After all, it was a one-room schoolhouse. In fact, all of the desks and schoolbooks are still there. How soon can you be ready to move?"

Beth's mind spun in turmoil, as she considered the difficulty of making a home for her family in such a setting. The kitchen, the living area, and the sleeping quarters for the four of them would all have to be organized in some way within that one large room! There certainly wouldn't be much privacy for any of them!

A week later, after much help from the people of their church, the Frazier family was settled in their new home. The desks and books which had belonged to the school had been replaced with household furnishings. Beth's cookstove, a kitchen cabinet, a table, and four chairs were placed in the back portion of the big room, and two double beds and a bureau were moved into the front part. However, due to a lack of closet space, most of their personal belongings had to be stored in an assortment of boxes, which were pushed under the beds or stacked up against the walls.

After several frustrating hours of trying to bring order out of the chaos surrounding her, Beth finally walked outside. She sank down on the front steps, exhausted. "I think I could use a little fresh air!" she murmured to herself.

Across the yard, she could see their dog, Laddie, excitedly wagging his tail, as Eberly pushed Lowell back and forth in the swing which hung from the spreading branches of a giant oak tree. As a light breeze cooled her flushed cheeks and gently lifted a damp curl from her forehead, she felt her tension gradually ebbing away.

"Well, Clifford was certainly right about one thing! This is a really beautiful piece of property!" she thought. Rising from the steps, she walked a little way into the woods. Her artistic nature exulted in the ever-changing patterns of sunlight and shadow that filtered through the trees onto the leafy carpet at her feet. Looking around, she saw massive oaks, tall hickory nut trees, spreading dogwoods, and low-growing sassafras and sumac bushes. Mingled among them were a few stately cedar trees, whose fragrant dark green needles made a striking contrast to the lighter green foliage of the other trees.

Each open space was a garden of beautiful wildflowers—bold yellow black-eyed Susans, dainty white Queen Anne's lace, bright sunny goldenrod, and colorful morning glories in a myriad of shades, ranging from deep pink to blue and violet. She turned and walked back toward the house, her soul refreshed by the beauty around her. "Thank You, Father, for giving us this lovely place!"

she breathed. It wasn't until the next day, when her ankles were covered with an itchy red rash, that Beth realized that their idyllic woodland garden was spoiled by at least one weed—an abundance of poison ivy!

On a bright, sunny morning in that fall of 1952, Beth and Lowell stood by the roadside and waved goodbye, as Eberly boarded the school bus for her first day at school—in another one-room schoolhouse. Beth had already learned that Eberly would be the only child in first grade, and that the thirty-one students, in grades one through eight, would be taught by just one teacher. "I'm really thankful that Eberly learned how to read before she started school," Beth mused, as she and Lowell walked down the long driveway leading to their house. "I'm afraid that it will be difficult for Mr. Van Parsons to give her much personal attention, since he has so many other students to teach."

As the days of September passed, Beth felt a deep contentment growing within her. The old schoolhouse in which they lived was gradually beginning to feel like home to her, and she was becoming more comfortable in her role as a pastor's wife. She rejoiced to see how the Lord was blessing Clifford's ministry, and she believed that they had found a place where they could serve the Lord together for many happy years to come.

However, she still longed for a chance to utilize her artistic talent. But how could she do that in this isolated place in rural southern Illinois? Puzzled by this problem, she poured it out to her Heavenly Father one morning. "Father," she murmured, "I know that You gave me this talent, and that You want me to use it. Please show me how I can!"

She rose from her knees and began vigorously sweeping the floor. Suddenly, as she wielded the broom, she thought, "Why, of course! That's the answer! I'll write to some Christian publishing companies and see if they have some free-lance artwork that I can do right here at home!"

Several weeks later, Beth received two answers to her inquiries. One was from the Bible Club Movement, which was publishing a set of lessons on the books of Exodus, Leviticus, Numbers, and Deuteronomy, and needed an artist to make the flannel-graph figures for the stories. The other was from Moody Press, which needed an artist to illustrate a book of children's stories, <u>Whiter Than Snow and Little Dot.</u>

For the next month, Beth pored over Bible commentaries, researching the details necessary for an accurate portrayal of Tabernacle furniture and priestly robes. Although she enjoyed the challenge of drawing the flannel-graph figures, she found an even greater delight in illustrating the children's book, because she had live models for it available right in her own family. When the pictures were completed, they bore an amazing resemblance to Eberly, Lowell, Clifford, and even Beth herself!

Several weeks after Beth sent the finished artwork to the publishers, she received a letter from Moody Press. Eagerly, she tore it open. "Dear Mrs. Frazier," she read, "We were greatly impressed with the quality of the work that you did for us recently. Therefore, we would like to invite you to illustrate another book for us. Enclosed is a copy of a manuscript recently completed by Mr. Ken Taylor. It is called <u>Stories for the Children's Hour</u>, and is designed to be used in family devotions."

It was while Beth was busily working on the pictures for this new book, once again using her family as models, that she made the joyful discovery that a new little Frazier would be joining their household early the following summer. She had never recovered completely from the grief of losing her dear little one just two years before, and the thought of having another child comforted her as nothing else could. Clifford was ecstatic when she told him the joyful news! "Well, Beth," he beamed, "the Bible says that 'children are a heritage of the Lord, and happy is the man who has his quiver full of them'!"

It was a cold, dreary, rainy December day, several weeks after Beth had completed the illustrations for the children's devotional book. Outside, the familiar sounds of a roaring engine and spinning tires alerted Beth to the fact that Clifford's car was again stuck in the mud. A moment later, the noise stopped, and Clifford burst through the door, not even pausing to wipe the mud from his shoes. "I've just got to take the car to town today to get it fixed, but it's all bogged down in that mud-hole! I think that the only way I'll ever get it out is if we put some rocks under the tires. Then I can drive it out over them."

Grabbing her coat, Beth followed Clifford out into the drizzle. He jacked up the car, and for the next few minutes, they both hauled rocks and positioned them carefully under the wheels. At last, Clifford lowered the car, climbed in, and started the motor. Carefully, he eased the car forward. The tires gripped the stones, the engine strained, and gradually the car made its way out of the mud and up onto solid ground.

Half an hour later, as Beth was building a fire in the cookstove in preparation for making supper, she was suddenly gripped with an excruciating pain in her abdomen, and an overwhelming and uncontrollable urge to urinate. She hurried to sit on the commode, and was startled to feel a great gush of warm liquid leaving her body. Rising unsteadily, she looked into the commode and was horrified to see that its contents had turned bright red from her blood.

"Oh, no! I must be having another miscarriage!" she thought sorrowfully. "I should never have tried to carry those rocks to help Clifford!" Then terror struck her, as she realized the seriousness of her situation. She was home alone with Eberly and Lowell, far from neighbors, with no knowledge of when Clifford would return! "Oh, Lord!" she cried silently. "Please protect us! Help me to know what to do, and help Clifford to come home soon!"

As she turned and walked weakly toward the bed to lie down, she caught a glimpse of Eberly standing in the middle of the floor, her face pale, with her wide eyes fixed on Beth. She realized too late that her daughter had also seen the contents of the commode. "Mommy, what's wrong?" Eberly asked fearfully.

Beth managed a faint smile. "I'm not feeling very good, Honey, and I've got to lie down for a while. I need you to watch Lowell for me until I start feeling better."

"I will, Mommy!" Eberly promised solemnly, her little face still white with fear.

Night was fast approaching, and still Clifford had not returned. "Oh, where could he be?" Beth thought in alarm. "I was sure that he would be home by this time!"

"Mommy, when are we going to have supper?" Lowell cried. "I'm hungry!"

Wearily, Beth dragged herself out of bed and hobbled unsteadily to the table. Settling herself gingerly into a chair, she lit the oil lamp and turned to Eberly. "Honey," she tried to say cheerfully, "could you please bring me the bread and the peanut butter and jelly out of the cabinet? I'm going to fix us some sandwiches for supper."

After supper, she tucked Eberly and Lowell into their bed, and staggered over to her own. "Father, help me!" her heart cried out, as she lost her balance and fell onto her bed in utter exhaustion.

For Beth, the dark hours of that endless night dragged by in a blur of pain and weakness. Sometime in the wee hours of the morning, she realized that she must make a trip to the commode. As she rose slowly from the commode, the room spun crazily around her, and then everything went black.

Sometime later—how long, she didn't know—she awakened to find herself lying on the floor, her head throbbing from the impact of having hit the wooden floor when she had fainted. Not trusting herself to rise, she dragged her body across the floor and back up into her bed. Then once again, she lapsed into unconsciousness.

When she awoke again, sunlight was streaming through the window, and she could hear her children beginning to stir. "They'll be waking up soon, and they'll need breakfast, but there's no way that I'll be able to fix it for them!" she thought.

A moment later, she heard footsteps, and opened her eyes to find Eberly anxiously peering down at her. "Mommy, are you all right?" Eberly asked in concern.

Beth smiled weakly. "I still don't feel very well, Honey. How would you like to fix breakfast this morning?"

"Yes, Mommy! I'd love to! Just tell me what I have to do!"

From her bed, Beth gave Eberly detailed instructions for making the fire, cooking oatmeal, and baking biscuits. It was a laborious process, but at last the food was prepared. When Eberly brought the finished products for Beth to sample, she exclaimed with as much enthusiasm as her weakened condition would allow, "You did a great job, Eberly! I'm so thankful that you're here to help me!"

The morning hours dragged by, but still Clifford did not return. Beth could feel herself steadily growing weaker, as her bleeding continued. "I need help!" she admitted to herself. "If only I could get word to the neighbors! But how can I do that? Oh, how I wish that we had a telephone!"

She considered her options. Their nearest neighbor was an old bachelor named Cyrus Newton, who lived across the road, on the other side of the creek in which Beth and her family had spent many enjoyable hours swimming during the summertime. "I could send Eberly over to Mr. Newton's house," she thought, but then she realized that the creek was probably swollen from the previous day's rain. "I can't send her over there," she thought in alarm.

"She might fall in while she's crossing it and be swept away and drowned!"

Suddenly, she remembered the old school bell, which still sat outside in the yard, left over from the days when their home had been a schoolhouse. "If only I could get to that bell and ring it, someone might hear it and realize that something is wrong!" she thought.

"Eberly, I need your help again," she addressed her small daughter.

"Yes, Mommy," Eberly responded eagerly. "What do you want me to do?"

"I need to go outside and ring the big bell to let our neighbors know that we need help, but I don't feel strong enough to walk out there all by myself. I need you to hold onto me and keep me from falling down when I go out there."

"Okay, Mommy!"

With Eberly's help, Beth managed to rise from the bed. Once again, the room whirled around her, and she feared she might faint. Breathing a quick, silent prayer for strength, Beth took a wobbly step toward the door, leaning on Eberly for support.

Slowly, they made their way out the door, down the steps, and around the house toward the bell. Leaning against the bell, Beth and Eberly pushed with all their might to move it back and forth. Finally, their efforts were rewarded with a loud, clanging sound. Then, her meager strength entirely spent, Beth allowed Eberly to lead her back into the house.

For the next several hours, Beth waited hopefully for an answer to her S. O. S. At last, she heard the welcome sound of a car coming up their driveway. A car door slammed, and she heard someone running up the steps. The door burst open, and Clifford walked into the room. "Beth, I'm sorry that I couldn't get back sooner, but they couldn't fix the car until today." Then seeing her pale form lying exhaustedly on the bed, he exclaimed in alarm, "Beth, what's the matter? Are you sick?" It was then that Beth realized that, in spite of all her effort, no one had heard her call for help.

"Oh, Clifford," Beth sobbed, as he stooped to gather her into his arms, "I'm afraid I've lost our baby!"

"Well, we're going to get you to the hospital right away! Surely there's something they can do to help!"

"No, Clifford. I'm afraid that it's already too late," Beth protested. "I'm not bleeding much anymore, so I think I just need to rest and get my strength back. Anyway, when I had my other miscarriage, the doctors couldn't do anything to help. There's no need to run up a big hospital bill!"

For the next week, Beth remained in bed, and the kind ladies of their congregation took turns bringing in meals and watching Lowell and Eberly. At last, on Christmas Day, Beth finally felt well enough to be out of bed for a short time.

However, early the next morning, the excruciating cramps suddenly returned, and Beth began hemorrhaging again. "This time, we're going to the doctor, Beth!" Clifford insisted. Doubled over with pain, Beth tried to agree, but before Clifford could even help her out to the car, she had delivered an extremely tiny, but perfectly-formed, stillborn baby boy.

"Oh, Clifford," she sobbed, brokenheartedly. "If only I had listened to you and gone to the hospital last week, they might have been able to save our baby!"

Clifford stroked her hair. "You didn't know, Beth," he soothed her. "You thought that you had already lost the baby!"

After several hours of sobbing out her grief to her Heavenly Father, Beth finally fell into an exhausted sleep. As her eyelids closed, her only comfort was found in the assurance that her dear little son was "safe in the Arms of Jesus".

The cold, dreary winter months of early 1953 dragged slowly by, and spring came at last, with tiny purple violets shyly peeking their lovely faces out from underneath the past year's fallen leaves. As soon as the danger of frost was past, Beth threw herself into planting a garden. She loved the soothing warmth of the spring sunshine on her back, and the feel of the rich, brown earth sifting through her fingers. She planted beans, peas, potatoes, carrots, corn, onions, lettuce, and tomatoes, dreaming of the day when she would reap a bountiful harvest as a reward for her labors.

Although Beth loved gardening, she also had a more practical reason for trying to grow her own vegetables. With the meager salary that Clifford received as a pastor, it had taken all of Beth's ingenuity to keep enough food on the table and to make sure that their car payments were paid, so she hoped to supplement his wages by growing some of their own food.

One day, about a week after her seeds had been planted, Lowell and Eberly came bursting into the house. "Guess what, Mommy!" Lowell exclaimed. "There's some little baby plants growing in your garden!" Excitedly, Beth followed her children out to the little garden plot, and rejoiced to see the first tiny bean leaves bursting forth from their protective prisons.

Each day, Beth lovingly watered and weeded her garden, finding satisfaction in the neat, orderly rows of tiny plants. However, after a month had passed, she became concerned because, in spite of her faithful care, her vegetables remained small and spindly. "What else can I do?" she wondered. "I think I'll ask Uncle Whit for advice. He's been a farmer for many years. I'm sure he'll know what the problem is."

The following week, after Uncle Whit and Aunt Lillie had enjoyed a delicious dinner with her family, Beth led Uncle Whit out to her garden patch. He took one look at the anemic-looking plants and began shaking his head. He pointed to the large oak trees that surrounded the field. "This just ain't a good place for a garden, Beth! Them trees are suckin' up all the nourishment from the soil. There ain't nothin' left for your plants. I'm afraid that you ain't gonna get much of a harvest here."

Beth continued to faithfully tend her garden, but unfortunately, Uncle Whit's prediction proved true. In spite of all her hard work, she only harvested enough produce to prepare a few meals for her family, rather than the abundant amount which she had hoped to preserve for their use during the coming winter months.

One afternoon in late summer, Clifford returned from a trip to town and walked excitedly into the house. "I think I've found the answer to our money problems, Beth! I just heard about a government construction job in Paducah, Kentucky that needs workers. Roy Lauderdale told me that he's found a job there, and he wants me to apply too, so that we can ride back and forth together. He doesn't have a car, you know, so he'll even help pay for my gas."

"But what about the church work, Clifford?" Beth inquired in concern. "How are you going to have time to do both?"

"I can study in the evenings, Beth," Clifford reassured her. "And since I have weekends off, I'll still be able to preach."

The next morning, Clifford drove to Paducah, and returned later that day with the good news that he had gotten the job and would begin work the following Monday. Though Beth was concerned about the long hours that Clifford would have to work, it was a great relief to her to know that their financial needs would be met at last.

One evening, several weeks later, Beth opened the front door and peered anxiously down the driveway, looking for the approaching headlights of Clifford's car. "Where could he be?" she wondered anxiously. "It's nine o'clock, and he's always been home by eight o'clock at the latest. I hope that he hasn't had an accident!"

Another half-hour dragged by, and Beth heaved a sigh of relief as she heard the familiar sound of Clifford's car pulling into the yard. A moment later, he burst through the door, enveloped her in his arms, and gave her a lingering kiss. "I really missed you today, Sweetheart! It's so good to be at home with you again!"

As he released her, she was astonished and repulsed as she detected the sour odor of beer on his breath. "Clifford," she exclaimed in shocked amazement, "have you been drinking?"

"Aw, I just had one beer," Clifford shrugged. "Roy wanted to stop at the tavern in Eddyville on the way home, and he offered to buy me a drink because he appreciates me letting him ride with me to work."

"But, Clifford, you're a minister!" Beth protested in concern. "What kind of a testimony do you think it is for you to be drinking—especially to a new Christian like Roy? He's only been saved for a few months, you know! And suppose some of the people from church saw your car outside the tavern? What would they think? They wouldn't have any way of knowing that you only had one beer."

"There's nothing wrong with drinking, as long as you don't get drunk!" Clifford retorted. "After all, even Jesus drank wine when He was here on earth."

Beth had no answer for that, but she was still deeply concerned about the effect which Clifford's unwise behavior would have on the effectiveness of his ministry.

The following Sunday morning, as Beth walked into the church, she noticed a small group of women engaged in an earnest discussion near the rear of the sanctuary. When they saw her, however, their conversation came to an abrupt halt, but not before Beth overheard Wilma Jackson exclaim indignantly, "…saw his car parked in front of the tavern last Thursday night!" Her cheeks flushed with embarrassment, Beth guided Eberly and Lowell down the aisle, settled them in the front row, took her customary place at the piano, and began playing a hymn.

Just as Beth had feared, Wilma Jackson had seen Clifford's car parked outside the bar. Soon the ugly gossip that Preacher Frazier was a drinking man had spread throughout the entire congregation and the whole Eddyville area.

Several weeks later, at Wilma's insistence, a congregational meeting was called to discuss the charges against Clifford and to decide whether he should continue as pastor. "Rev. Frazier, what possible excuse can you give to justify such reprehensible behavior?" Wilma demanded angrily.

"Roy invited me to stop for a drink, and I was just trying to be sociable," Clifford attempted to defend himself. "And I only had one beer!"

"Preacher Frazier," John Jackson, the chairman of the church board, said reluctantly, "We've all enjoyed your ministry here, but we just don't think that it's right for a minister of the Gospel to drink. It's not a good example—especially for our young people."

Before anyone could say another word, Clifford jumped to his feet. "Well, if you folks feel that way, I have no choice but to resign as pastor of this church—effective immediately!"

Beth's heart sank. In one horrible moment, her dream of their enjoying many fruitful years of ministry at the Boulden and Old Home churches, and of raising their children out in the country, near the quiet little town of Eddyville, evaporated. She sat in stunned silence, her head spinning from the unexpected turn that their lives had taken.

For the next month, Clifford and Beth and their children continued living in the old schoolhouse, and Clifford continued working at his construction job, but they did not attend church anywhere. Beth missed having fellowship with other Christians, and she felt extremely awkward whenever she met any of the people who attended the churches that Clifford had previously pastored.

One night in late September, Clifford burst through the door excitedly. "I've got great news, Beth! I met a guy named Tom Sanders on the job today. He attends Gilead Church near Metropolis, Illinois. Right now they're without a pastor. When he heard that I'm a preacher, he called one of his friends, and they've invited me to come and candidate there next Sunday!"

"Why, Clifford, that's wonderful! Maybe this is how the Lord will provide another place of ministry for you!"

"Yes. If Gilead calls me to be their pastor, we can move to Metropolis. You know, Metropolis is just across the state line from Paducah, so I won't have to make such a long trip to go to work each day, and we'll be close to the church too! That will be ideal!"

Beth's heart sank at the thought of moving, especially since Eberly had just begun another year of school, but she rejoiced at the prospect of Clifford finding another pastorate.

The following Sunday, Clifford preached at Gilead, and within a week, they received word that the congregation had voted to call him as their pastor. The next week flew by in a whirlwind of house-hunting and moving, and soon the Frazier family was settled in a tiny house on the outskirts of the small town of Metropolis.

Several weeks later, Beth felt a familiar queasiness in her stomach, and rejoiced with the knowledge that once again, she was going to be a mother. However, her happiness was short-lived, because just two weeks later, she once again lost her baby. This miscarriage was not as traumatic physically as her previous ones had been, because she was only about six weeks pregnant. It was over quickly, with just a few hours of cramps and a brief episode of heavy bleeding.

However, it devastated her emotionally. "I'm thirty-seven years old, and now I've lost three children in a row," she sobbed broken-heartedly, as she poured out her grief to the Lord. "I wonder if I'll <u>ever</u> be able to bear another child! Oh, Father, if it's Your will, please enable me to have another baby someday!"

The following Sunday, the Frazier family was invited over to the Sanders' farm for dinner after church. Beth brought along her art supplies and asked permission to paint a picture of the beautiful fall scene that was visible from their front porch. Her hosts seemed delighted with her beautiful watercolor painting of their barn, surrounded by trees flaming with their bright foliage of red and gold. However, she also noticed a strange reserve in Mr. Sanders' manner.

On the way home, Clifford exploded angrily. "I can't believe what Tom Sanders said to me this afternoon! He said that any man who is pastor of their church has to be a Mason, and he asked me to join his lodge. I told him that I didn't believe that Christians should be members of secret societies. Then he told me that if that's the way I feel, maybe the church should begin looking for another pastor! So I told him, 'Fine! You'd better start looking then, because I'm not going to change my mind!' "

"Clifford, that's terrible! He has no right to require that of you. Surely none of the other church members share his feelings, do they?"

"I'm afraid they do, Beth," Clifford answered grimly. "All of the men on the church board are Masons, just like Tom. But I'm not going to compromise what I believe to satisfy them, even if it means losing this pastorate."

"You're right, Clifford!" Beth encouraged him. "You're responsible to do what the Lord wants you to do, no matter what people say!"

So it was, that at the next board meeting, faced with the demand of the church leaders that he become a Mason, Clifford resigned as pastor of Gilead Church. "What do you have for us now, Lord?" Beth questioned, as she lay in bed that night. "We've lost two pastorates within just a few months! Please show us where we should go from here!"

# Chapter 11—Yankees in Dixie Land

Several weeks later, Clifford trudged slowly into the house after work, a glum expression on his face. "We got word today that our job in Paducah is almost over," he sighed. "Next week will be our last week of work. How on earth are we going to be able to pay our bills?"

"I don't have any idea, Clifford!" Beth commiserated. "But I do know that the Lord has never let us down yet. This is something that we need to pray about."

"You're right!" Clifford agreed, and they knelt together beside their bed and poured out their need to their Heavenly Father.

However, long after Clifford's steady snoring proclaimed that he was sound asleep, Beth lay awake, thinking of the huge car payment which came due every month. "If only we didn't have those car payments," she thought. "How I wish Clifford would be satisfied when we get one car paid for, instead of always trading it in for the latest model! And I wish that we could discuss major decisions and make them <u>together</u>, like Mother and Dad used to do, instead of Clifford making them all by himself and then telling me about it afterwards!"

The following Monday, Clifford burst through the door after work, a big grin lighting up his face. "Well, it looks like the Lord has already answered our prayers, Beth! Jim Barnes, one of the guys at work, told me that he just heard that they need workers in the pulpwood industry down in southern Alabama. He and some of the other men are going to Alabama next week to look for jobs, and they invited me to go with them! If we get those jobs, I'll probably have to stay down there by myself and work for a while, but I'll come back and get you and the kids as soon as I can."

Although Beth was thankful to hear about the possibility of a new job for Clifford, her heart sank when she heard how far away it was. If Clifford got the job, then she, Eberly, and Lowell would be left all alone, without any transportation, in a community in which they had lived for only a few months, and where they knew few people! "Do you have to go all the way to Alabama, Clifford?" she questioned. "Surely you could find something closer!"

"Jobs are hard to find right now, Beth," he reminded her. "A man has to take what he can get!"

The next day, Clifford kissed Beth goodbye and headed south to Alabama. With a lump in her throat, Beth waved as his car pulled out of sight, wondering how long it would be before she would see him again. Feeling a tug at her hand, she looked down to see Eberly looking up at her with worried eyes. "When is Fahfee coming back, Mommy?" she questioned seriously, using the pet name that she and Lowell had used for their father ever since Lowell had invented it as a toddler.

"I don't know, Eberly." Beth turned away quickly, to hide a tear which insisted on trickling down her cheek. "But I do know that Jesus is with us even though Fahfee isn't, and Jesus will take good care of us!"

Satisfied with this answer, Eberly turned and skipped out the door to join Lowell in playing with Blazie and Blackie, their puppies. Glad for a few moments of solitude, Beth fell to her knees beside the bed and poured out her concerns to her Heavenly Father, remaining there until His peace had calmed the storm of fear and loneliness which raged in her heart.

For the next three weeks, Beth heard nothing from Clifford. She waited anxiously each day for the mailman, and at last the long-awaited letter arrived. Eagerly, she tore it open and sank into a kitchen chair to read it. "Dearest Beth," she read, "The Lord has answered our prayers beyond our wildest dreams! Not only do I have a job in the pulpwood industry, but God has also opened up a new door of ministry for me! The first Sunday that I was here, I attended a little country church called Liberty Church. They, and their sister church, Indian Creek Church, are presently without a pastor. When they heard that I'm a preacher, they invited me to preach at Indian Creek Church the next Sunday, and they've called me to be the pastor of both churches. I'll be a 'circuit-riding preacher', just like I was at Boulden and Old Home, preaching at Liberty two Sundays a month and at Indian Creek the other two Sundays, on alternating Sundays. There's a parsonage right next door to the church at Indian Creek, so we already have a place to live! Start packing, because not long after you receive this letter, I'll be back to get you and the kids and take you to our new home in Alabama!"

Unable to read any further, Beth sank to her knees beside her chair, her eyes brimming with tears of joy and thankfulness. "Thank You, Father! Oh, thank You so much for answering our prayers in a greater way than we could ever have imagined!" she breathed in love and gratitude.

Several days later, Clifford returned, and he and Beth crammed all of their belongings into the car. When everything was packed, there was barely enough room for Clifford and Beth to squeeze into the front seat, and for Eberly, Lowell, and the dogs to lie lengthwise, flat on their stomachs, in the back seat, wedged between the car's roof and the assortment of boxes and bags that contained all of their family's possessions.

After two days of exhausting travel, with just a few brief stops by the roadside, so that Clifford could sleep when he was too exhausted to drive any further, they finally pulled into the front yard of their new home. It was a newly built house, set in a grove of huge Southern pine trees, right next door to a little white church. Clifford gestured toward the church. "That's Indian Creek Church, Beth, and this parsonage is brand-new. In fact, the inside of the house isn't even finished yet. There used to be three churches in this circuit, but the congregations decided that they needed a place for their pastor to live, so they voted to tear down one of the churches, use the lumber to build this parsonage, and have the folks from that congregation begin attending either Indian Creek or Liberty Church. I'm afraid that some of the people from the church that was torn down are still pretty angry about that decision!"

"I can imagine why they would be!" Beth sympathized. "I hope that their hurt feelings won't cause trouble in the other two churches."

With the help of several strong men from the church, the car was soon unloaded, and Beth began unpacking. After having lived in a one-room schoolhouse, Beth felt that even this small house, with its living room, kitchen, and two bedrooms, was spacious, although it lacked electricity, running water, or an indoor bathroom.

The following Sunday, Beth took her place at the piano and began to play. As she pressed the pedal of the piano, she happened to glance down at her feet, and was mortified to see that she was wearing a black shoe on her right foot and a red shoe on her left one. As she had hurried to get ready on time, she had reached into the darkness of their bedroom closet and grabbed what she thought were two matching shoes, without even noticing the difference.

"Well, there's nothing I can do about it now," she thought, her fingers flying across the keys, even as her face reddened with embarrassment. "I'll just have to hope that no one notices, and then hurry home and change right after the service. It sure is a good thing that we live next door to the church!"

Clifford delivered an impassioned sermon, warning sinners of the fiery judgment of God, and as soon as the final "Amen" was uttered, Beth edged down the aisle and crept out the door past Clifford, who was shaking hands with a burly farmer. "Purty good sermon, Preacher—for a <u>Yankee</u>!" he remarked condescendingly.

As Beth slipped across the churchyard toward her home, she passed a huge pine tree. Several men of the congregation were leaning up against the tree trunk, smoking cigarettes. They were engrossed in animated conversation, and didn't even notice her as she walked by. As she hurried homeward, snatches of their conversation followed her. "…can't believe that they called a Yankee to be our preacher!" one was saying angrily.

"Me neither!" another agreed. "We don't need no fool Yankees down here! They ought to stay up <u>North</u> where they belong!"

"That's right!" a third man added indignantly. "Yankees ain't nothin' but troublemakers! Why, I must've been twelve years old before I learned that 'd___ Yankee' was two words instead of one!"

Beth hurried up onto the porch of her house, her cheeks flaming, trying to shut out the sound of the loud guffaws that followed that last remark. Although they had been in Alabama for less than a week, she had already noticed that the people there continually referred to their family as "Yankees". "I wonder why they hate Northerners so much?" she mused. "They act like they're still fighting the Civil War. I'm afraid that it is going to be a real challenge to win the friendship of these people!" Suddenly, she felt like an alien, living in a hostile foreign country!

After changing her shoes, she hurried back to join Clifford in greeting the congregation. After the rest of their parishioners had left, one couple still lingered—Myrtle and Hilary Lee Byrd. It was the custom for a different one of the church families to invite the preacher and his family over for dinner each Sunday, and this week, it was the Byrds' turn. "Y'all just follow our pickup," Hilary Lee instructed, "and we'll show you the way to our place."

As they sat around the table enjoying a meal of Southern fried chicken, cornbread, collard greens, and sweet potato pie, Myrtle Byrd, who was Eberly's third-grade teacher, remarked, "I'm so glad to have Eberly in my class at school. She's really a good reader! But she's so quiet that you hardly notice that she's there!"

Later, after they had finished eating dinner, Mrs. Byrd rose from her chair, left the room for a moment, and returned with a sheet of paper in her hand. Turning to Clifford, she remarked, "That was a good sermon this morning, Preacher Frazier, but I noticed that you made quite a few grammatical errors, such as using the word 'ain't' quite frequently. I've listed your mistakes for you here on this paper. I'll be doing this for you every Sunday, and I hope that you will look over my corrections and improve your speech. Since I am a schoolteacher, I feel that it's my duty to help you in this way."

Beth was flabbergasted at Myrtle's audacity, and she watched Clifford to see how he would handle this uncomfortable situation. She was not surprised to see his face turn red with a combination of embarrassment and barely concealed anger, although he mumbled a polite, "Thank you."

In the early days of their marriage, she herself had thought that it would be helpful to Clifford if she corrected his grammar, but had soon realized that it was not worth the strife that it created. However, Mrs. Myrtle Byrd was not troubled by any such second

thoughts about her meddlesome behavior. Each Sunday morning after church, as she shook hands with Clifford, she handed him a sheet of paper on which all of his grammatical errors were neatly listed
.

As Clifford and Beth spent each Sunday afternoon in a different home, they became better acquainted with the various families of their congregation. Each time, as they were leaving after a visit in one of their parishioners' homes, their hosts would bid them farewell with a big smile and a warm invitation, "Y'all come back soon now, ya hear?"

However, as the weeks went by, both Clifford and Beth began to sense that this "Southern hospitality" was being offered out of obligation, rather than sincerity, and once Clifford even remarked from the pulpit, "When some of you invite me to your house, I get the feeling that I need to ask you if you really want me to come, or if it's just a 'courtesy invitation'."

One home in which they felt genuinely welcome, however, was that of their nearest neighbors, the Nichols, who lived just down a short, dusty lane from the parsonage. "Mr. Jim" and "Miz Ethel", as they were called, out of respect for their age, didn't attend church, but they often invited Beth and Clifford and their children to share meals with them.

At the Nichols' house, Beth was introduced to several Southern foods—hoe-cake, (which was a rather tasteless pan-fried bread composed of cornmeal, salt, and water), "pot-likker", which seemed to be any type of broth in which the hoe-cake could be dipped, and grits. "Grits is an extremely versatile food," Beth mused to herself one day, as they sat around the Nichols' table together. "It tastes like whatever you put on it!"

One thing that Beth especially enjoyed about visiting Mr. Jim and Miz Ethel was the love that she could feel radiating between husband and wife. Mr. Jim never tired of describing the first time he had seen Miz Ethel.  She had been about fourteen years of age, and he had never met her before, although they were first cousins. "She was the purtiest girl I ever seen!  I fell in love with her as soon as I seen her," he would remark, looking lovingly at her. "And she's still just as purty!"

As she looked at Miz Ethel's faded blue eyes, set in a wrinkled face, and saw the tobacco juice continually running down the corners of her mouth, from the wad of snuff that was always tucked in her cheek, Beth thought, "Now, that's real love!"

As the two families spent more time together, a genuine friendship developed between Clifford, the Yankee preacher, and Mr. Jim, the old Southern farmer.  Late in the fall, when it was "hog butcherin' time", Clifford and Beth were invited to help the Nichols.  Clifford worked alongside Mr. Jim, while Beth helped Miz Ethel in the kitchen.

One day, several weeks later, Clifford burst excitedly through the parsonage door and into the kitchen, where Beth was making biscuits for supper.  Swooping her up in his arms, he spun her around and around.  "Beth, I've got great news—the best news ever!  This afternoon, Mr. Jim asked the Lord to be his Savior!"

"That's wonderful, Clifford!  Praise the Lord!" Beth exulted, rejoicing with her husband over this first visible fruit of his ministry in "the heart of Dixie".

Several weeks later, as they were eating supper, Beth approached Clifford with an idea that she had been considering since they had moved to Alabama.  "Clifford," she suggested, "don't you think it would be a good idea for me to learn to drive? Suppose something ever happened to you?  The kids and I would be stranded way out here in the country with no transportation."

Clifford thought for a moment.  "That's a good idea, Beth.  I'll give you your first lesson tomorrow."

The next morning, Beth sat nervously behind the wheel of their shiny new car, which was parked in their yard, as Clifford pointed out the gas pedal, the clutch, and the brake, and explained the function of each.  Then he instructed her in how to start the car, shift into first gear, and release the clutch.

Beth succeeded in getting the engine started, struggled to shift into first gear, and began gingerly releasing the clutch.  However, although she tried to do it smoothly and gently, the car lurched violently back and forth like a bucking horse, as it sped directly toward a giant tree.  Beth jammed on the brake, and the motor abruptly died—just inches from the tree trunk.

"Watch where you're going!" Clifford yelled.  "You almost wrecked my brand-new car!"

Beth broke out in a cold sweat.  Driving a car was not nearly as simple as Clifford made it appear!  "Now you'll have to shift into reverse and back up, Beth," Clifford instructed.  Carefully, Beth followed Clifford's instructions, shifting into reverse, stepping on the gas, and trying to gradually ease her foot off the clutch.

What followed was a repeat performance of her earlier attempt, except for the fact that the car was now jerking unevenly backward.  To Beth's horror, as she looked in the rearview mirror, she saw a tree looming behind the car, right in its path!  Clifford saw it too.  "Stop, Beth, stop!" he screamed.  In panic, Beth felt for the brake with her left foot and missed it.  She only succeeded in pressing down harder on the gas pedal with her right foot, gunning the engine, and backing directly into the tree with a crash!

"Oh, no!" Clifford exploded at her.  "Just look what you've done!  You've ruined my beautiful car!"  And Beth instinctively knew, the moment that the car collided with the tree, that her driving lessons had also come to an abrupt halt!

About a month later, as Beth and Clifford were greeting their parishioners after church, Austin Compton, a stocky gray-haired farmer, paused and said to Beth, "Miz Beth, we're havin' a fiddlin' convention over at the Dozier School next Saturday night, and we'd like you to come and bring along that big fiddle of yours. Most folks around here ain't  never seen a fiddle like that before, and I think they'd like to hear you play it."

Beth stifled a giggle, as she heard Austin refer to her cello, on which she often played special music at church, as "that big fiddle".  She smiled at him, and replied enthusiastically, "I'd love to come and play, Mr. Compton."  But she was also puzzled. "What on earth is a fiddlin' convention?" she wondered to herself. "Well, I guess I'll just have to wait till next Saturday to find out what it is!"

The following Saturday, Beth joined a gathering of men, standing backstage at the Dozier High School auditorium.  All were carrying violins, (or "fiddles", as they called them).  Beth was the only woman there, and all the fiddlers gawked in amazement at her cello.  "What in tarnation is that thing?" she heard a thin, white-haired man with a wrinkled face ask a friend.  "Biggest fiddle I ever did see!  Wonder what it sounds like?"

For the next two hours, the fiddlers stepped out onto the stage, either singly or in groups, and performed what sounded to Beth like a prolonged session of tuning their instruments.  They repeatedly used their bows to saw rapidly back and forth on the open strings of their instruments.  The raucous sounds that proceeded from those violins were like no other music that Beth had ever heard!  However, judging from their enthusiastic clapping, foot stomping, and cheering, the people in the audience were enjoying it immensely.  Finally, Beth ventured to say timidly to the man standing next to her, "Excuse me, sir.  When are they going to stop tuning their violins and begin playing?"

He looked back at her with a look of utter amazement on his face, as if he couldn't believe what he had just heard.  "What do you mean, 'When are they gonna start playin'? They <u>been</u> playin' breakdowns for the last two hours! The fiddlin' convention is almost over."

Beth's face reddened in embarrassment at her ignorance, but she couldn't help thinking that "breakdowns" was an appropriate name for the music that she was hearing. She felt that if they didn't stop soon, her musical ears would have a breakdown!

At last the music stopped, and Austin Compton strode out onto the stage. "We have a special treat to end our fiddlin' convention tonight, y'all! Miz Beth Frazier, our preacher's wife, is going to play for us on her big fiddle." He beckoned her out onto the stage. "What do you call it, Miz Beth?"

"It's called a cello," Beth replied, as she walked out onto the stage, carrying her instrument. She took a seat in the chair provided for her, touched her bow to the strings, and began playing a classical melody, which she knew was just as foreign to her listeners as the "breakdowns" had been to her. She had never felt so out-of-place in her life!

After Beth finished playing, the audience applauded politely, but without much enthusiasm. Before she could rise from her chair, she saw Clifford striding across the stage to join her. "Before we leave tonight, I'd like to ask my wife to play for me, as I sing one of my favorite songs, 'The Stranger of Galilee', and I'd also like to invite you all to join us in church tomorrow morning."

As Beth drew her bow across the cello's strings, accompanying Clifford, and his beautiful tenor voice proclaimed the story of Jesus' ministry, she vowed that she would never again accept an invitation to a fiddlin' convention! "I'll probably never have to worry about that," she thought ruefully. "I'm sure they'd never invite me again anyway. I fit about as well here as collard greens and grits would fit on the menu of a fancy New York restaurant!"

The dreary winter months dragged past, and spring finally came. With the warmer weather came an abundance of rain, which turned roads and fields into a sea of mud. Of even greater concern to the local residents, however, was the swelling of the nearby Patsaliga River, which threatened to overflow its banks and spill onto the neighboring farmland.

One sultry spring Sunday, the Frazier family, along with Mr. and Mrs. Austin Compton, was invited to have dinner and spend the afternoon at the home of the Comptons' son and daughter-in-law. Annabelle, the younger Mrs. Compton, served a delicious dinner of ham, cornbread, sweet potatoes, mustard greens, and pecan pie.

After dinner, the hours passed swiftly as they all relaxed and visited in the spacious living room. Suddenly, Annabelle gave a start as she glanced at her watch. "My goodness, it'll be time for the evening service to start in just an hour. I'd better hurry if I'm going to get those dishes done before it's time to go!"

Immediately, Beth jumped to her feet. "Let me help you with the dishes, Annabelle. We appreciate your hospitality so much!"

Half an hour later, when the women were almost finished washing the dishes, Clifford hurried into the kitchen. "Are you ready to go yet, Beth?" he questioned anxiously. "We need to leave for church right now!"

"We're nearly done here," Beth replied. "We'll be through in another five minutes."

"Why don't you just go on to the church with Daddy Compton, Preacher Frazier?" Annabelle suggested. "I'll bring Miz Beth and your kids with me when I come."

"That's a great idea, Annabelle," Clifford agreed. "I'll see you all at church."

A few minutes later, Beth, Eberly, and Lowell climbed into Annabelle's new station wagon and started down the road. Beth glanced at her watch anxiously. "I hope that we make it on time!" she worried. "I'm supposed to play the piano for the service."

"We'll be there in plenty of time!" Annabelle assured her. "We'll take the river road. That's the shortest way from our house to the church."

About a mile from Annabelle's house, Beth noticed a young man standing by the side of the road. His thumb was raised, indicating that he needed a ride. Immediately, Annabelle pulled to the side of the road and stopped. Beth recognized the man as David Bergens, one of their church members. David came running over to the car. "Could I hitch a ride with y'all to church? My car's broke down!"

"We'd be glad to take you!" Annabelle replied, so David quickly got into the car and they continued on their way.

As Annabelle turned onto the river road, Beth noticed that the sky was growing ominously darker. Suddenly there was a deafening clap of thunder, and the next instant, a brilliant flash of lightning split the sky. The wind roared through the trees, and the rain poured down in torrents. It was difficult to see where they were going.

At last the rain began to lessen. As Beth peered through the rain-streaked window, she could see that they were approaching a gigantic puddle of water, extending as far as she could see. It was not only in front of them, but also on each side of the road. It was impossible to tell how deep it was. Annabelle slowed the car to a crawl. "Maybe we should turn around and go the other way, Miz Beth," Annabelle said hesitantly. "This doesn't look very safe! I can't tell how deep that water is!"

"Yes, I think we should do that, Annabelle," Beth agreed.

"Aw, Annabelle, don't be such a scaredy-cat!" David teased. "The water's not that deep! Go ahead! You can make it!"

"I don't know, David," Annabelle replied doubtfully, as she slowly eased the car into the edge of the water.

At that moment, they were all startled by a loud horn blast, coming from a large truck that had pulled up behind them. "See, Annabelle," David encouraged. "He wants you to go. He knows you can make it! Hurry up! Let's go!"

Annabelle stepped on the gas and drove further along the flooded road, to the accompaniment of the truck's continued frantic honking. Looking out, Beth could see that the water was getting deeper. Already, the car's tires were half-submerged in the water. Glancing behind her, Beth could see that the driver of the truck was now rapidly turning his lights on and off, as if he were trying to signal them. Annabelle noticed it too. "I don't know, David," she said in confusion. "Maybe he's trying to tell us to turn around!"

"Naw, Annabelle," David replied confidently. "He's telling us to go—," but his words were cut off by the sickening rush of water entering the car, as the station wagon dropped into a deep hole in the road, and the engine died with a swoosh and a gurgle!

Instantly, the water that had rushed into the car reached the height of the seats, and Beth wondered if they would be swept away by the flood. "Quick, kids! Climb up onto the seat!" she ordered. Eberly and Lowell instantly obeyed, their eyes wide with fear.

"Mommy, are we going to drown?" Eberly cried in terror.

"No, Honey! We're going to be all right. Jesus will take care of us." Beth tried to soothe her daughter, although she feared the same possibility herself.

"I'll walk back to that truck and ask them to help us," offered David. He opened the car door and stepped out into the rushing water. Beth was horrified to see him immediately sink down into the water, which was chest-high! David struggled to walk in the direction of the truck, but Beth could see that he was having difficulty keeping his footing.

Just then, Beth saw the doors of the truck burst open, and two men jumped out. One of them was carrying a coil of rope. He threw one end of the rope to David, who grabbed it and held on tightly. With all their strength, the two men pulled David out of the water. Peering through the gathering darkness, Beth suddenly realized that the two men were Austin Compton and Clifford!

As soon as David reached dry ground, Austin secured the rope to the bumper of his pick-up. Then, each of the three men took turns tying the rope around their waists and struggling through the floodwater until all four of the remaining occupants of the marooned car were rescued!

As Beth watched the rescue of her two children, she breathed a prayer of thanks that the water had never risen above the level of the seats, and that the car had not been swept away in the torrent. "Thank You, Father, for keeping us safe!" she murmured.

After everyone had been brought to safety, Austin turned to his daughter-in-law in exasperation. "Why on earth did you keep driving into that water, Annabelle? Didn't you hear me honking at you to turn around? When Clifford and I got to the church, we heard that the river road was flooded. We were afraid that you'd go this way, so we came looking for you to warn you!"

"David thought you were telling us to go ahead." Annabelle turned angrily to face David. "I never should have listened to you, David!" she blazed at him. "Thanks to you, my brand-new car is ruined!"

"Hey, I was wrong, and I'm sorry!" David replied remorsefully. "Can you ever forgive me, Annabelle?"

"Yes, I forgive you," Annabelle said grudgingly.

Just then, Clifford spoke up. "Folks, I think that instead of blaming each other for what happened, we need to thank the Lord that no lives were lost in this mishap!"

"Me too!" Beth agreed heartily. So they all bowed their heads, as Clifford led them in a prayer of heartfelt gratitude to the Lord for His protection.

The warm, wet spring of 1954 turned into a hot, humid summer. Although Clifford and Beth had been in Alabama for months, they still felt like outsiders among the people to whom they ministered. For some reason they couldn't comprehend, their parishioners could never seem to forget the fact that they were Northerners. They often overheard snide remarks conveying the sentiment that "Those Yankees should go back up North where they belong!"

One hot July day, the mailman delivered a parcel addressed to "Pastor, Indian Creek Church, Dozier, Alabama". The return address was the main headquarters of the Congregational Church of America, the denomination to which Indian Creek Church and Liberty Church both belonged.

Beth ripped the package open and saw that it contained a stack of adult Sunday School study books, containing lessons for the next quarter. On top of the books was a letter. "Dear Pastor," she read. "Since your church is a member of the Congregational Church of America, we are sending you some copies of our adult Sunday School literature. From now on, in order to standardize what is being taught in the churches of our denomination, we have decided to require that all churches use our denomination's official Sunday School lesson materials. Thank you."

Beth laid the letter aside and glanced at the Sunday School quarterlies. "Jesus, Our Great Example" was emblazoned in bright red letters on the cover of each book. With an uneasy feeling in the pit of her stomach, she opened the top book, turned to the introduction, and began reading. "Jesus is regarded by all educated people to be one of the greatest moral teachers of all time. Our goal should be to please God by following his example. If we faithfully strive to pattern our lives after his, we can have good reason to hope that God will one day accept us into heaven."

"Though in the past," the book continued, "much emphasis has been placed on Jesus' deity, his virgin birth, and the necessity of his death on the cross to pay for the sins of mankind, many modern theologians question whether these things are actually true. They feel that Jesus' followers may have incorporated these stories into his teachings to give greater authority to his words. The details of Jesus' birth, life, and death are unimportant in comparison to the moral principles of his teaching…"

Beth had read enough! She was appalled! Slamming the book shut in disgust, she tossed it onto the floor. "Why, those are the same lies that I heard at the Unitarian Church where Mother and Dad sent me when I was a little girl," she thought in dismay. "I've got to show Clifford this immediately!"

Quickly, she grabbed the letter and one of the lesson books and ran out the front door and across the yard to the church. Bursting into the little Sunday School classroom which Clifford used as a study, she exclaimed, "Clifford, you've got to read this! It's terrible!"

Clifford took the book from her outstretched hand, opened it, and read silently for a moment. "You're right, Beth!" he agreed in alarm. "It looks like the leaders of this denomination have forsaken the doctrines of true Christianity and become 'modernists'!"

"What are you going to do?" she questioned.

"I'm going to call a meeting of the leaders of both churches and show this to them. Surely they won't want to stay in a denomination that denies the deity of Jesus Christ, His virgin birth, and the way of salvation!"

However, at the meeting, Clifford and Beth met with unexpected opposition. "But, Preacher Frazier, we can't withdraw from our denomination!" Don Bell, a member of the board of Liberty Church protested. "The Congregational Church owns our church buildings, the parsonage, and the land they are built on. If we tried to leave the denomination, they would take our churches away from us. Besides, our families have been members of the Congregational Church for the past two hundred years!"

"Yes," Austin Compton agreed. "Besides, I don't see what's so bad about those Sunday School books anyway. Personally, I'd like to hear a little more about following Jesus' example and a lot less of your 'hell-fire and damnation' preachin', Preacher Frazier!"

"But I'm preaching the truth from God's Word, and these books deny it!" Clifford protested. "Can't we at least agree not to use this Sunday School material?"

Just then, "Mr. Jim" Nichols spoke up. "I don't know about the rest of y'all, but I never did know how I could have my sins forgiven and go to heaven till Preacher Frazier explained that Jesus died on the cross for me. I make a motion that we don't use them books." A vote was taken and the motion passed, although by a very narrow margin. Both Clifford and Beth left the meeting with a distinct feeling that although they had won this battle, the "civil war" within their church was far from over!

Several weeks later, at the conclusion of the Sunday morning worship service, Don Bell rose to his feet and made an announcement. "As most of y'all know, there's been some disagreement recently about whether or not we should use our denomination's Sunday School books. We've all heard what

Preacher Frazier thinks, but some of us would like to hear the other side of the story. So Austin Compton and I have invited Rev. Thomas Butterworth, who works at the Congregational Church headquarters, to come and speak to us next Sunday morning here at Liberty Church. We've invited the congregation of Indian Creek Church to join us for that service. I think that after we've heard what Preacher Butterworth has to say, we'll be able to make a more intelligent decision about this matter."

Clifford was furious when he heard that Don and Austin had invited Rev. Butterworth without even consulting him, but there was nothing that he could do to change it. "How could they do that to me?" he fumed to Beth on the way home from church. "It looks like we're heading for a real showdown now! If that Butterworth preaches false doctrine from my pulpit, I'm just going to speak up and start preaching the truth, and the people will have to decide who they're going to listen to!"

Although Beth admired Clifford's courage in being willing to stand up for what was right, she couldn't imagine that he would be able to accomplish anything constructive by engaging in a shouting match with Rev. Butterworth. "We don't even know the man," Beth cautioned. "Perhaps he doesn't even agree with what is written in those quarterlies. Why don't you just listen to him, and then if he does say something heretical, you can preach against it in your sermon the following Sunday? You could invite the people from Liberty Church to join us at Indian Creek for another joint church meeting."

"No, Beth!" Clifford insisted. "The time for false teaching to be confronted is when it is preached—not later!" So Beth said no more on the subject, knowing well that it was futile to disagree with her husband when he had made a decision.

In addition to her apprehension about the coming confrontation, Beth also felt a growing concern about her husband's health. For the past few weeks, Clifford had been troubled with a throbbing ache in his left shoulder. It seemed to grow worse at night, often becoming so excruciatingly painful that it disrupted his sleep. She feared that he might be having trouble with his heart! "What would we do if something happened to Clifford?" she wondered. For the next few days, she spent much time on her knees, pouring out her heart to her Heavenly Father.

Long before dawn on Sunday morning, Clifford and Beth were roused from sleep by an insistent pounding on their front door. "Who on earth could that be at this hour?" Clifford muttered, as he rolled out of bed and stumbled through the darkness into the living room.

Beth hastily pulled on her bathrobe and groped for the oil lamp. By the time she had gotten it lit and joined Clifford, he was already talking to Hilary Lee Byrd, one of the few people in their neighborhood who had a telephone. "I just got the call, Preacher Frazier," Hilary Lee was saying to her husband. "The Powell family was in a terrible car wreck down in Jacksonville, Florida last night. Their boy Elihu was hurt bad, and he's in the hospital there. They want you to come right away!"

"Thanks for letting me know, Hilary Lee," Clifford responded. "I'll leave just as soon as I can get ready!"

As Clifford hurriedly dressed for the trip, he remarked, "I know I've got to go visit the Powells, but this couldn't have happened at a worse time! Now I won't even be here when Butterworth preaches!"

"I'll get a ride to Liberty Church with Mr. Jim and Miz Ethel, and I'll take notes on Rev. Butterworth's sermon and let you know exactly what he says," Beth promised.

Several hours later, Beth sat in a pew at Liberty Church, her pen poised above the pad on her lap. How thankful she was that she knew shorthand, so that she could quickly record the exact words of their guest speaker! Rev. Butterworth rose and stood behind the pulpit, a broad smile on his face. "It is a great pleasure to be with y'all this morning. As I look out over this congregation, I can see that there are many fine families represented here—leading citizens who are pillars of this community. I know that God Himself must be very pleased to see so many wonderful people gathered here in His house today!"

"Well," Beth thought to herself with a wry smile, "Rev. Butterworth is certainly living up to his name! He's really 'buttering up' these people!"

"My subject today will be 'Jesus, the Great Teacher'," he announced, and then he proceeded to preach a sermon that sounded as if it had been taken directly out of the offensive Sunday School book. "In conclusion," he finally said, after an address full of flowery phrases and flattery, "our God is a God of love! He would never be so cruel as to send anyone to hell! If we sincerely try to do the best we can in following Jesus' example, we can be assured that God will welcome us into heaven."

Beth laid down her pen in disgust after she had recorded his final words. "Well, now I know what the Bible means when it talks about false teachers who tickle people's ears!" she thought. Looking around at the smiling faces of the congregation, she could see that most of them had enjoyed the sermon immensely.

"Great sermon, Preacher Butterworth! We need more preachin' like that!" she heard several of the leading men in the church comment, as they shook the visiting minister's hand heartily.

The following Sunday, after reading Beth's notes on Rev. Butterworth's sermon, Clifford once again proclaimed the truth from God's Word about the way of salvation and Who Jesus is. "The Bible says that the road to hell is wide and that many people are walking on it, but the path to eternal life is narrow, and only a few find it. Jesus said, 'I am the Way!' He is the only Way to heaven. We are all sinners who deserve to go to hell, and there is only one way we can escape that terrible punishment! It is to believe that Jesus, God's only begotten Son, died on the cross for our sins!"

As Beth glanced around at the congregation, she couldn't help contrasting the expressions on their faces with the looks that she had seen on those same faces the week before. For the most part, angry frowns replaced the happy smiles which had been there the previous Sunday. However, she was encouraged to see Mr. Jim nodding approvingly and occasionally calling out a hearty "Amen, Preacher!" to the points that Clifford was making.

The following Tuesday evening, Beth heard a knock at the door, and opened it to find Don Bell and Austin Compton standing there. "Is Preacher Frazier here?" Don inquired.

"Yes, he's here. Won't you men come in and have some coffee?" she invited

.

"No, thank you, ma'am." Austin replied. "We just need to talk to him for a minute."

When Clifford came to the door a moment later, Don said brusquely, "Some of us had a meeting last night, and we've called a full congregational meeting for tomorrow night at Liberty Church. There's some things we need to discuss with you, Preacher Frazier!"

With that, the two men abruptly turned and walked down the porch steps and out into the night. Beth looked at Clifford, an uneasy feeling in the pit of her stomach. "They had a secret meeting last night, Beth," Clifford sighed. "I'm afraid that our ministry here may be coming to an end!"

The next night, Clifford sat next to Beth in the pew at Liberty Church, while Don Bell acted as chairman of the meeting. Without spending any time on preliminaries, he stated, "The purpose of this meeting is to inform y'all, and especially you, Preacher Frazier, about some decisions that were made by the leaders of this church when they met together last night. First, we agreed that we prefer Rev. Butterworth's type of message, rather than Preacher Frazier's. If modern scholars have made some new discoveries about the true meaning of the Bible, we need to know about them. After all, this is the twentieth century!"

Looking pointedly at Clifford, he continued, "If you plan to stay on as our pastor, we will expect you to teach our denomination's beliefs when you preach. The second thing we decided is that we will be using the Sunday School materials which were sent to us by the Congregational Church headquarters."

Without waiting to hear any more, Clifford rose to his feet. "If that's the kind of pastor you want, you'll have to find yourselves another man," he said firmly. "I can't remain in a place where I am forbidden to preach the truth of the Word of God! I resign, effective immediately!" And with those words, Clifford's brief ministry in "the heart of Dixie" came to an end.

Later that night, as Beth lay in bed, her heart cried out, "What do you have for us now, Lord? We haven't even been here for a year, and now we'll be moving again! Please show us what you want us to do!" As she continued praying, her troubled thoughts gradually grew calm, and at last she drifted off into a peaceful sleep.

# Chapter 12—American Gypsies

The next morning, as they sat around the breakfast table, Clifford announced, "I spent most of last night praying, Beth, and I believe that the Lord wants us to move to California. We'll leave as soon as you can get packed."

Beth's mouth dropped open in amazement, and the spoon she had been holding clattered to the table, splattering oatmeal everywhere. "California?" she questioned incredulously. "What on earth would we do in California? We don't even know anyone there!"

"My brother Earl and his wife Mildred live in Glendale. I'm sure that we could stay with them until we find a place to live and I get a job."

"Shouldn't we write to them first and ask if that would be convenient for them?"

"Nah! They're family. We don't need to ask ahead of time. They'll be thrilled to see us!" Clifford assured her.

The following morning, after a frenzied day and night of packing, the Frazier family crowded into their car and began the long trek to the West Coast.  Beth was wedged in the front seat, unable to move, her feet crowded between bags of their belongings.  Eberly and Lowell peered out of the back seat, as they lay prone in the small space left between a stack of boxes and the roof.  And between Beth and Clifford, two wriggling, panting dogs competed for what little space was left.  As they sped down the highway, Beth's head spun from the rapidity with which their lives had changed.  Even after more than nine years of marriage, she still had not become accustomed to her husband's swift and unpredictable decision-making!

Beth's thoughts were rudely interrupted by Clifford's irritable voice. "Get those dogs out of my way, Beth!  I don't even have room enough to drive!"

"I'm sorry, dear."  She slid Blackie over onto her lap, and encircled Laddie with her left arm.

The next several days were a blur of heat and weariness.  The summer sun beat down mercilessly on the roof of the car as it inched its way across state after state.  Clifford drove until he was exhausted, only stopping to park on the side of the road and sleep for a few hours when he could continue no longer.

Late one afternoon as they were driving through the middle of the Arizona desert, Clifford suddenly pulled off the road and gripped his left shoulder, grimacing in pain. "Clifford, what's the matter?" Beth cried in alarm.

"It's that awful pain!  It started bothering me again this morning, and it's gotten worse all day!" he groaned. "I don't see how I can drive any longer."

A cold fear gripped Beth. "Maybe Clifford is having a heart attack!" she thought in panic. "If something happens to him, we could be stranded out here in the desert! Oh, if only I knew how to drive!" In desperation, she cried out silently to her Lord, "Father, help us! Show us what to do!"

A moment later, she recalled having just seen a billboard advertising a motel that was located only ten miles down the road. "Clifford, there's a little town just a few miles from here. Do you think that you could manage to drive just a little bit further?"

"I'll try," he agreed, gritting his teeth from the pain.

As Clifford drove and Beth prayed, their car crawled the few remaining miles into town. Never had such a short time seemed so endless to Beth! At last, they pulled into the parking lot of a small motel. "We're going to have to stay here tonight," Clifford sighed wearily. "I can't go any further."

Beth breathed a silent prayer of gratitude. "Thank You, Father, for getting us here safely! And Father, please heal Clifford!"

That night, Clifford's pain became so excruciating that he was unable to sleep. He tossed, turned, and moaned, and couldn't find any position that was comfortable. Finally, he got out of bed, went in the bathroom and reclined in the tub. For some unknown reason, he seemed to feel a bit better there. Beth stayed close by his side, fearful that he might not survive until morning.

At last, the first faint rays of dawn shone through the window, signaling the end of that interminable night. "Clifford," Beth urged, "I think that you need to get to a doctor as soon as possible and find out what's the matter with you!"

"I'm afraid you're right, Beth," he conceded reluctantly. "We can't afford it, but I can't go on like this. I've got to get some help!"

Several hours later, Clifford and Beth were seated in the examination room of Dr. Stone's office. The doctor listened carefully to Clifford's heart and breathing, and then moved Clifford's shoulder up and down. As the doctor moved his shoulder back and forth, beads of sweat formed on Clifford's face, and he grimaced in pain.

At last, Dr. Stone released Clifford's shoulder, and smiled at him encouragingly. "I've got good news for you, Rev. Frazier. Your heart is fine. Your shoulder pain is caused by an inflammation in your joint. The medical term for it is bursitis. Rest, ice packs, and medication should help alleviate the pain."

"But we're on our way to California, and we need to get back on the road," Clifford protested. "How soon will I be able to drive again?"

"You're in no condition to drive right now," Dr. Stone replied firmly. "If you do, it will only aggravate your problem. You need to rest for a day or two until the pain subsides and then you can continue your trip."

Later that afternoon, while Clifford was resting in their motel room, Beth took Eberly and Lowell outside for a walk. It was a sweltering summer day and even the sidewalk felt hot beneath Beth's feet. "You know, kids," she remarked, "I once heard someone say that it gets so hot here in the Arizona desert that you can fry an egg on the sidewalk! It sure feels like you could do that today, doesn't it?"

"Let's try it, Mommy!" Eberly suggested eagerly.

"Yes, let's see if it will really work!" Lowell begged.

"All right," Beth agreed impulsively. She hurried into their room and returned with an egg from their small supply of food. Cracking open the eggshell, she let its contents drip out onto the sidewalk. It sizzled briefly and gradually turned slightly white around the edges. However, after fifteen minutes of waiting and enduring the amused looks of passersby, Beth finally cleaned up the still-raw egg, and disposed of it. "Well, kids," she said, her cheeks pink with embarrassment, "I guess that should teach us that we can't believe everything we hear, shouldn't it?"

After a day of rest, Clifford's pain subsided enough that they could continue their journey, and they finally arrived at Earl and Mildred's house late the next afternoon. Earl was busily watering his lawn as they drove into his driveway. Dropping the hose, he ran over to the car. "Clifford," he gasped in amazement, "What on earth are you doing here? I thought you were in Alabama."

"We've decided to move to California, and we figured that we could stay with you until we can find a place of our own."

Earl's face reddened in anger. "Well, you figured wrong! You've got a lot of nerve to just barge in on us like this, without even asking us if it was all right!" he yelled. "I have a wife and two kids of my own, you know, and we only have a small house. Honestly, I don't know where we can put you."

At this angry outburst, Beth shrank down in her seat and wished that she could make herself invisible. However, Clifford's face instantly turned a brilliant shade of crimson, which exactly matched that of his brother's. "So, this is the kind of welcome we get after we've come all the way across the country to see you?" he roared. "Just in case you've forgotten, we're family! I thought family members were supposed to help each other, but I can see I was wrong!"

"All right, I guess you can stay with us for a few days," Earl agreed grudgingly, "but you'd better be out of our home by the end of this week!"

Beth's heart sank. The meager funds with which they had begun their trip were almost totally depleted. Even if they were fortunate enough to find a house to rent within such a short time, they didn't have enough money to pay for it! In desperation, she silently poured out her burden to the Lord, "Father, You know our need! Please provide a place for us to live, and show us what You want us to do now!"

The next few days were a time of great tension between the two Frazier families. The anger that continually smoldered in Clifford and Earl's hearts needed only the smallest spark to cause it to suddenly burst forth in a flaming battle of words. Although Earl's wife Mildred graciously tried to make them feel welcome, Beth knew that having them there was putting a tremendous strain on her sister-in-law.

At supper one evening, Mildred announced, "I think I may have found the answer to your housing problem! I was talking with our neighbor today, and I mentioned that you folks needed a place to live. When she heard that Clifford was a preacher, she told me that her church operates something called a 'missionary colony'. It's a place where missionaries can live rent-free while they are home on furlough. She said that since Clifford is a minister, they might let you stay in one of their houses. She suggested that you should go see her pastor tomorrow."

"That sounds like a great idea, Mildred!" Beth exclaimed gratefully.

The next morning, Clifford and Beth sat in the office of Paul Browning, the pastor of Calvary Christian Missionary Alliance Church. After hearing their story, Pastor Browning said encouragingly, "I believe that we can help you folks. Our denomination has received an extremely generous gift from a wealthy Christian lady who lives here in Glendale. She donated her entire estate for the purpose of building houses on it to provide places for missionaries to live while they are on furlough. I'm sure that she will agree with me that you deserve the use of one of the homes in the missionary colony."

"Praise the Lord!" Beth cried, overflowing with thanksgiving for the way He had met their need.

What a relief it was to both Clifford and Beth to be able to move their family into a beautifully furnished cottage in the middle of a Christian community! As they lay in bed that night, Clifford remarked, "Isn't it wonderful how the Lord has provided a place for us to live? But we're almost out of money. I sure hope that I can find a job soon, but I don't know how I'm going to be able to work with this terrible pain in my shoulder."

Beth shared his concern. Although Dr. Stone had assured Clifford that he should be feeling better within a few days, the excruciating pain had continued, making it impossible for him to use his left arm and causing him to have many sleepless nights. "How will Clifford ever be able to work if his arm hurts so badly and he is getting so little sleep?" she wondered. Long after Clifford had fallen asleep, she lay awake pondering the problem and consulting her Heavenly Father about it.

The next morning as they sat around the breakfast table, Beth said hesitantly, "I think I may have a solution to our financial needs. I believe that I should get a job and work until your bursitis gets better."

She had expected Clifford to protest vigorously, so she was surprised to hear him admit reluctantly, "I'm afraid you're right, Beth. I hate the thought of you having to support our family, but I don't see any way that I can hold down a job right now."

Later that morning as Beth was having her prayer time, she whispered, "Father, please guide me to the right job. How wonderful it would be if I could find an art job!" Suddenly she jumped up from her knees, as an exciting possibility occurred to her. "Why, Gospel Light Press is located right here in Glendale!" she thought. "They're the company that produced the Sunday School and Vacation Bible School materials that we used when we were in Illinois! Maybe they need an artist! Perhaps I can serve the Lord with my artistic ability!"

The following day, Beth sat in the office of Miss Eleanor Doan, the art director of Gospel Light Press. Miss Doan leafed through Beth's portfolio, and then looked up with a smile. "Your work is outstanding, Mrs. Frazier, and we do need another artist right now. We've recently begun work on our Vacation Bible School materials for 1955, and one of the ladies in the art department has just resigned because she is expecting a baby. Could you begin work next Monday?"

"I certainly could!"

The summer and fall flew by in a happy flurry of busyness! Beth was overjoyed to be using her artistic talents to illustrate literature that would be used to teach God's Word to children. "Oh, Father," she breathed thankfully one morning as she prepared for work, "You truly have done 'exceeding abundantly above all that we could ask or think'! Only You could have provided me with a job that not only meets our needs, but also gives me such a wonderful opportunity to serve You!"

Early in November, Beth realized that she was pregnant once again. However, although she was overjoyed at the thought of having another baby, her happiness was mingled with fear. "I've already lost three babies," she thought sadly. "Suppose I lose this one too! I'm thirty-eight years old now, and by the time this baby is born, I'll be thirty-nine. This is probably my last chance to have another child." She determined that this time she would seek medical help <u>before</u> she developed any problems. If there was any way to prevent another miscarriage, she was determined to find it!

Beth made an appointment to see an obstetrician the following week. "Mrs. Frazier," Dr. Danforth said soberly after he had finished examining her, "since you have already had three miscarriages, you have a great risk of losing this baby also. However, there is a treatment available now that has had good success in preventing miscarriages in women who are at high risk of having one."

"What is it?" Beth asked hopefully.

"You would receive a hormone shot each month until the critical first few months of your pregnancy are past. I can give you the first shot today if you wish to try this treatment."

"Yes, please do!"

After getting the shots for several months, Beth was able to welcome the new year of 1955 with the joyous knowledge that the most dangerous part of her pregnancy was over, and with eager anticipation of the birth of a new little Frazier in early June!

By the end of January, Clifford's bursitis pain finally began to lessen. Beth could see that he was getting restless after his period of forced inactivity. One evening as they lay in bed, he remarked, "Beth, I'd like to get back into the pastorate again. I want you to write to Moody Bible Institute again and see if they can recommend a church where I can candidate."

"Yes, Clifford, I'd be glad to!" How she thanked God that Clifford again desired to pastor a church! He had been so terribly discouraged by the events in Alabama that she had feared he had given up on the idea of ever being a pastor again. Although Beth thoroughly enjoyed her job, she knew that she wouldn't mind leaving it if Clifford found a church to pastor. Besides, she had only planned to work for a few more months anyway, since the baby was coming.

In mid-February, a letter arrived from Moody, recommending that Clifford contact Grace Bible Church in rural Nebraska. After several weeks of corresponding with the church leaders, they invited Clifford to come and speak at their church. "Beth," Clifford exclaimed excitedly, waving the letter in the air, "this could be our next place of service for the Lord. Tell Miss Doan tomorrow that next Friday will be your last day at work, and then start getting ready to move to Nebraska!"

"But, Clifford, don't you think that we should stay here until we're certain that they're going to call you to be their pastor?" Beth questioned in dismay. "It's wonderful that they want you to go up there and preach, but I don't think that we should plan on moving until we know for sure that you have the job!"

"Well, even if it doesn't work out, I don't want to stay here in California any longer anyway!" Clifford retorted angrily. "I'm sick of having people looking at me and wondering why my wife is working and I'm not! It's time now for you to quit your job and let me support this family again like I'm supposed to!"

Beth sighed. She had learned during their ten years of marriage that when Clifford made up his mind about something, it was useless to discuss it any further. "Even if I could convince him to change his mind, he wouldn't really agree with me about it, and if anything went wrong, he would blame me for it," she mused. "It's just like Mother used to say, 'A man convinced against his will is of the same opinion still'!"

The following week, the Frazier family began the long journey to Nebraska. Their car snaked its way across California, Arizona, Utah, and into Colorado. Soon after they entered the mountainous high country of Colorado, ominous gray clouds blotted out the sun and huge snowflakes began to fall, driven furiously before an icy wind. The snow obscured Clifford's vision and rapidly covered the highway. The landscape became a continuous expanse of white, making it nearly impossible to discern where the highway ended and the roadside began.

In the gloom of the early twilight of the winter day, Beth peered at the map and realized that they were approaching the ascent to a mountain pass that rose to a summit of ten thousand feet. "If the road is this bad down here, what must it be like at the top of the pass?" she thought in alarm. Just then, she glanced out the window, and noticed a sign by the side of the road. She could barely read it through the swirling snow and the gathering darkness. "Warning!" It proclaimed in bold letters, "All vehicles traveling beyond this point must have chains!"

"Clifford, did you see that sign?"

"No, Beth," he answered irritably, "It's taking all my concentration just to keep this car on the road. It's getting slippery out there! What did it say?"

"It said that we must have chains on our tires in order to go any further on this road. We're coming to a mountain pass!"

"Well, I want to get over that mountain before it gets any darker, and there's no place here to stop and buy chains," Clifford said firmly. "I'm sure we'll be fine if I just drive slowly and be careful."

"I don't think we should try to go any further tonight," Beth cautioned. "It's too dangerous. We just passed through a little town. I think we should go back and spend the night there. Then tomorrow we can buy chains and be on our way."

"Nah, we'll be fine!" Clifford assured her.

"No, Clifford. We should stop now!" Beth argued with uncharacteristic firmness. "If we go on tonight, we'll be risking our lives!"

Finally, Clifford gave in to her pleas and reluctantly turned the car around. At the outskirts of the small town, he pulled into the parking lot of a gas station that had already closed for the night. A sign in the window advertised, "Chains for sale!"

"We'll spend the night here in the car," he announced. "That way, as soon as the station opens tomorrow morning, we can buy some chains and get on the road."

"But it's below freezing out there, Clifford," Beth protested. "How are we going to keep warm if we stay in the car?"

"I'll turn the heater on for a while whenever we get too cold. We'll be fine."

Beth bundled herself and her family up in blankets and settled down to endure the long cold night. Just when she felt that the night would never end, the first faint rays of dawn glowed in the eastern sky. Several hours later, the proprietor of the filling station arrived and opened it for business. Within a few minutes, Clifford had bought the chains and had them put on the tires, and they were on their way.

As the car inched its way along the icy, snowpacked road, Beth was appalled as the morning light revealed the tremendous danger they would have been in if they had tried to continue their journey the night before. The highway was perched on the edge of a sheer drop-off, with no guardrails to prevent travelers from plunging thousands of feet into the chasm below. Hairpin turns snaked their way back and forth as the road proceeded up the mountain, and signs proclaimed that even in the best of times, it was unsafe to exceed a speed of ten or fifteen miles per hour.

As they rounded yet another tortuous bend, Beth gasped in horror at the terrifying sight that met her eyes. To her right, a car had slid off the road. Its front wheels were suspended in mid-air, hanging out over a cliff, and its rear wheels were stuck in a snowbank. As they passed by, she could see the white, panic-striken faces of the family of four who sat motionless in the car, fearful that their slightest movement would loosen the car from its precarious position of safety and hurl them over the edge of the precipice to their deaths.

Instantly, Beth breathed an urgent prayer for the family in distress. "Why that, or something even worse, could have happened to us!" she realized, suddenly feeling weak all over. "Thank You, Father, for your protection!"

Clifford had also seen the grave plight of the family. He turned and smiled gratefully at Beth. "You probably saved our lives by insisting that we needed to stop last night, Beth!" he said thankfully. "I have to admit that you were right and I was wrong!"

"Well, let's just praise the Lord that we're safe!" Beth responded with a shaky smile.

They arrived safely in Nebraska that Saturday night, and on Sunday Clifford preached in the little country church. Beth played the piano for the services, and she and Clifford sang a duet. As Beth blended her soft alto voice in harmony with Clifford's rich tenor, she looked out over the congregation, and wondered whether this place might be their next place of ministry.

After the Sunday morning service, the people of the church had planned a special dinner so that they could become better acquainted with Clifford and Beth and their family. "That was a great sermon, Preacher Frazier," a red-faced farmer remarked, around a mouthful of fried chicken. "When you preach, you don't beat around the bush! I like that!"

After lunch was over, several of the ladies of the church invited Beth to join them on a tour of the parsonage, which was located next door to the church. Beth was pleasantly surprised to see that, unlike the house where they had lived in Alabama, this one had electricity, running water, and an inside bathroom! As they walked into the kitchen, one of the ladies announced, "We're planning on redecorating this place for our new pastor." She picked up a book of wallpaper samples, which was lying on the kitchen table. "Which ones do you like best, Mrs. Frazier?" For the next few minutes, Beth paged through the book and indicated her preferences for wallpaper for the living room, kitchen, and the three bedrooms.

During the next few days, the Frazier family visited in several different homes. They enjoyed getting to know various members of the congregation and were impressed by their warm-hearted friendliness. On Wednesday evening, as they sat around the table enjoying a dessert of blueberry pie, Mrs. Edith Sloane, their hostess, beamed at them. "Well, tonight's the big night! After prayer meeting, we'll be voting on whether we should call you as our pastor, Rev. Frazier. If it goes the way I expect it to, you folks can begin moving into the parsonage tomorrow. It's really wonderful that you brought all your things with you!"

After prayer meeting was over, Clifford and Beth and their family returned to the Sloanes' house and eagerly awaited the outcome of the vote. At last they heard a car pull into the driveway. The front door opened, and Mrs. Sloane entered, accompanied by her husband Allen, who was the chairman of the board of elders. Mr. Sloane twisted his hat nervously in his hands, looked at the floor for a moment, and then cleared his throat. "I'm afraid that we have bad news for you, Rev. Frazier," he reported sadly, "Much to our surprise, the congregation voted not to call you as our pastor. The vote was close though. We're so sorry! We were looking forward to having you as our minister."

Clifford and Beth both stood there speechless with shock. From the reception they had received from the church people, both of them had expected that Clifford would be called as their pastor. "Lord, what do you have for us now?" Beth wondered in confusion.

The next morning, as Clifford and Beth were getting dressed, Clifford announced, "I think that we should go to Florida. When we were living in Alabama, I heard that there were a lot of jobs available in the vegetable packinghouses in Florida."

"Florida?" Beth questioned unbelievingly. "But Clifford, that's so far away! Don't you think that you could find a job someplace closer?"

"Well, I need to get a job as soon as possible, since our new baby is coming in just a few months, and since I know I can find a job there, that's where we're going."

After a grueling but uneventful trip, the Frazier family arrived in Florida at last. They found a place to live in a government housing project in Pahokee, a small town on the shores of Lake Okeechobee, and Clifford soon found a job in a packinghouse. Every day, he worked long hours sorting and packing tomatoes, green beans, and other vegetables for shipment to markets throughout the United States. The work was tedious, and the pay was low, but it provided for their basic needs.

Several months passed. One warm April night as they sat around the supper table, Clifford remarked, "I think that we should move before the baby is born. Since you have to have another Caesarian, you need to be in a big city where you can get top-notch care."

"Do you want to go back to Chicago again? I got good care there."

"No, I don't have any desire to go back to Illinois after all the trouble we've had there. Since your family is in New Jersey, I think that we should move to Newark."

Once again, the Fraziers packed their belongings and piled into the car. By the end of the week, they had moved into a small second-floor apartment in downtown Newark, and Clifford had found employment as a desk clerk in a hotel nearby. Beth soon found a good obstetrician, and the birth of her baby was scheduled for June 6th.

Although Beth was thankful that Clifford had gotten a job and that they were living near her family, she felt concerned about the effects which such an unsettled life was having on her children.

Although Eberly continued to do well in her studies, Beth could see that she was becoming painfully shy and withdrawing into a world of books. Lowell, however, had the opposite problem. Although he never had any difficulty making new friends, he was having great difficulty in learning to read and was struggling with his schoolwork. "It's no wonder that they're having problems," she thought ruefully. "After all, they started this school year in California, moved to Florida, and ended up in New Jersey!"

Also, the environment in Newark was the exact opposite of what her children were used to. Instead of having acres of land on which to run and play, their playground was now the city streets and the miniscule yard behind their apartment building. However she turned these concerns over to her Heavenly Father.

As the time approached for the new baby to be born, Lowell and Eberly became tremendously excited. "I can't wait for the baby to come! I sure hope it's a girl! I want a little sister!" Eberly announced firmly one day.

"No!" Lowell protested. "It better be a boy, because I want a brother!"

One night, as Clifford and Beth were lying in bed, Clifford said, "If we have another boy, I'd like to name him Raymond, after my good friend Ray Boulden."

"That sounds like a great idea, Clifford. And if it's a girl, I'd like to name her Ramone, after my French friend Ramone, who worked with me at Norcross."

"What about a middle name?" Clifford questioned.

Beth was silent for a moment, shocked that Clifford had not already made a decision on that issue. "I'd like to give my maiden name, 'Conrad', to our baby as a middle name, in honor of Dad and Mother," she replied thoughtfully. "They've done so much for me!"

"Okay. Raymond, or Ramone, Conrad Frazier, it is, then!"

When Beth awoke from the anesthesia on that hot afternoon of June 6, 1955, she was greeted by a nurse who was holding a bundle wrapped in a blue blanket. "I'm glad to see that you're awake, Mrs. Frazier," she smiled. "Your son is eager to meet you!"

Beth reached out and took her baby into her arms. "Hello, Raymond!" she breathed joyfully. As she looked into his wide blue eyes and gently smoothed back his soft blond hair, her heart overflowed with a song of thanksgiving. "Thank you, Father, for answering my prayer and giving me another child!"

"Amen!" Clifford agreed heartily, as he stood by her side, beaming with pride at their new son.

Several days later, when Beth brought Raymond home, he was greeted by a very excited big sister and brother. Although Eberly had hoped the baby would be a girl, she instantly fell in love with her new baby brother! And Lowell was ecstatic! When he found out that the baby was a boy, he jumped up and down, clapped his hands and yelled, "We won! We won!"

One hot day in late July, Clifford burst excitedly into their small apartment, and grabbed Beth by the hand. "Come downstairs with me! I have a surprise for you!"

Brimming with curiosity, Beth scooped Raymond out of his crib and hurried down the stairs, with Lowell and Eberly trailing behind. Clifford escorted them out the door, and pointed to a shiny new car parked by the curb. "We've got a new car," he announced proudly, "a 1955 Rambler station wagon!"

It was all that Beth could do to keep from groaning out loud. "Oh, no!" she thought in dismay. "How could Clifford do this when we still owe so much money to the hospital for Raymond's birth, and we hadn't even finished paying for our old car yet? Clifford must have traded it in on this new one, and I'm sure that the payments for this one will be much more expensive!" However, she forced a faint smile to her lips. "It's a beautiful car, Clifford, but how can we ever afford to pay for it?" she asked doubtfully.

"That's no problem, Beth!" he replied confidently. "I just quit my job at the hotel, and I've got a new job that will pay a lot better! Of course we're going to have to move to Philadelphia as soon as you can get packed, but with this station wagon, moving will be no problem! We'll have plenty of room for all of our things, and the kids won't be nearly as crowded as they've been whenever we've moved before!"

Beth's mouth dropped open in amazement, and she was momentarily speechless. Her head whirled as she tried to absorb the impact of all the changes which Clifford had so rapidly sprung upon her. To steady herself, she reached out and grasped the metal railing that was beside the steps leading up to their apartment building. If she hadn't been holding Raymond, she was sure that she would have collapsed onto the sidewalk in a heap. Still recovering from major surgery, the thought of having to pack up all of their belongings and move to another state overwhelmed her! Once again, she was dazed by the speed with which her husband could make major decisions, which dramatically altered their lives, without even consulting her! When she finally found her voice, she asked weakly, "What kind of job is it, Clifford? And how soon do we have to move?"

"It's a sales job, Beth! Ralph Barnett, one of the guests at the hotel, works for a company that sells cleaning supplies directly to people in their homes. He says that the products are easy to sell, and that I should be able to make a lot of money at it. His firm needs someone to be their sales representative in the Philadelphia area, so I took the job. I needed to get a new car because this job will involve traveling all over eastern Pennsylvania, and I will have to carry the merchandise around with me! That car will pay for itself in no time!  You just wait and see!  I start work next Monday, so you need to start packing right away."

Beth's heart sank.  It was now Friday afternoon.  That gave them only two days to pack, move, and find a place to live in a strange city!  Suddenly another concern occurred to her.  "Are they paying you a regular salary, Clifford, or do you have to depend on the commissions from what you sell?" she inquired apprehensively.

"Well, the amount I make will be based on how much I sell, but that won't be a problem."  Clifford assured her.  "Ralph says that the products are so good that they practically sell themselves!"

Beth sighed.  Although she was sure that Clifford, with his friendly personality and gift of gab would be an effective salesman, she dreaded to think of their entire income being dependent on the uncertainty of a door-to-door selling job.

The following Monday found the Frazier family crowded into a small, stiflingly-hot apartment on the third floor of a run-down brick building in downtown Philadelphia.  As the next several weeks crawled by, Clifford left for work early every morning and returned home late each evening.  However, in spite of his diligent efforts, Beth's worst fears about his new job were confirmed.  No matter how hard he tried, he just wasn't able to sell enough cleaning products to pay their bills and support their family.

One night as he sank wearily into bed, he admitted, "This job just isn't working out like I thought it would!  I've been thinking and praying about what we should do, and I've decided that we should move back down to Florida.  At least I know that I can find work there!  Can you be ready to leave the day after tomorrow?"

Beth stifled a groan as she thought of re-packing all of their belongings, piling them into the car, and making the long, hot trip to Florida.  "Well, at least I hadn't finished unpacking everything from our last move yet, so maybe it won't be so hard to pack after all!" she thought with a wry smile. However, all she said aloud was, "Yes, dear."

The following evening, when Clifford came home for supper, he was not alone. "Set another place at the table, Beth. This is Ed Bly. He'll be joining us for dinner and staying here with us tonight."

Beth stole a curious glance at the balding, paunchy, middle-aged man whom her husband had brought home. "Why on earth did Clifford bring home a guest when we are right in the middle of moving?" she wondered as she laid another plate on the table. How she hoped that their meager meal would stretch to feed another hungry mouth!

As they lay in bed that night, her question was answered. "I met Ed when I was giving out tracts in the park today," Clifford explained. "He's a Christian, but he has a drinking problem. I suggested to him that it might do him good to get away from his old buddies and make a new start, so he's going to go to Florida with us tomorrow. He'll probably be staying with us for a while."

Beth gasped in horror. How could Clifford even think of bringing a strange man into their family like this? For all they knew, he could be a dangerous criminal! "Are you sure that's wise?" she questioned. "You just met him, and we don't know anything about him!"

"I believe that God led me to Ed, and that He wants me to help him, so we'll just have to trust the Lord," Clifford countered confidently. "Anyway, I'm sure he's totally harmless. It will be all right. You'll see."

Several days later, the Frazier family, with the addition of Ed Bly, arrived in the little town of Tice, Florida, near Fort Myers, and rented a small house. Both Clifford and Ed soon found work in a vegetable packinghouse nearby.

The remainder of the summer passed quickly, and the time soon came for school to start.  As they sat around the supper table after Eberly and Lowell's first day of school, Clifford announced, "I have a surprise for all of you.  Today I heard about an opportunity that was just too good to pass up.  I met a man who is selling lots near Punta Rassa, about fifteen miles from Fort Myers, for a really good price, so I put a down payment on one.  We're going to have a place of our own, and we'll be moving over there tomorrow!"

"But, Clifford, the kids just started school today!" Beth protested.  "It isn't fair to make them change schools when they've attended this one for only one day!  And what are we going to live in?  Is there a house on the property already?"

"No, there isn't," Clifford admitted reluctantly.  "but we can stay in the station wagon for a few days until we can find a trailer or something to put on it."

"Live in the station wagon?" Beth echoed in shocked horror.  "How can we possibly do that?  There are six of us, counting Ed, and besides that, where are we going to put all of our belongings?"

"We'll figure out a way," Clifford assured her confidently.  "Besides it will only be for a few days until we can make some other arrangements.  The important thing is that I want to get moved onto our property right now!"

Beth opened her mouth to object, but quickly shut it again.  She knew that it would be pointless to continue the argument.  To do so would only cause Clifford to lose his temper and expound angrily to her on the duty of wives to "submit to their husbands in everything, as unto the Lord".

 Late on the following afternoon, the Fraziers, plus Ed Bly, with all of their assorted belongings piled into the car, turned off the highway, drove down a sandy lane and stopped in front of their new "home". "Well, this is it!" Clifford announced proudly. "Isn't it great? How do you like it?"

Beth crawled out of the car's front seat and surveyed her surroundings. The land that Clifford had bought was a small lot covered with weeds, scrub palmetto bushes, and pine trees. There were several similar vacant lots between it and the highway, but on the property adjoining theirs on the other side, a rundown shack had been built. As she looked in that direction, she was greeted by the ferocious barking of a mean-looking black dog who was straining to escape from his chain. On the lot across the street, a dilapidated trailer was parked haphazardly, and two shabbily dressed children were playing tag among the palmettos. The sandy road continued around a bend and she could see several similar dwellings in the distance. Looking behind her and in the direction of the highway, she could see more trailers. The only decent-looking buildings in the entire area were a comfortable-looking house located behind one of the vacant lots, and another situated just across the highway. Her heart sank. "How can we possibly live here?" she thought in dread.

Within the next few hours, Beth found out the answer to that question. Clifford and Ed unloaded their belongings, stacked them on the ground, and covered them with a piece of canvas. They then proceeded to dig a hole for an outhouse, and construct walls, a roof, and a door for it out of some scrap pieces of metal roofing which they had found at the dump which was located just down the road. With that done, Clifford stepped back to survey their handiwork. "Well, that's taken care of," he remarked with satisfaction, pointing to the outhouse. "As for sleeping arrangements, Ed can sleep in the front seat of the car, I can sleep in the back seat, and we can make up a bed for you and the kids in the back of the station wagon."

For the next few days, the Frazier family lived in their station wagon. Each morning, Beth roused Eberly and Lowell from their bed in the back of the car and helped them get ready for school. Beth cooked their meals over a campfire. Since they had no water on their own property, she had to walk across several vacant lots and haul water in buckets from a faucet that protruded from the ground on someone else's land. Unfortunately, this water had a sulfurous, rotten-egg taste that gave its horrible flavor to anything that Beth mixed with it.

After several days of living under these miserable conditions, Clifford was finally able to obtain a tent which they could set up on their land and into which they could move their belongings. Even though their living arrangements were still extremely primitive, Beth was thankful that they finally had a place that gave them a little more privacy than the station wagon had provided!

However, several days later, a torrential downpour turned the "floor" of their new "home" into a sea of mud and soaked most of their belongings, proving the tent to be totally inadequate for a permanent dwelling. As Clifford, Beth, and their family disconsolately surveyed their soggy possessions, they suddenly noticed a man approaching from across the field. Upon reaching them, he introduced himself. "I'm Elmer Hand, and I live right over there," he said, indicating one of the fancier houses that Beth had noticed. "I couldn't help seeing that you folks have a problem here, and I think that I might have a solution for you."

By now, even Clifford could see that living in the tent was not going to be practical, so he asked eagerly, "What is it, Mr. Hand?"

"Well, I just happen to have a small place nearby that I would be glad to rent to you. It used to be an old chicken coop, but I've fixed it up a lot, and it will certainly be a better place for you to live in than that tent!"

Beth groaned inwardly, even as she admitted that almost anything would be better than the tent. "What else are we going to have to live in?" she wondered. "First a station wagon, then a tent, and now a chicken coop!"

"We'll take it!" Clifford decided. "Anyway, it will only be temporary. As soon as possible, I want to buy a trailer and put it on our property. Then we'll have a permanent place to live."

The "chicken-coop" apartment was located on the lot just behind the one which Clifford had bought, so it was a simple matter to move their belongings into it. Although it was nothing fancy, it seemed like a palace compared to their two most recent living arrangements! Beth was thankful to have a roof over her head, a real floor under her feet, and four walls to shut out both the elements and the prying eyes of her neighbors!

One day, several months after they had moved into the "chicken-coop", Clifford burst excitedly through the door and announced, "Get ready to move again, Beth! Today, Ed and I bought two trailers and they will be moved onto our land tomorrow!"

"Two trailers?" Beth asked in surprise. "Why did you get two trailers?"

"Because neither one of them is big enough to fit all of us and our stuff. We can live in one trailer, and Ed can live in the other one, and we can store some of our things in that one too."

The following day, the Frazier family moved into their trailers. Although their living conditions were still primitive, with no electricity, plumbing, or running water, Beth was thankful that they were finally settled on their own property.

A few weeks later, Clifford went to Fort Myers to get their car fixed, leaving Ed, Beth, and the kids at home. In the middle of the afternoon, Beth realized that she hadn't seen Ed for several hours. "I wonder where he could be," she thought. "Maybe he went out for a walk."

Just then Lowell ran through the door of the trailer. "Mommy! Mommy! Mr. Bly is in the outhouse, and he has his hands all chained together, and he can't get them loose. He called me and told me to tell you that he needs help!"

Beth almost burst out laughing at the ridiculous picture of Ed sitting in the outhouse, with his hands bound together, unable to free himself. He had been trying for some time to perform an "escape artist" trick with chains, but he had never been able to accomplish it. She had never dreamed that he would practice it in the outhouse!

Then the awkwardness of the situation dawned on her. Clifford was gone to town, and Ed was a prisoner in the outhouse! How on earth could she help him? Would he have to remain there until Clifford returned? "Father, give me wisdom," she breathed, and immediately an idea occurred to her. Going to a drawer, she opened it, pulled out a file, and handed it to Lowell. "Go take this to Mr. Bly, and help him use it to cut through those chains."

Half an hour later, a very red-faced, sheepish Ed Bly emerged from his smelly prison, freed of his shackles. "Thanks, Beth," he muttered as he handed the file back to her.

Since they had no running water or indoor plumbing, it was only practical to bathe once a week, so every Saturday night was "bath night" in the Frazier household. It was a laborious task for Beth to haul bucket after bucket of water from the faucet on their neighbor's property, heat it up on the stove, and then fill and refill the round galvanized wash tub, as each member of her family took their turn in it.

One Saturday night, as Eberly was bathing by the dim light of the oil lamp, Beth was startled to hear their dog Trixie barking ferociously just outside the trailer door. "What on earth is the matter with her?" she wondered. Going to the door and peering out, she saw that Trixie was scratching at the door with her paws and tearing at the door frame with her teeth, trying frantically to get inside the trailer. "What is it, girl?" she asked curiously, opening the door. Trixie rushed past her in a furry blur, ran over beside the tub, picked up something from the floor in her teeth, and began shaking it violently.

Beth ran to the table, grabbed the oil lamp, and hurried to see what Trixie had found. Trixie wagged her tail excitedly, dropped the object on the floor, and looked up at Beth expectantly. Beth bent down, and the lamplight illuminated the now-dead body of a poisonous coral snake! The snake had been lying on the floor right beside the tub where Eberly was bathing!

Trembling, Beth returned the lamp to the table and then sank to the floor beside the washtub, gathering her daughter in her arms. "Thank you, Father, for sending Trixie to save Eberly's life," she prayed with tears of gratitude. Then turning to Trixie, she threw her arms around the dog and buried her wet face in Trixie's ruff. "And thank you, Trixie, for being such a good dog!"

As she looked up, she saw Eberly watching her with round, frightened eyes. "Oh, Mommy, I saw the snake's eyes shining in the dark, and I almost reached out and touched it to see what it was! It would have bitten me, wouldn't it?"

"Yes, it probably would have, Honey," Beth agreed, her voice shaking, "but Jesus kept you from doing that, and He caused Trixie to know that the snake was there so that she could kill it! Let's thank Him!" So, together, mother and daughter bowed their heads and praised God for His protection.


During the cold winter months of early 1956, Raymond developed a terrible cold that rapidly went down into his chest, filling it with thick phlegm. Beth desperately tried every home remedy she knew. She rubbed his little chest with Vicks Vaporub, she placed pans of steaming water beside his bedside, and she made hot onion poultices, and placed them on his chest to try to loosen the congestion. However, in spite of Beth's best efforts, Raymond's fever skyrocketed, his body was racked with coughing, and his breathing became more and more labored. She stood anxiously beside his crib, watching as he struggled for every breath. "Oh, Father," she pleaded through her tears. "I asked You for this child. Please don't let me lose him now! Please heal him, if it's Your will!"

At that moment, Clifford walked into the room. "How is Raymond doing?" he asked anxiously. "Is he any better?"

"Oh, Clifford," Beth wept, collapsing in his arms. "I'm afraid that Raymond has double pneumonia, and everything I've tried to do to help him hasn't worked! We've got to get him to a doctor as soon as possible."

"Let's take him right now then!"

Quickly, Beth bundled Raymond up in blankets and hurried him, Lowell, and Eberly out to the car.

An hour later, they were seated in Dr. Blake's examining room, watching as he listened to Raymond's lungs with a stethoscope. The doctor looked up at them, his face grim. "Your baby has a severe case of pneumonia, but I believe that he will survive. I'm going to give him a shot of penicillin, and prescribe some medicine which will need to be given to him four times daily for the next two weeks. You brought him in just in time. If you had waited till tomorrow, it would have probably been too late!"

Although Raymond's recovery was slow, the doctor's prognosis proved to be correct, and several weeks later, he was completely well. "Thank You, Father, for sparing Raymond's life," Beth murmured in gratitude as she stood beside his crib, watching him sleeping peacefully.

"Amen!" Clifford echoed heartily as he stood by her side.

With the coming of spring, Beth noticed that Ed seemed to be getting increasingly restless. One morning, he said, "I sure do appreciate you folks letting me stay with you for such a long time, but I think that now it's time for me to be hitting the road!"

"What are you going to do, Ed?" Clifford asked.

"I think that I'll see if I can get a truck driving job again." So, after breakfast, Ed packed up his things and walked over to the highway and out of the life of the Frazier family.

Several weeks later, as they sat around the supper table, Clifford announced, "Beth, we've got a serious problem. As long as Ed was here and we were both working, we had enough money to pay our bills, but now with just one paycheck, we don't have enough to pay for our property, make the car payments, and keep food on the table. I'm afraid that the only solution is for you to begin working at the packinghouse with me."

"I know that we need more money, but I hate to be away from the kids. And besides, with both of us working, who is going to take care of them?" Beth asked in concern. "We can't afford to pay anyone to baby-sit."

"I'm sure that our next-door neighbors, the Fosters, will be glad to keep an eye on them for us. They have a couple of kids who are about the same age as Eberly and Lowell are. It shouldn't be any trouble for them to let our kids play with theirs during the daytime, and when bedtime comes, Eberly and Lowell and Raymond can come back to our house and go to sleep."

The following day, Clifford approached the Fosters concerning this arrangement, and they agreed to watch over the Frazier children while Clifford and Beth were at work. Reluctantly, Beth joined Clifford in working long shifts at the packinghouse. The hours dragged by, as an endless array of tomatoes rolled past her on a conveyer belt. As she mechanically performed the monotonous job of sorting them according to size and ripeness and throwing out the "culls", she thought continually of her children and grieved that she was forced to leave them in the care of people who were almost total strangers to them. "Father," she prayed fervently, "please keep my children safe, and please soon make it possible for me to be at home with them once again!"

Late one night, several weeks later, Clifford and Beth walked into their trailer after a long, hard day at work and found Lowell and Raymond sound asleep, but Eberly gone! Before they could recover from the shock of this frightening discovery, they heard a knock at their door. Rushing to answer it, Beth saw their neighbor, Mrs. Hand, standing there, with Eberly by her side. A huge bandage covered the lower part of Eberly's right leg. "Eberly, what happened?" Beth exclaimed in concern. "Where have you been? Are you all right?"

"Oh, Mommy!" Eberly rushed into Beth's outstretched arms. "Please don't make us stay over at the Fosters anymore! They've got a really mean dog, and he bit me on the leg today!"

"He certainly did!" Mrs. Hand chimed in indignantly. "And those people didn't even have the decency to see that Eberly got proper medical attention after their dog bit her! Mrs. Foster just poured a bottle of methiolate on her leg and then told her to take her brothers and go home and go to bed. A couple of hours ago, Eberly came and knocked on our door and said that her leg was hurting and that she felt weak. When I let her in, I was horrified to see that that dog had taken a huge chunk out of her leg, and that the wound was still bleeding, and it hadn't even been bandaged! My husband and I took her right in to the doctor, and it took several stitches to close it up!"

"How can we ever thank you for all your help, Mrs. Hand?" Beth cried gratefully, as she held her precious daughter close in her arms. "You are truly a good neighbor!"

Later that night, as she and Clifford lay in bed, Beth asked worriedly, "What are we going to do now, Clifford? I know we need the money, but who is going to take care of our kids? We certainly can't leave them with the Fosters anymore."

"I've been thinking about that, and I don't believe that we need to find anyone else to watch the kids. I think that Eberly is old enough to look after Lowell and Raymond by herself now."

"But she's only ten years old!" Beth protested. "And Lowell is not quite seven, and Raymond is only one! I really think that that is far too much responsibility to put on her!"

"I'm sure that she can handle it!" Clifford said confidently. "And, anyway, if an emergency should come up, she can always go over to the Hands' house and get help! They've proved that they are really good neighbors!"

Reluctantly, Beth agreed, but she spent her entire shift each day silently beseeching the Lord to watch over her dear children and keep them safe.


A few weeks later, as Beth was leaving for work, she reminded her young daughter, "Now be sure and sweep the floor before we get home tonight, Honey. It's really dirty!"

"Yes, Mommy, I will," Eberly promised as Beth and Clifford climbed into their car and drove away.

Later on that night, as they pulled into the driveway, Beth was shocked to see a crowd of people standing in their yard, gathered around what appeared to be a smoldering pile of rubbish. She jumped from the car and ran across the yard, searching the group with her eyes and frantically calling for her children. With relief, she observed that Eberly and Lowell were standing beside Mrs. Hand, who was holding Raymond in her arms.

Upon seeing her mother, Eberly erupted from the crowd, and grabbed her mother around the waist, wailing, "Oh, Mommy, I'm so sorry! I didn't mean to set the bed on fire!"

Gently, Beth tried to quiet her hysterical daughter. "Calm down, Honey, and tell Mommy all about it," she soothed her
.

Eberly's story poured out, punctuated by sobs. "Well, Lowell and I were playing 'pillow fight' this afternoon, and I threw my pillow at him, but it missed him and hit the oil lamp chimney and broke it. Then Lowell and his friend Connie and I were playing 'tag', and all of a sudden I realized that it was getting dark and I hadn't swept the floor yet, like you asked me to. I knew the oil lamp wouldn't work, so I got a candle and lit it and put it on the floor so I would be able to see where I was sweeping. Lowell and Connie were still playing tag, and when he was running away from her, he accidentally kicked over the candle, and it went under the bed and caught the bed on fire. Lowell and I hurried and hauled some water and dumped it on the bed and we thought that we had put the fire out, so we went to bed. But I couldn't sleep, and a little while later, I opened my eyes and the whole trailer was full of smoke! So Lowell and I went over to the Hands' house and told them about it, and there was a fireman visiting them, and he came over and got Raymond out of the trailer, and then he hauled the mattress out of the trailer and threw it on the ground and poured a lot more water on it! Oh, Mommy, I'm so sorry! Can you ever forgive me?"

"Of course, I can!" Beth assured her trembling daughter. "The only important thing is that you kids are all safe!" Overwhelmed with gratitude, Beth bowed her head and thanked the Lord for His protection and for their kind and helpful neighbors!

That night as Clifford and Beth sat wearily together at their dining room table, Beth turned to Clifford and said firmly, "I was afraid that we were putting far too much responsibility on Eberly, and now I know that we were. We could have lost all of our kids tonight! I am not going to leave them at home alone here for even one more day!"

"You're right, Beth. Tomorrow we'll take them with us and they can stay in the station wagon while we're at work. Eberly can watch the boys out in the car. That way, you can go out and check on them during our lunch hour and our break times."

"But, Clifford, I don't think it's safe for them to be cooped up in that hot car all day either!" Beth protested. "And, besides, they'll really be bored. What on earth can they do all that time?"

"Well, Eberly likes to read, so she can take some books along and read to Lowell, and they can take along some toys for Raymond to play with. And of course we'll leave the windows rolled down so that they can get plenty of fresh air!"

"All right," Beth agreed dubiously, "I'm willing to try it for one day, but if it doesn't work out, I'm quitting my job and staying at home here with the kids where I belong!"

The following day showed abundantly that Beth's concerns were completely justified. Every time she went to check on her kids, she found them in the same miserable condition. Eberly and Lowell were hot, tired, bored, and cranky, and Eberly was trying frantically to comfort Raymond, who was squirming and screaming in her arms.

That night she said resolutely to Clifford, "It is totally wrong to put our kids in the situation they were in today. Their being safe and well cared for is much more important than any money I could make, so I will not be going to work with you tomorrow. I am quitting my job and staying home with our children from now on!"

"You're right. The kids do need you to be at home with them! We'll just have to make it somehow without your paycheck, but I sure don't know how we're going to do it."

One night several weeks later, when Clifford returned from work, he was not alone. He had another man with him. "This is

Jim Johnson. I met him at work today. He's new on the job, and he needs a place to stay, so he'll be staying with us for a while."

Beth looked up to see a tall, slender, balding, bespectacled man who was in his mid-thirties. "Glad to meet you, Mrs. Frazier," he smiled cordially. But as Beth looked into his eyes, she shivered involuntarily as she felt a chill pass throughout her entire being. She couldn't explain why, but she felt an instant distrust and dislike of this stranger who would now be sharing their home.

Although she had never become totally accustomed to having Ed Bly living with them as a part of their family, and had been relieved when he had left, she had adjusted to his presence and become reasonably comfortable with having him there. He had treated their children much as a kind uncle would, and had enjoyed playing with them, since he himself was a bit childlike. But in the presence of Jim Johnson, she felt an uneasy premonition of danger. Somehow she sensed that she would never feel that she and her children were safe when he was around.

That night in bed, she expressed her concerns to Clifford. "Are you sure that we should invite Jim to stay with us, Clifford? I know that Ed was a total stranger when he came to live with us and that that worked out all right, but this time we might not be so fortunate. For all we know, Jim Johnson could be wanted by the police! For some reason, I just don't trust him."

"Aw, Jim is a great guy. Of course he needs the Lord, but we can be a witness to him," Clifford reassured her. "Once you get to know him a little better, you'll like him fine. And besides, it will really help us to have another paycheck coming in!"

A few days later, a new school year began. As Beth observed her children's progress in school, she saw once again, with concern, that even though Eberly excelled academically, she was steadily becoming more shy and withdrawn, and that while Lowell had a multitude of friends, he was still struggling desperately to learn the basics of reading.  Also, she noticed that Eberly had no friends of her own age in their neighborhood.  Her only playmates were Lowell and his friends.

One day in the late fall, a new boy came over to play.  Beth noted that he was almost as old as Eberly, and she hoped that finally Eberly would find a friend who was nearer her own age.  As the children engaged in a lively game of "hide-and-seek" among the palmetto bushes, Beth could hear them laughing and shouting as they ran across the yard.  Suddenly, the playful shouts turned into angry yells.  Leaving the tub of clothes that she had been vigorously scrubbing on the washboard, she hurried over to see what was happening.

As she rounded the side of the trailer, she was horrified to see her daughter pelting the new boy with pinecones.  "Don't you ever throw pinecones at my dog again, Pete Beach!"  Eberly was screaming angrily.  "Go home!  We don't want you here!"

Grasping her squirming, furious daughter by the arms, Beth restrained her from further violence.  Meanwhile, Pete ran from the yard, calling menacingly over his shoulder, "I'll get you back for that, Eberly!  You just wait and see!"

"Eberly, what in the world got into you?" Beth questioned in amazement.  "Why did you treat Pete like that?  He was your guest!"

"He's the meanest boy in the world, and I hate him!  He was throwing pinecones at Lassie, so I just threw some at him, so that he would know how it feels!"

"Well, he shouldn't have hurt your dog," Beth conceded, "but that still didn't give you the right to treat him that way.  The Bible says that we are supposed to be kind to others even when they are unkind to us."

"I don't care," Eberly muttered sullenly.  "I'm glad I hurt him!"

One day, several weeks later, Eberly brought home a note from Mrs. Barnes, the principal, requesting that Clifford and Beth meet with her as soon as possible. "What could possibly be wrong?" Beth wondered anxiously. "Eberly has never been in trouble at school before!"

The following afternoon, Mrs. Barnes ushered them into her office and motioned for them to be seated. "Your daughter Eberly is an excellent student, and until recently she has been a model of good behavior, but lately we have been having some serious problems with her."

"What kind of problems?" Clifford asked.

"Well, several times, she has thrown stones at one of girls in her class during recess. And just the other day, she pulled the hair of two girls who were sitting in the row in front of her during a school assembly, and yesterday morning, she was involved in a fight with a boy during recess! She has been punished by her teacher, and forced to apologize to the other students involved, but I believe that you need to talk to her at home and see if you can find out what is causing her to misbehave."

For a moment both Clifford and Beth sat there in shocked silence. Then Beth murmured quietly, "Thank you for letting us know about it, Mrs. Barnes. You can be sure that we will deal with her at home!"

Later that afternoon, at home, Beth motioned to Eberly. "Come here a minute, Honey," she said gently. "I need to talk to you."

"What is it, Mommy?" Eberly asked curiously.

"We had a meeting with Mrs. Barnes today, and she said that you've been mean to some of the other kids at school lately. Could you tell me about it?"

"Well, ever since that ol' Pete Beach has been in school, he's been telling all of his friends to pick on me, and they do," Eberly sobbed, tears running down her cheeks. "That's why I got in a fight with Butch Robinson yesterday. Pete told him to hit me, and he did, so I just hit him back! And then we fell down on the ground and rolled around hitting each other until finally I got him down and sat on him! He's so big and fat that I never thought that I could beat him up, but I did!" At the memory, Eberly's tears vanished, and were replaced by a smile of satisfaction at her unexpected victory.

"Well, I can understand that you had to defend yourself if Butch started the fight," Beth conceded, "But why did you throw stones at that girl?"

"I threw stones at SueLynn because I don't like her. Everybody likes her, and nobody likes me. I wish I had blue eyes and golden curls like she does. Then maybe people would like me," Eberly replied sadly.

"You know, Honey," Beth said gently, drawing her unhappy daughter into her arms. "God is the greatest Artist there is. He makes each person different, and each one has hair, eye, and skin colors that go together perfectly. I imagine that SueLynn has pale skin that fits with her blond hair and blue eyes, just like you have darker skin that blends well with your beautiful hazel eyes and brown hair. And God doesn't want us to be jealous of other people. He wants us to be satisfied with the way He has made us."

"I know you're right, Mommy," Eberly admitted, "but I just wish I had some friends."

"Well, if you want friends, you need to be kind to others, and pulling those girls' hair in the auditorium the other day was certainly not kind. What on earth made you do that?"

"But I only pulled those girls' hair because they told me to. I just did what they said, and then they got me in trouble with the teacher!" Eberly replied with a puzzled look on her face.

"Honey, just because a person tells you to do something, that doesn't mean that you have to do it," Beth admonished her. "It sounds to me like those girls asked you to do that just so they could tell on you! The next time someone tries to get you to do wrong, don't pay any attention to them."

"Okay, Mommy," Eberly agreed, snuggling into her mother's arms.

At that moment, Beth looked up and realized with a start that Jim Johnson had quietly entered the room while she and Eberly had been talking and had probably overheard their entire conversation. "Couldn't he see that I needed some privacy to talk with my daughter?" she thought in annoyance. "Why did he have to stay in here and listen? He's not part of our family!"

"Aw, Beth, your kid doesn't just need to be talked to. She needs discipline!" Jim announced sternly. "She's a spoiled brat—that's what she is! Let me show you how to teach her to behave!" And before Beth could even utter a protest, he scooped Eberly up into his arms and deposited her in Raymond's crib, instructing her loudly, "If you're going to act like a baby, Eberly, you belong in a crib. And you're going to stay there until you start acting your age!"

Instantly, Eberly's face turned a brilliant shade of crimson, as she tried to climb out of the crib, but was restrained by Jim Johnson's firm hands. "Let me out of here, you mean old man!" she yelled angrily. "I hate you! I hate you!"

Hearing Eberly's screams, Clifford hurried into the room. "What's going on here?" he demanded.

"I'm just trying to help you folks discipline your daughter, Clifford, but as you can see, she's being very disrespectful to me. I don't think that you should allow her to get out of that crib until she apologizes to me."

"Eberly, you have no right to talk to Mr. Johnson the way you've been doing," Clifford said firmly. "Tell him you're sorry, and then you may come out of the crib."

"Will not!" Eberly exploded. "Why is <u>he</u> punishing me? He's not my father!"

"That doesn't matter," Clifford retorted. "He's an adult, and I never want to hear you talk like that to a grownup again! You need to learn to respect those who are older than you are."

Beth watched the scene before her in horrified amazement, helpless to do anything. "Eberly's right," she thought angrily, "Jim has no right to discipline her! He just butted into a situation that was none of his business, but I can't contradict Clifford in front of Eberly."

So for the next two hours, Beth unwillingly enforced Jim's brand of "discipline". At last Eberly gave in, with a grudging, "Sorry, Mr. Johnson," but Beth was certain that the only reason she said it was so that she could be liberated from her prison.

A few weeks later, Jim announced at supper, "I'll be leaving you folks tomorrow. Time for me to move on."

The following morning, Beth heaved a sigh of relieved thankfulness as she watched him walk around the bend in the road and out of sight. How good it was to have only her own family in her home again, free from the presence of this unwelcome intruder.

The next day, Clifford walked through the door, his face grim. "I'm afraid that you were right about Jim, Beth," he admitted ruefully. "I heard at work today that he is running from the law. He's wanted for several sexual crimes!"

Beth sank weakly into the nearest chair, as she realized that she and her children could have become victims of this evil man! "Thank You, Father, for keeping us safe!" she whispered.

"Amen!" Clifford agreed.

# Chapter 13—Moving Around in Cycles

The rest of the school year passed uneventfully, although it was a continual struggle for Beth to stretch Clifford's meager paycheck to pay the bills and put food on the table.

One night in early summer, as they lay in bed, Clifford said, "Beth, I've just got to get a better job. I think I'm going to drive over to Miami tomorrow and look for one there. When I find work, I'll be back to get you and the kids."

"What kind of job are you looking for, Clifford?"

"Well, I've been thinking and praying lately about what I should do, and this morning the Lord reminded me that I got some medical training when I was in the army. I think I'll try to find work in a hospital as a male nurse or an orderly."

"That sounds like a great idea, Clifford," Beth encouraged him. "It certainly will be more interesting than working in a packinghouse, and I'm sure that you'll get better pay too. Besides, you'll probably have a lot of chances to witness to the patients and the people you work with."

A week later, Clifford returned from his trip, and burst triumphantly into the house. "Start packing, Beth! We're moving to Miami. I've got a job working as an orderly at Dade County General Hospital!"

"That's wonderful, Clifford! Were you able to find us a place to live too?"

"Not yet," he admitted. "When we first get over there, we'll have to stay with Dave Reynolds and his family. I met Dave at work, and he said that we could live with them for a while. But we'll have a place of our own in no time—you just wait and see!"

For the first few weeks that they lived in Miami, the five Fraziers crowded into the small house already occupied by the three members of the Reynolds family. Though Beth appreciated their hospitality, it was a great relief to her when they finally found a house to rent.

They had hardly gotten settled in their new home when Beth received the sad news that her father had died suddenly, as a result of injuries suffered in a fall. "If only I were sure that Dad knew Jesus, I could bear to lose him, because then I'd see him in heaven again someday," she thought sorrowfully, tears streaming down her face. "I tried so many times to tell him about the Lord, and Clifford did too, but he just didn't want to listen."

As she sat recalling the many happy memories of her times with her dad, she thought to herself, "This must be even harder for Dot than it is for me. At least I still have my husband, but she lost Bake four years ago, when he fell off that ladder when he was working on their roof. And besides, she doesn't even have the Lord to comfort her in all of her sorrow." She turned from her own sorrow to breathe a fervent prayer for her sister's comfort and salvation.

However, as she remembered Bake's tragic death, her grief was compounded by the fact that now both her brother-in-law and her father might have passed into eternity without knowing Christ. "Well, I'll just have to leave them in God's Hands," she concluded sadly. "They both knew the way of salvation, so maybe they each finally accepted the Lord as their Savior before they died, even though they weren't able to tell anyone about it."

The remainder of 1957 sped by, and New Year's Day of 1958 found Beth sitting contentedly at her kitchen table, reflecting on the many blessings that God had given them during the previous year. "Father," she whispered gratefully, "How thankful I am that Clifford has a good job, and is making an adequate salary at last, and that we are living in a house that has electricity, running water, and an indoor bathroom! And thank You, also, for all the good times that we've had as a family this past year—especially being able to go to the beach and go swimming together!" How she hoped that Clifford had finally found a place where he could settle down and be content to stay.

The spring of 1958 passed uneventfully. As summer approached, however, Beth noticed that Clifford seemed restless. One night at supper, he announced, "It's been a long time since we've been at our property in Illinois. I think we need to go up there and make sure that everything is all right. We could spend the summer there. It would really be nice to get out of this hot city and be out in the country again! Start packing, Beth! We'll leave as soon as you can get ready."

"But Clifford, can't we at least wait until school is out?" Beth protested, "It's only a couple of weeks until summer vacation begins! We should let the kids finish their school year and not take them out early."

"Aw, it won't matter if they miss a few days of school. They don't do much schoolwork at the end of the year anyway."

Beth knew it was useless to discuss the matter further, so she dropped the subject and began preparing to move once again. How she hated to leave the comfortable home that they had been renting with an option to buy! And she couldn't help wondering how Clifford was going to be able to find a job that would adequately support their family in rural southern Illinois.

A few days later, the Frazier family pulled into the rutted road that led to the old schoolhouse that they had left nearly five years before. The driveway was overgrown with weeds, but the building was still in good condition. Although Beth's heart sank at the prospect of living under such primitive conditions, she had to agree that it was refreshing to be out in the country again.

Her artistic soul drank in the beauty of the colorful wildflowers that carpeted their property. She especially loved the morning glories, with their varied shades of pink, blue, and purple. "It's been so long since I've done any artwork!" she mused. "I think that this summer would be a perfect time for me to begin drawing and painting again." So as soon as they were settled in their home, Beth ventured out into the field, with sketchbook, pencils, and palette in hand, to capture the lovely flowers on paper. As the days passed, Beth made sure that a part of each afternoon was spent in doing what she loved best—using her artistic talent to create realistic portrayals of the work of the Master Artist.

Just as Beth had feared, Clifford found it difficult to find employment in the area. One morning, as she was praying about their financial needs, she thought of a way that she might be able to help in supporting their family, and still stay at home with her children. "I think I'll put an ad in the paper, offering to do oil paintings by using photographs to work from," she thought. "Perhaps people who would like to have a portrait of themselves or their family members, but who wouldn't want to take the time to pose for it, might be interested in having one made from a photo." The following day, she went into Harrisburg, and placed an advertisement in the newspaper, offering her services. However, she only attracted a few clients—certainly not enough to make a significant contribution toward their living expenses.

As the summer drew to a close, it became obvious to both Beth and Clifford that it would be impractical for them to remain in southern Illinois any longer. The few odd jobs that Clifford had found had not provided even enough money to buy an adequate supply of food for their family. In fact, there had been at least one night when Beth had had the heartbreaking experience of seeing her children go to bed hungry because there was no more food in the house. Also, they had already missed more than one payment on the new car that Clifford had purchased shortly before they left Florida.

One hot summer night as Beth lay in bed unable to sleep, her mind drifted back over the years since Clifford had left the pastorate. "How I wish Clifford could get back into the ministry again," she thought wistfully. "The happiest times in our married life have been when we've been serving the Lord together. But ever since we left Alabama, he hasn't even been willing to go to church with the kids and me on a regular basis, and sometimes we've had to stay home because we couldn't get a ride to church and he wouldn't take us. I understand that he's been deeply hurt by the way the church in Alabama treated him, but I also know that the way he's acting isn't pleasing to the Lord!" Her musings soon turned into a prayer, as she turned her burdens over to her Heavenly Father. "Father, please work in Clifford's heart!" she implored. "Please draw him closer to Yourself, and show us what we should do now!"

The following morning, during Beth's daily prayer time, an idea occurred to her. "Perhaps Clifford needs to go back to Bible school," she thought. "He never really completed his training for the ministry. Maybe the teaching and fellowship that he would receive at a Bible institute would help him to get back on track again." As she thought more about it, she felt that returning to either Moody Bible Institute or Philadelphia Bible Institute would be out of the question. "Clifford needs a place where he can make a fresh start," she reasoned. "And now that we have children, it would be so much better to live in a rural area, rather than in a big city. I think I'll send for some information about that school that the Clarity boy has been attending down in Arkansas—Ozark Bible Institute."

That very day, Beth sent out a letter requesting information concerning the Bible school. For nearly two weeks, she awaited an answer, but decided that she was not going to mention it to Clifford until she had received a reply. When the catalog and application arrived, she eagerly tore open the envelope and began to read. She learned that Ozark Bible Institute was a small Bible school located in a rural area of northwestern Arkansas, and rejoiced to see that its tuition was very reasonable.

That evening at the supper table, she hesitantly broached the subject to Clifford. "I got something in the mail today that you might be interested in," she began tentatively.

"Oh, really?" Clifford questioned curiously. "What is it?"

"Well, I've been thinking recently that you might be interested in returning to the pastorate, and I thought that perhaps getting some more Bible school training might be helpful to you, so I sent for some information about that school in Arkansas that Tommy Clarity has been attending. Would you like to look at it?" she asked hopefully
.

"You know," Clifford replied thoughtfully, "Lately I've been thinking about how much I miss being in the Lord's work fulltime. I'd really like to pastor a church again. Maybe I should consider going back to Bible school and finishing my education."

After looking carefully at the material that the school had sent, Clifford and Beth agreed that they should plan to move to Ozark, Arkansas as soon as they could get packed. The school year would be starting in just a few weeks, so they needed to get there as soon as possible so that Clifford could find a job and they could find a place to live. "For once, I'm actually enjoying packing to move!" Beth thought happily as she went about the familiar task of stuffing their belongings into boxes.

Just as Beth finished filling a box with her children's clothes, she heard their dogs barking furiously outside. A moment later she heard the sound of a car turning off the main road and starting up their driveway. "I wonder who that could be?" she wondered curiously. "I can't imagine why Clifford and Ray would be coming back so early." That morning her husband had driven off with his best friend Ray Boulden in Ray's old pickup truck to spend one last day together at their favorite swimming hole.

Looking out the window, she saw a fancy and unfamiliar car, which was occupied by two men, stop in front of their house. A tall man dressed in a suit and tie jumped out of the car, hurried up the steps, and knocked decisively on her door. "Is Clifford Frazier here? I need to talk to him!" the man demanded as soon as Beth had cautiously opened the door a crack.

"No, my husband isn't here right now," she replied reluctantly, "but I expect him back later today. What did you need to see him about?"

"Well, I'm from the American Motors Finance Company, and because you've missed your last two car payments, they've sent me to repossess your car. Since you are Mrs. Frazier, I won't need to see your husband after all. I can just take the car right now. Could you get the keys for me? My coworker will drive it away."

For a moment Beth was speechless. They were getting ready to move, and now their car was about to be taken away! How would they ever get to Arkansas? When she had regained her wits, she pleaded, "But we need our car! Surely something can be worked out! Couldn't you come back later when my husband gets home and talk to him about it? He should be home in a few hours."

"No, ma'am, I can't!" the man replied firmly. "I've been sent to get your car, and I've got to take it back now."

"Isn't there any other alternative?" Beth questioned as she thought about how upset Clifford would be if he returned and found his car gone.

"No, there isn't!" the man answered curtly. "Now, may I have the keys?"

Reluctantly, Beth strode to the dresser where Clifford had left his car keys, picked them up, and handed them to the man. A moment later, she stood at the window, tears streaming down her face, as she watched their car being driven away. "Oh, Father, we're stranded out here in the wilderness without a car!" she cried. "We've never been in a situation like this before! What are we going to do now?"

Beth dreaded Clifford's homecoming that night. Just as she had expected, he ran up the steps and burst through the door asking, "Where in the world is our car?"

Quickly she recounted the events of that miserable day to him, hoping that he would understand that she had had no choice but to surrender the car to the finance company. However, before she could even finish telling him what had happened, he interrupted her angrily. "It's all your fault that we're without transportation, Beth!" he yelled furiously. "You should never have allowed that man to take our car! You should have insisted that he come back later and talk to me about it! Why did you ever give him the car keys anyway?"

"I didn't feel that I could do anything else, Clifford," Beth responded quietly. "After all, we have missed our last two car payments. The finance company did have the right to take our car back. I wish that you had been home, but even if you had been here, I don't think that there's anything you could have done about it!"

"Well, I would have figured out something to do!" Clifford retorted angrily. "I wouldn't have let him take my car!"

Later, after Clifford had calmed down a bit, he and Beth discussed the problem of how they could move to Arkansas, now that they had no car. "I think that the only thing I can do is to hitchhike down to Ozark and find a job and a place for us to live. Then, as soon as I'm able, I'll send you some money and you can buy bus tickets for you and the kids to come down and join me. I'm afraid that by the time I can do all of that, it will be too late for me to start Bible school this semester, though," Clifford concluded reluctantly.

Beth nodded in sad agreement. "Perhaps you can begin school the second semester, Clifford," she encouraged him.

The next morning Clifford walked down the driveway and out onto the main road to seek a ride. As she watched him disappear from view, the seriousness of her situation weighed heavily upon her mind. Her husband was gone for an indefinite period of time, she was stranded in an isolated rural area with her three young children, and she had very little money and no transportation. She had never felt so alone in her life! "But I'm not alone!" she reminded herself firmly. "Jesus has promised that He will never leave me nor forsake me, and He also said that He would supply all of our needs!"

The weeks before Clifford's first letter came dragged endlessly. When an envelope bearing his familiar handwriting finally arrived, Beth tore it open eagerly. "Dearest Beth and children," she read, "Praise the Lord! I have found a job and a place for us to live. I am working for a man who owns a motel and a farm on the outskirts of Ozark. In return for my working on his farm, he says that we can live in one of the kitchenette units of his motel. Within the next few days, I will be sending you money for bus fare and to pay for shipping our things down here, so that you and the kids can all join me in our new home. I love all of you so much, and can hardly wait until we can be together again as a family. You are so precious to me, my Beth, and I miss you so much. Truly, you are a virtuous woman like the one mentioned in Proverbs chapter thirty-one, whose 'price is far above rubies'! Love, Clifford."

Beth pressed the letter to her heart, a smile lighting her face, as a tear of joy at Clifford's loving words trickled down her cheek. "It's so wonderful to know that Clifford still loves me, even though he gets so mad at me at times! Why is it that he does so much better at expressing his feelings in writing, or on the phone, than he does when he is with me?" she wondered. For a moment she stood, lost in thought, as she fondly recalled all the romantic letters he had written to her during their wartime courtship.

A week later, Beth and her children boarded a Greyhound bus in Harrisburg, Illinois for the long trip to Ozark, Arkansas. Their belongings, packed in boxes, were loaded into the freight compartment. Day turned to night as the bus crawled along winding country roads, making stops at each tiny town. Beth dozed fitfully throughout the night. In the wee hours of the morning, she woke with a start as the bus jerked to a stop somewhere in rural Missouri. She was just in time to see Lowell leave his seat and begin to sleepily walk down the aisle, following a heavyset black woman who had reached her stop and was preparing to get off the bus. "Stop, Lowell! Come back here!" she called frantically. "This isn't our stop."

"Aren't we there yet, Mommy?" Lowell mumbled drowsily, as he returned to his seat beside her.

"No, son," she replied softly. "We won't be there until sometime tomorrow morning. Try to go back to sleep."

"Okay, Mommy." A moment later he fell asleep, his head leaning against her shoulder.

How happy Beth was when the long trip was finally over, and she fell into Clifford's welcoming arms at the bus station! "Beth,

I'm so thankful we're together again at last!" Clifford kissed her tenderly.

"So am I!"

"Now let's go home!" Clifford led her to a pickup truck that he had borrowed to come and meet his family at the bus station.

The kitchenette unit at the motel proved to be tiny, but adequate. Beth rejoiced that once again she had modern conveniences, rather than having to live under nineteenth century conditions. However, it was a very small space in which to crowd a family of five people, plus all of their possessions.

The fall months passed quickly, with Clifford working long hours on Mr. Simmons' farm to help harvest the crops. During one week, the farm work involved the entire Frazier family, as they all pitched in to pick endless rows of peas. Even three-year-old Raymond trailed behind Beth as she worked her way down each row, occasionally picking a few peas and tossing them into her bucket.

One night in late October, Clifford came home for supper with a sober look on his face. "Mr. Simmons told me today that he can't afford to let us live here after the harvest is over. He said that this was just a temporary living arrangement so that I could help in harvesting his crops. I need to find a new job, and we're going to have to find another place to live."

For the next two weeks, Clifford used all of his spare time to try to find another job, but the search was fruitless. One night as he and Beth were lying in bed, he remarked, "There just isn't any work to be had in this town. I think that the only solution is to move somewhere else!"

"But how are we going to do that?" Beth inquired in surprise. "We don't even have a car."

"I know that, but I met a man today who may be able to provide us with a place to live and a way to get there. His name is Don Mitchell, and he's from the town of Plumerville, which is about eighty miles southeast of here. His mother just died, and he's looking for someone to live in her house out on the farm and look after things, until he can sell the place to someone. He said that he would move us over there, if we would be willing to stay there. He's got a good-sized truck that should be able to fit all of us and our things."

"All right, Clifford," Beth agreed reluctantly. "It seems like this is our only choice right now." Sadly, Beth realized that their plans for Clifford to resume his Bible school studies would probably never materialize now.

The following day, all of the Frazier family's belongings were piled haphazardly in the back of Don Mitchell's battered pickup truck. Because there was only room enough in the cab for Don, Clifford, Beth, and Raymond to fit, Eberly, Lowell, and the two dogs were forced to ride in the back of the truck, perched precariously atop several mattresses which had been tied on the top of the load. "Clifford, are you sure that the kids will be safe back there?" Beth worried.

"Aw, they'll be fine!" Clifford assured her confidently. "In fact they'll love it—especially Eberly. You know she's been complaining ever since we decided to move, because she's going to miss going on a hayride with the church youth group. Well, she should be happy now, because she's getting to go on an eighty-mile hayride!"

However, in spite of Clifford's assurances, Beth found herself spending the whole trip silently imploring her Heavenly Father to keep her dear children safe! When they were about halfway to their destination, Beth was startled by a loud banging on the roof of the pickup. Don hastily pulled to a stop at the side of the road, and Clifford, Don, and Beth, who was holding Raymond, jumped quickly out of the truck and hurried to see what was wrong.

As she looked up at the back of the pickup, she was greeted by Eberly and Lowell's terrified cries. "Oh, Mommy," Eberly screamed. "We thought that we and the dogs were all going to fall off onto the highway! The mattresses started moving around, and we yelled and yelled, but you didn't hear us, so finally Lowell crawled up by the top of the truck and banged on it. We're so glad you finally stopped!"

To Beth's horror, she saw that the mattresses had shifted to such a dangerous angle that the only way her children had managed to stay on the truck was by clinging to the ropes which secured the mattresses to the pickup. Each child was desperately holding onto a rope with one hand, and clutching a frenziedly panting dog with the other arm. Beth suddenly felt weak as she realized how close she had come to losing her beloved children. "Praise the Lord that Lowell was able to get up there and bang on the cab!" she murmured. "If he hadn't, we probably would never have stopped until it was too late!"

"Amen!" Clifford echoed. "Thank You, Lord!"

A few minutes later, as a light drizzle began to fall, the Frazier family resumed their journey, with the mattresses tightly secured, and six people and two dogs jammed tightly into the cab of Don's pickup. An hour later, to everyone's relief, they finally halted in front of the old farmhouse that was to be their new home. Beth was so busy thanking the Lord that they had reached their destination safely, that she barely noticed the well in the front yard, the outhouse in the back, and the lack of electrical lines coming from the road to the house. The fact that she was once again returning to primitive living conditions seemed minor compared to the fact that she had almost lost two of her children that day!

For the next few months, it was a struggle for Clifford to find enough odd jobs to keep food on the table. Fortunately, Beth was able to buy a few chickens from a neighbor, so they had a daily supply of eggs. They also enjoyed an occasional chicken dinner, courtesy of the roosters in the flock. However, Beth was reluctant to sacrifice any of her laying hens in this way.

The new year of 1959 dawned cold and dreary. As January slowly dragged by and was replaced by February, Beth couldn't help contrasting the circumstances in which they were presently living with those of just one year ago. Clifford must have been having similar thoughts, because one afternoon, he remarked, "This just isn't working, Beth! I've got to find a decent job so that I can provide for you and the kids! And we need to get a car again too! I think that the only solution is for me to hitchhike down to Miami. I know that I can get a good job there. I'll send you some money to live on here, and as soon as I can, I'll come back and get you and the kids, and we'll move back down there. We should never have left and gone up North!"

Reluctantly, Beth agreed. She knew that it was the only sensible plan, although she dreaded once again being left alone out in the country with her children. But she took comfort in knowing that they were all in their Heavenly Father's care. Early the next morning, she watched Clifford walk down the road and out of sight, wondering how long it would be before she saw him again. She knew that it might be months before he would be able to earn enough money for a down payment on a car, so that he could come back and move them to Florida.

For the next few weeks, Beth waited eagerly for a letter, but none came. She hurried out to the mailbox as soon as the mailman came each day, only to return to the house disappointed. "I hope that Clifford is all right!" she thought anxiously. "He's never been gone for this long before without writing me."

By the time that Clifford had been gone for almost a month, a new problem joined Beth's concern for her husband's safety. She was now totally out of money, and their meager food supply was almost exhausted. One cold March day, she took a quick mental inventory of what little food she had left. "All I've got in the house is eggs, rice, and margarine!" she thought in dismay. "I don't even have any salt to put on the eggs or the rice! And we ate the last rooster for supper a week ago. Of course, I could start killing the hens and cooking them, but then we wouldn't get any more eggs! Oh, Father, what should I do?"

At that moment, Lowell burst excitedly through the screen door, carrying the limp body of a rabbit in his hand. "Guess what, Mommy! You know that bow and arrow I made yesterday? Well, I just shot this rabbit with it!"

"That's wonderful, son! I'm so proud of you!" Beth praised him. "And you know what? The Lord just used you to provide our dinner for tonight."

And that evening, before they partook of a delicious dinner of succulent rabbit meat and gravy, served over rice, Beth gathered her children around her and thanked their Heavenly Father for His faithful provision for their needs. Later that night, as she lay alone in her bed, she marveled at how God had used her nine-year-old son, with his homemade bow and arrow, to provide food for his entire family!

The next afternoon, Beth was standing beside the mailbox as the mailman approached. He waved as he drove past, but then came to a screeching halt in the middle of the road, as he noticed that she was signaling him to stop. He backed up his car, rolled down the window, and asked politely, "Can I help you, ma'am?"

"Yes. My name is Mrs. Clifford U. Frazier, and I've been waiting for almost a month for an important letter from my husband. Are you sure that you haven't seen any mail for me from him?"

"No, ma'am. I'm sorry, but I haven't," the mailman answered sympathetically. "There's been no mail of any kind for this address for weeks, but I'll certainly be on the lookout for that letter. Perhaps it will come tomorrow."

Beth walked slowly back down the driveway toward the house, wondering what they could have for supper that evening. The rabbit had been delicious, but it was gone! "Oh, Father, please provide for us again!" she implored.

Suddenly, she heard excited barking coming from a grove of trees to her left. Eberly burst out of the woods excitedly. "Mommy, come here quick, and see what Trixie's doing!"

Beth ran after her daughter and was amazed to see Trixie standing at the bottom of a slanting fallen tree, barking furiously at a squirrel that was perched, frozen in terror, on its topmost branch. Trixie was clawing frantically at the log, trying to get a foothold that would enable her to reach the squirrel, but was repeatedly sliding back down to the ground. Breathing a quick prayer for help, Beth hurried over to the dog and gave her a boost up the log, pushing and supporting her as she struggled upward after her prey. "Go get it, Trixie!"

Within a few seconds, Trixie had managed to scramble her way up the log and seize the terrified squirrel in her mouth. "Good girl, Trixie!" Beth commended her, as she reached to take the squirrel from the dog's mouth. However, before Beth could even touch the squirrel, she was knocked away from Trixie by a flash of white fur, as Snowball stole Trixie's prize from her and ran off triumphantly, wagging her tail. "Eberly, run and see if you can catch Snowball and take that squirrel away from her. We need it for our supper tonight."

Eberly frantically pursued Snowball for several minutes, but the dog managed to stay just out of her reach. Finally, Eberly jumped forward and pounced on Snowball, grabbing the dog with one hand and the squirrel with the other. Just as she wrenched the squirrel from Snowball's mouth, it turned its head, and in desperation, sunk its teeth into Eberly's little finger and hung on. A moment later, it lost its battle for survival, and dangled limply from Eberly's bleeding hand.

"You did a great job, Eberly!" Beth praised her daughter enthusiastically. "I'm so sorry that you got bitten, though. Let's go into the house and get your hand taken care of, and then we're having squirrel for supper!"

The squirrel proved to be just as delicious as the rabbit had been. However, as Beth lay in bed that night and thanked the Lord again for His provision, she also came to a decision. "Tomorrow, I'm going to walk over to the Rainwaters' house and ask Sunny Faye Rainwater to give me a ride into town. I want to go to the post office in person and check to see if there's a letter there for me from Clifford. We can't go on like this anymore."

The following afternoon found Beth standing in the post office, listening as the man at the window shook his head and said, "No, I'm sorry, Mrs. Frazier. There's no mail of any kind here for you. In fact, I don't believe that any mail has come addressed to the old Polly Mitchell place since y'all have moved in there."

"Well, my husband left for Florida more than a month ago, and he promised to write me as soon as he got there, and I haven't heard anything from him. Perhaps the letter has been misplaced somewhere. Could you just take another look around the post office and see if it's here?" Beth pleaded in desperation.

The bored look in the man's eyes changed to one of pity as he regarded Beth. Instantly she knew what he was thinking. "He thinks that my husband has deserted me and is never coming back, but I know that's not true!" she thought indignantly. "Either something terrible has happened to Clifford or his letter has gotten lost in the mail!"

"All right, ma'am, if it'll set your mind at rest, I'll look around here one more time," he sighed reluctantly. As he turned from the window, his shirtsleeve caught on a large bulky envelope, knocking it to the floor and revealing a smaller envelope, which had been concealed on the counter beneath it.

As he bent to pick up the letter he had dropped, Beth peered through the window and saw her name written in Clifford's familiar handwriting on the small envelope which had just been uncovered. "There it is! That's my letter right there on the counter!"

"Where did that come from?" the man asked in confusion. "It wasn't there just a minute ago!"

"It was hidden under that letter that fell on the floor!"

Puzzled, the man looked from the large letter to the smaller one. "Oh, Mrs. Frazier, I'm so sorry!" he exclaimed apologetically, as he read her name from the envelope. "This letter from your husband was sent from Miami a month ago, and it was accidentally placed under this other letter, which was marked 'Please hold for one month'! It's been sitting here in our post office for almost a month!"

Thanking the Lord, Beth walked joyfully out of the post office. She eagerly tore open her precious letter, and began to read. In it, she found an adequate supply of money for their next month's expenses, as well as the encouraging news that Clifford had found a good job as a private nursing attendant, caring for an elderly rich man in Miami. He closed by telling her how much he loved and missed all of them, and assuring her that he hoped to be able to buy a car and come for them as soon as the school year was over! Beth's next stop in town was the grocery store, and that night, she rejoiced that she was able to put an adequate meal on the table for her family.

As winter turned into spring, Beth heard increasing reports of people who had contracted a dangerous illness that had apparently been brought into the United States from Asia. This "Asiatic flu", as it came to be known, was characterized by severe vomiting and diarrhea, and was taking the lives of numerous victims across the country. "Father, You know that I'm all alone out here with the kids and that I have no transportation. Please protect us, and keep us well!" she prayed fervently.

However, one morning, several weeks later, Eberly awakened feeling sick and aching all over. When Beth placed her hand on her daughter's forehead, she found to her alarm, that Eberly was burning up with fever. A few hours later, the almost-continuous vomiting and diarrhea began, and for the next week, she could do little but watch, as Eberly's strength slowly drained away.

Beth tried all of the home remedies she knew, to no avail. At last, Eberly became so weak that she was no longer able to get out of bed by herself to use the commode. Since Beth couldn't stay in the house all of the time, she brought Eberly a bell that she could use to summon Beth if she had to be outside for some reason. "Oh, Father, am I going to lose my only daughter?" she cried silently in agony as she stood beside Eberly's bed and gazed down at her pale face. "Show me what I should do!"

Instantly, she knew what she must do! Eberly needed the help of a doctor, as soon as possible, but Beth didn't know how to get in touch with one. "I know what I'll do," she decided quickly. "I'll walk over to the Rainwaters' house and ask if I can use their phone. I'll call the school and ask if they can help me find a doctor!"

With that settled, she called Lowell to her side. "Son, I really need your help! I'm going to walk over to Rainwaters and call a doctor to come out here and help Eberly. You will have to take care of Raymond until I get back."

"I will, Mommy! I'll take real good care of him!" He hesitated a moment and then looked up at her, fear filling his eyes. "Oh, Mommy! Is Eberly going to die?"

"I hope not, son!" Beth tried to reassure him, although she feared the same possibility herself. "Let's take just a minute to pray for her before I leave." Seated at her daughter's bedside, Beth encircled Eberly with one arm and Lowell with the other, as she balanced Raymond on her lap. "Father," she murmured, "Please heal Eberly, and please enable me to find a doctor that can help her. And please keep all of the kids safe while I'm gone."

Several hours later, Beth again sat by her daughter's bedside, anxiously awaiting the doctor that the Plumerville School principal had promised to send. At last, she heard a car pull up and stop in front of the house. Beth hurried out the door to greet the two women and one man who were getting out of the car. She recognized the two women. One of them was Eberly's English teacher, Mrs.Pierce, and the other was Mrs. Branson, the principal's wife. However, she didn't recognize the man who had come with them. "Mrs. Frazier, this is my father, Dr. Pope," Mrs. Branson explained. "We hurried out here just as soon as we heard about Eberly."

"Thank you so much for coming, Dr. Pope!" Beth exclaimed. "Come right in!"

However, as the trio approached the porch, Beth noticed that their friendly smiles were suddenly replaced with expressions of shock and barely-restrained curiosity. Following their gaze, she saw with horrified embarrassment that their eyes were fixed on a granite tombstone with the name "Frazier" engraved on it in ornate letters. The Frazier family had been hauling that headstone all over the country ever since they had removed it from the Wohner family cemetery plot in Kankakee, Illinois when their friendship with Mrs. Wohner had ended. Beth had completely forgotten that it was sitting in their front yard, and she didn't even want to imagine what her guests were thinking! "This way," she encouraged them.

Tearing their eyes from the incongruous spectacle of the tombstone waiting in readiness for the untimely demise of the patient inside, her three guests hurried through the front door and into Eberly's bedroom. Dr. Pope quickly examined her. "She's becoming dehydrated. We must give her something that she can keep in her stomach. In my experience with this illness, the only things that most of my patients have been able to tolerate are Coca-Cola and saltine crackers. We'll see how she does with that." Then turning to his daughter, he instructed, "Edith, please go out to the car and bring in several bottles of Coke and a box of crackers."

Reaching into his black bag, he withdrew a needle and quickly gave Eberly a shot. "I've given her a shot of penicillin. Normally penicillin has no effect on this flu, but I believe that Eberly has developed an additional infection, and that she needs an antibiotic."

For the next few hours, Dr. Pope remained at Eberly's bedside, coaxing her to take small sips of Coke and tiny bites of crackers. Beth stood nearby, fervently praying that this nourishment, small as it was, would remain in her daughter's stomach. When several hours had passed without a recurrence of the vomiting and diarrhea, Beth could see Dr. Pope begin to relax. Leaning back in his chair, he gave a sigh of relief. "You called me just in time, and I think that she's going to be all right. But it's a good thing that you didn't wait any longer…" His voice trailed off. "Have her keep trying to take small amounts of food and liquid as often as she is able, and don't hesitate to call me again if she takes a turn for the worse."

"Thank you so much, Doctor! How much do we owe you?"

"No charge!" he answered kindly. "It will be payment enough when I see your daughter healthy and back in school again."

Over the next two weeks, Eberly slowly regained her strength, and at last the happy day arrived when she once again walked down the lane with Lowell to catch the school bus. As Beth watched the bus drive away, she brushed tears of joy and thankfulness from her eyes. "Thank You, Father! Oh, thank You for sparing my precious daughter's life!" As she turned to go back into the house, her eyes fell on the still-unused grave marker. "And thank You, Father, that there was no need for that!" At that moment, she came to a firm decision that that tombstone had made its final trip with the Frazier family, and that when they moved to Florida, they would leave it behind to "rest in peace" in Arkansas!

The remaining months of school flew by, and at last the long-awaited day came when Clifford pulled into the driveway in their new car. As soon as they could get packed, the Frazier family joyfully piled into the car and headed for Florida. Several days later, after a long, hot, and tiring trip, Clifford pulled into the driveway of a duplex in a residential section of Miami. "Well, here's your new home, Beth!" he beamed.

Beth's eyes took in the attractive house and spacious yard. "It's beautiful, Clifford. I know that we're going to love living here, but the best thing is that our family is finally all together again!"

"Amen!" Clifford agreed fervently, as he gently drew her into his embrace and kissed her tenderly.

The remainder of 1959 flew happily by, and the beginning of a new year ushered in the decade of the sixties. One night in early February, as Clifford and Beth lay in bed, Clifford remarked, "You know, Beth, I hate putting out money for rent here in Miami when we have a place of our own over in Punta Rassa. I think that we should move back there."

"But, Clifford, how are you going to make a living over there?" Beth questioned in concern. "You know that you can't make enough money to support our family by working in a packinghouse!"

"Well, I've been thinking about that, Beth, and I think I have the solution. I'm sure that I can get a job at the hospital in Fort Myers. That's only about fifteen miles from our property. I want you to start packing tomorrow morning. We'll leave as soon as you can get ready."

Just as Clifford had hoped, he was able to find a good job as an orderly at Lee County Hospital in Fort Myers. Although Beth didn't relish returning to primitive living conditions once again, she was thankful that this time, there was adequate money to put food on their table and pay their bills.

As summer approached, however, Beth could sense that Clifford was becoming restless and dissatisfied with his job. One Thursday night, he suggested, "Let's take a quick trip to Alabama this weekend and visit Mr. Jim and Miz Ethel Nichols. We haven't been up there to see them for years!"

That Saturday afternoon, when the Fraziers' car pulled into the Nichols' yard, they were greeted enthusiastically by their two old friends. As they sat around the supper table that night, after enjoying a delicious dinner of Miz Ethel's fried chicken, cornbread, collard greens, black-eyed peas, and sweet potato pie, Mr. Jim exclaimed, "I sure do wish that y'all still lived here, Preacher Frazier! I ain't heard no good preachin' since you left!"

"I've always felt bad that we had to leave here like we did," Clifford agreed. "I know that there are a lot of people here who need the Lord, and I'm sure that they're not hearing the Gospel at Indian Creek Church!"

"You're right! They sure ain't!" Mr. Jim replied. "Y'all know what? I just got a great idea. I own some land that's right across the road from that church. It's about two and a half acres. Right now, it has cotton planted on it, but I'd like to give you that property to build a church on! If I do that, would you move up here?"

"I sure would! I've been wanting to get back into the Lord's work for a long time, and this sounds like a wide-open door to me!

We'll go down to Florida tomorrow, and as soon as we can pack up our things, we'll be back!"

Beth was flabbergasted at this sudden turn of events. Questions swirled through her head like dry leaves swept up by the whirlwind of change that had suddenly appeared out of nowhere to dramatically alter the course of their lives. "Where will we live? Where will we have our church meetings? How can we build a church? And how will we ever make enough money to survive up here?"

Yet, even in the midst of these perplexing thoughts, she rejoiced that God was providing an opportunity for Clifford to get back into the ministry! She knew that he had never been truly happy doing anything else. "I know that You will provide for us, Father!" she whispered, as she let her anxious soul relax in her Heavenly Father's loving Arms.

The day before they were to leave for Alabama, Clifford drove into Fort Myers to get some packing boxes. When he returned, he was not alone. He had brought with him a slender, red-haired man who was in his mid-thirties. "Beth, this is Red McCloskey. He used to work with me at the hospital. I met him in town, and when I told him about what we're doing, he offered to go with us! He's going to help us build our church!"

Beth's heart sank. Although she was thankful that her husband had found someone to help him build the church, she felt uneasy about once again having a strange man living with them, especially now that Eberly was a teenager! However, she knew that it would be useless to protest. "Father, please protect my family!" she implored silently. "You kept us safe from Jim Johnson, and now we need Your help again!"

Upon arriving in Alabama, Beth was appalled to find that the living accommodations for the six of them consisted of just one room in Mr. Jim's weather-beaten old barn! Their new home had only one door and no windows at all! "Well, I suppose it could be worse!" Beth thought grimly. "At least it has a wooden floor instead of a dirt one, but how on earth are we all going to fit in there and still have any privacy?"

It took all of Beth's ingenuity to figure out how to fit their belongings into their cramped living quarters, and of course she also faced the continuing challenge of making a home without the benefits of electricity or running water. With Clifford and Red's help, however, she was able to fashion partitions out of blankets to divide the kitchen area in the front of the room from the bedroom section in the back, and to separate Red's sleeping quarters from those of her family.

The day after they moved in, Mr. Jim walked over and surveyed the results of their efforts. "I know it's mighty crowded in there for y'all, but it's only temporary, you know. I've got a house up the road a piece that y'all can move into just as soon as the sharecropper moves out of it. I told him that he would have to leave at the end of the cotton harvest."

Beth breathed a sigh of relief. She had been afraid that they were going to have to live in the barn indefinitely! However, her relief was short-lived, as she realized, with a sick feeling in the pit of her stomach, that this was only the end of April, and the cotton wouldn't be fully harvested until early November!

Each morning, Beth's face burned with embarrassment for her children, as they left the barn to go to school. Although they hurried across the dirt road and stood in front of the Nichols' house to wait for the bus, vainly hoping that the other kids wouldn't guess where they actually lived, they fooled no one, and Lowell soon acquired the derisive nickname of "Barney"!

As the hot summer days of 1960 dragged by, Beth found that it was a daily struggle just to find enough food to feed her family. Fortunately, she was able to supplement their meager provisions with eggs from the Nichols' chickens, milk from their cows, and fresh vegetables from Miz Ethel's garden. In addition to this, she and her children spent hours picking blueberries in the Nichols' blueberry patch, figs from the tree in their yard, and wild blackberries and pokeweed leaves from the nearby fields. It always amazed Beth that, although the berries and stems of the pokeweed plant were poisonous, the leaves made a tasty dish when combined with scrambled eggs in what the local people referred to as "poke salad". Beth spent many long days canning fruit and vegetables, knowing that the summer's bounty would soon be over, and that she needed to make preparations for the lean winter months ahead.

With the cooler days of fall, harvest time came, and with it, a demand for farm workers of all kinds. For several days, the Frazier family stacked peanuts from dawn to dusk. It was backbreaking work to gather up the peanut vines with pitchforks and then drag them across the field and pile them on top of each other in stacks so that they could dry. Eberly, who was now fourteen years old, and Lowell, who was eleven, worked faithfully alongside their parents throughout each long, hot day. However, when the farmer paid them, Beth was infuriated to learn that, because they were just kids, he had given her children only two dollars and fifty cents per day, rather than the wage of five dollars daily that he had given each adult. Angrily, Beth determined that they would never work for him again!

Other days found Beth and her family taking burlap sacks and going into Mr. Lee Byrd's pecan orchard to pick up the nuts that had fallen to the ground. At the end of the day, Mr. Byrd weighed the pecans and paid them five cents a pound for the results of their hard work.

However, most of their time was spent in doing the work that was most in demand during the fall in rural southern Alabama— picking cotton. Day after weary day was spent dragging their long canvas cotton sacks down endless rows of cotton plants. As Beth and her family picked, the rough stalks of the dying plants scratched their hands and faces, and burrs from the cockle-burr plants that grew among the cotton became entangled in Beth and

Eberly's long hair. Sweat streamed down their faces as they slaved under the mercilessly hot Alabama sun. Beth had never imagined that something as light as cotton could feel as heavy as lead as she hauled her sack up one row and down another! She was also amazed, however, to see how little her sack weighed each time it was put on the scale. In spite of her best efforts, she could rarely make even three dollars per day, since the pay for picking cotton was only three cents a pound! In order to earn three dollars, a worker had to pick one hundred pounds of cotton in a day!

As the weeks went by, the cotton stalks became increasingly dry and brittle, and it became much more difficult to pull the cotton from the boll without breaking off part of the plant along with it. Late one afternoon, Beth was puzzled by a singsong chant that began among a group of Negro workers in another part of the field. "Rotten cotton! Cotton rotten!" they repeated over and over again.

That night, as the cotton was being weighed, Benson Williamson, the farmer, remarked, "I heard what y'all were saying today, and y'all are right! The cotton is rotten. Starting tomorrow, you'll be pulling cotton instead of picking it."

"Pulling cotton?" Beth thought in puzzlement. "What on earth does he mean by that?"

The next day she found out exactly what he meant. Rather than picking the cotton out of the boll, they were allowed to pull both the cotton and the bolls off the brittle stalks. However, because the bolls added weight to their cotton sacks, they were only paid two and a half cents per pound for pulling cotton!

Even though working in the cotton fields was exhausting, backbreaking labor, Beth was thankful for it, because it enabled her family to have food on their table. However, as the cotton harvest ended, and winter approached, Beth wondered how they would make it financially through the long, cold months to come.

True to his word, Mr. Jim asked his tenant farmer to leave at the end of the cotton harvest, and the Frazier family was finally able to leave the barn and live in a real house. Although they still had to haul water, cook on a wood stove, and use oil lamps for light, Beth felt like they were living in a palace, compared to their previous living arrangements!

The house was located right across the road from the property that Mr. Jim had given to Clifford to build the church. However, the church itself was still only a vision in Clifford's mind. All that could be seen in the field now was row after row of dry cotton stalks, trailing wisps of bedraggled cotton, which blew back and forth in the wind.

One day, shortly after they had moved into the small frame house, Beth found a letter in their mailbox bearing the familiar handwriting of her sister Dot. Eagerly, she tore it open. "Dear Beth," she read, "I have sad news for you. Mother passed away quietly in her sleep last night..." Tears blurred her eyes and prevented her from reading any further.

She hurried back into the house, sank down into a kitchen chair and began weeping inconsolably. "If only Mother had known the Lord, I could bear it, because then I'd know that I'll see her again in heaven!" she sobbed. "Oh, how can I stand the pain of losing her without knowing that she was saved?"

Gradually the violent storm of her weeping subsided, and two memories gently surfaced in her anguished soul. The first was of herself, as a teenager, shortly after she had received Jesus as her Savior. One day, she had found her mother's Bible and had paged through it, amazed to find that many verses which made plain the way of salvation had been underlined, and had notes written beside them in her mother's handwriting. The second memory was a much more recent one—of only a month ago, in fact. Her mother had written a letter to her—the letter that had now proved to be her last communication to Beth. One phrase from the end of the letter emblazoned itself in Beth's mind. "There is a way that is right. Pray for us!" her mother had written in her shaky handwriting.

Still crying softly, but now with tears of joy rather than sorrow, Beth murmured, "Thank You, Father! Oh, thank You for Your comfort! You've reminded me that my mother knew the way of salvation, and I'm going to trust You that she did finally come to know You in the end!"

Drying her tears, Beth picked up the letter that had fallen to the floor and continued reading. She was startled to read, "Mother and Dad have left you a small inheritance, Beth. They set up a trust fund for you. You will not be able to use the principal, but it will pay you fifty dollars per month from its interest for the rest of your life. Upon your death, whatever is in the fund will be divided among your three children."

Fifty dollars a month—why that would be enough money for them to live on while they served the Lord in Alabama! "Thank You, Father!" Beth cried gratefully. "You are always so faithful in providing for our needs!"

Even though the summer and fall of 1960 was a time of extreme privation and back-breaking labor for the entire Frazier family, Beth forgot their hardships each time that they gathered for meetings in various people's homes. For several nights each week, they met for worship and fellowship in the houses of different believers in the community. One night the service was held at Mr. Jim and Miz Ethel's house, another night it would be at Miz Polly Campbell's, a third night, they would meet at Miz Fannie Kilpatrick's, and yet another meeting would be held in the home of Mr. Jeremiah and Miz Ila Willams.

One night, Beth looked out over their little congregation, and thought, "This is worth it all, isn't it, Lord Jesus? It's worth all the hard work we've had to do to survive and the primitive conditions that we're living under! You know what it's like to live in a barn, don't You? And yet You were willing to do it for me! How can I do less for You?"

She watched Miz Fannie's glowing face as she sang enthusiastically, "I'll fly away—oh, glory! I'll fly away—in the morning!"

A few moments later, she listened to Roy Bell Kilpatrick, Miz Fannie's son, as he enthusiastically strummed on his guitar and sang in a slightly off-key, nasal whine, "Life is like a mountain railroad, with an engineer that's brave. We must make the run successful—from the cradle to the grave!"

She was overjoyed to see the group of teenagers who had joined the older folks for their meeting—not only Eberly's friends, Marilyn Davis and Agnes Duke, but also the unruly Powell boys, Elihu and I. V., who were notorious in the community for their bad behavior.

She loved playing her cello for the congregational singing and adding her soft alto harmony to their praises. And it was so encouraging to hear resounding "Amens!" from Mr. Jim and Mr. Jeremiah as Clifford enthusiastically proclaimed the truth from God's Word. If the Frazier family hadn't come back to "the heart of Dixie", how would this poorer class of Southerners, who were looked down on and called "poor white trash" by the more well-to-do, ever have heard the way of salvation?

Shortly after school was out in the summer of 1961, Clifford remarked, "Beth, I think that we need a little break from the work here. Let's go and spend the summer at our place in Illinois."

"But Clifford, where will we live?" Beth protested. "You know that last spring, when we needed money so badly, you sold the schoolhouse to a man who wanted lumber and that he tore it down and hauled it away!"

"Don't worry about that, Beth!  We'll figure that out when we get there.  Right now, I want you to start packing, because I want to get on the road as soon as possible!"

Several days later, the Frazier family's car pulled into the yard of what had once been the Boulden Schoolhouse.  Now however, the only structure left standing was the two-seater outhouse!  Beth's heart sank.  "Oh, no!" she thought apprehensively, "Are we going to be living in the car in an open field again?"

However, as soon as Clifford got out of the car, he strode to the outhouse, opened the door, and began measuring it with his eyes.  "Come over here, Beth.  I think that if we work it right, we can move a bed into the outhouse!"

At that moment, something inside of Beth snapped!  She heard a voice that she scarcely recognized as her own screaming furiously, "Clifford U. Frazier, we are <u>not</u> going to live in an outhouse!  We've lived in a car in an open field, we've lived in a tent, we've lived in a chicken coop, and we've lived in a barn, but we are <u>not</u> going to live in an outhouse!  The kids in Alabama called Lowell 'Barney', and that was bad enough, but I'm <u>never</u> going to let him be called 'Outhousey'!"

Shocked by her unexpected outburst, Clifford hurried away from the outhouse and held up his hands in surrender.  "All right, Beth.  We'll look around and find another place to live."  So the Fraziers, with the addition of Red McCloskey, spent that summer in an old farmhouse that was located a few miles away from their property.

As fall approached, Clifford said, "We need to get back to Alabama.  There's a lot of work to be done there.  We've still got that church to build!"  The following day the Frazier family piled into their car for the long hot trip down to Alabama.  However, as they were passing through the small town of Bethel Springs,

Tennessee, smoke began pouring out from under the hood of their car, and the engine suddenly died. Clifford was barely able to pull the car off the road before it ground to a halt.

Several hours later, at a local garage, a mechanic slammed the hood of the car down and shook his head sadly. "I'm sorry, Rev. Frazier, but your car's not fixable. The engine is burnt up. The only thing that your vehicle is good for now is to be hauled to the junk yard and used for scrap metal!"

Beth's heart sank. "Here we are--stranded in a strange town with no transportation, and hardly any money! We had just barely enough money for the trip back to Alabama, and we certainly don't have enough to buy another car! What on earth are we going to do now? Father, help us!" she implored.

A moment later, Clifford came to her side. "Well, I guess we're stuck here!" he exclaimed in frustration. "I think that the only thing that we can do is to find a place to live and stay right here until I can earn enough money to get us a car."

"Well, if you're going to do that, I think that's it's time for me to hit the road," Red McCloskey remarked. "I said that I'd help you build your church, but since it don't look like that's going to happen anytime soon, I'll be on my way."

At this announcement, Beth breathed a sigh of relief. At least in this new town, she wouldn't have to deal with the dangerous and embarrassing situation of having a man who was not even related to them living in the same house with her teenaged daughter! She had been mortified when someone in Illinois had assumed that Red and Eberly were married to each other and had referred to Red as "your son-in-law"! She hadn't even wanted to think about what that person might have thought when Beth had told her that Red wasn't Eberly's husband!

Fortunately, Clifford and Beth were able to rent half of a house that belonged to a widow lady named Cora Hendrix. Mrs. Hendrix and her adult grandson Bobby lived in the other side of the house.

Beth was overjoyed that their new home had electricity and also had one water faucet in the kitchen, although trips to the bathroom still necessitated a walk down the path behind the house!

However, when Beth took her children to the local school to register them, she was astounded to find out that the school year had begun six weeks earlier—in the middle of July. "We always start in the middle of the summer," Mr. Barker, the principal, explained. "That way, the kids can get out for their six weeks of 'cotton-pickin' vacation' when the cotton gets ripe. Around here, the farmers need every hand they can get to harvest their cotton crop. We've done it that way for years."

So it was that the Frazier children had missed six weeks of school before they even arrived, and it was extremely hard on all three of them. Eberly, who was a sophomore in high school, struggled hard to do her makeup work, but, in spite of her best efforts, she almost failed her typing class. Lowell, who had by now failed one grade in school, found himself so far behind the rest of his class that he was unable to catch up, ensuring the fact that he would fail this year also. And it was especially hard on Raymond, who was just starting school for the first time, and who was in the first grade!

The kids had barely started school when it was time for the "cotton pickin' vacation" to begin. The next month and a half was like a bad dream—a repeat of the nightmarish experience of the Frazier family's toiling in the cotton fields of Alabama. Each morning, they all piled onto a truck which took them to the cotton field for the day's work, and each night they returned home at dark—so exhausted that all they could do was to fall into their beds. Six days a week for those interminable six weeks they labored, and at the end of that time, all that they had to show for their labor was a meager fifty dollars each!

"Why on earth do they call that a 'cotton pickin' vacation?" Eberly complained on the morning that the kids went back to school. "It sure didn't feel like a vacation to me!"

"It didn't to me either!" Lowell chimed in, in hearty agreement.

Though he tried hard, Clifford was unable to find any work in the small town of Bethel Springs. Shortly before the new year of 1962 began, he announced, "I'm going to hitchhike down to Miami and find a job. I'll be back for you as soon as I can get a car and find a place for us to live."

As Beth watched him walk down the road once again, she reflected on the fact that for the past few years, their lives had followed a predictable pattern. It was a cycle that repeated itself over and over again. First, they would be living in Miami, in a modern house. Then, Clifford would get restless and move them out into the country, where they would live under nineteenth century conditions. Next, because he couldn't find a job, he would leave them and return to Miami and find work there. And, finally, he would come and move them back to Miami again, and the cycle would be complete—until the next time it happened! "How long will it be this time before I see Clifford again?" she wondered wearily.

The dreary winter months crawled by, and just as the new leaves of spring were beginning to appear on the trees, Clifford pulled into the driveway in his new car. "Pack up, Beth! We're heading down to Florida as soon as you can get ready!"

"Have you found a place to live?" she questioned anxiously.

"Well, not yet," he admitted reluctantly, "but we can stay with my friends Luke and Estelle DeBerry for a while. They offered to let us live with them until we can find a place of our own."

Beth groaned inwardly. She hated the thought of their family moving in with strangers and imposing on their hospitality.

"Sometimes it seems like Clifford takes advantage of people," she thought in embarrassment. "He just doesn't seem to know when he's worn out his welcome!"

Fortunately, though, a month after the Fraziers moved to Florida, they were able to find a house in Sweetwater, a small town that was located just a few miles away from Miami. However, this move also resulted in another change of schools for the children— this time only one month before their summer vacation began.

As Beth settled down in her new home, although she was thankful that once again they had adequate housing and enough money to pay their bills, she thought, "How I wish that we could just stay in one place like most families do! How I wish that Clifford would be content to do that, instead of wanting to move around all the time! He always says that the Lord is leading him to do what he does, but I'm afraid that many times, he is just being fooled into thinking that 'the grass will be greener on the other side of the fence'! And it never is!"

That summer, Beth was overjoyed to see that Eberly was finally beginning to make friends with some girls of her own age—for the first time in her life! And she was deeply thankful that her daughter's new friends were active in the youth group of a nearby Baptist church, which Eberly began attending faithfully. However, she was very concerned about Lowell's choice of friends. The companions that he chose were boys who seemed to be troublemakers in the community. It was even rumored that they had broken into a local store and stolen some merchandise! Burdened for her son, she poured out her heart to her Heavenly Father and asked Him to intervene in Lowell's life and rescue him from going any further in the wrong direction. How Beth rejoiced when, just a few weeks later, a local rancher offered Lowell a part-time job caring for his stock. Busy with this new responsibility, Lowell had less time to spend with his friends and soon lost interest in them.

As fall approached, Beth was thrilled to learn that there was a Christian school nearby. "It would be wonderful if our kids could go to school there, and receive a Christian education," she thought wistfully, "but how could we ever afford it?" Her wishful thinking was soon transformed into a prayer as she shared this desire of her heart with her Heavenly Father. Suddenly, a marvelous idea occurred to her! "I wonder if Miami Christian School needs an art teacher!" she thought excitedly. "Perhaps I could pay for the kids' tuition by teaching art!"

That very day found Beth in the office of Mr. Everett, the principal of the Christian school, offering to teach art so that her children could attend school there. "Mrs. Frazier, your coming here today is an answer to prayer!" he informed her enthusiastically. "We've wanted to start an art program in our school for several years, but until now, we've never been able to find anyone who is qualified to teach it. We would be glad to let your children attend school here in exchange for your services as an art teacher!"

The following school year flew happily by, as Beth shared her artistic abilities with students from kindergarten through twelfth grade. She reveled in the challenge of using her creativity as she prepared lessons for each age group, and introduced them to the fascinating world of art—teaching them to draw with pencils and pen and ink, paint with watercolors and oils, and model with clay. And she rejoiced that her artistic talent was being used to provide her children with a Christian education.

When Clifford came home from work one warm evening in the early spring of 1963, he was not alone. He brought with him a dark-haired, brown-eyed, fair-skinned young man who appeared to be in his mid-twenties. Clifford introduced their guest. "This is Don Warren, and he's going to be staying with us for a while. I decided to give out tracts at the band concert at Biscayne Park after I finished working tonight, and I met him there. He's from North Carolina and he needs a place to live."

Beth greeted Don cordially, even though inwardly her heart was filled with apprehension about how this might affect her teenaged daughter. "How can Clifford even think of having a young man living with us, now that Eberly is sixteen years old?" she wondered in shocked amazement.

Later that night, as they lay in bed, she voiced her concerns to her husband. "Clifford, do you think that it's wise to have Dom staying in our home? Eberly has grown to be an attractive young lady, and Don is only a few years older than she is! Suppose they become interested in each other! That would really be an awkward situation, with him living here!"

"Aw, don't worry about that, Beth," Clifford assured her. "Don is seven years older than Eberly. He's almost twenty-four years old. And he's a fine Christian young man. He is really lonely right now, and he needs friends and encouragement. I think that we could be a real help to him. Besides he won't actually be living with us. He'll only be eating his meals with us. He can stay in the apartment out back."

So it was that Don Warren moved into the small apartment which was attached to the rear of the house that the Fraziers were renting. After a while, Beth began to relax and feel that her fears had been groundless. Don was a cultured, polite, pleasant young man who truly loved the Lord. And besides that, he was a gifted musician who played both the clarinet and the alto saxophone! He was totally different from any of the other men that Clifford had brought home in the past. Beth enjoyed many musical evenings as she blended the rich music of her cello with one of Don's instruments and Eberly's violin. Soon the trio was providing special music for their church.

However, as spring turned into summer, Beth noticed that Don and Eberly were spending more and more time together. So she was not surprised when one night, shortly before her seventeenth birthday, Eberly announced, her face aglow, "Guess what, Mother!

Don and I are 'going together' now! Tonight he asked me to be his girlfriend!"

As the fall months passed, and winter approached, Beth's concern grew, as the young couple became inseparable, and their relationship grew more serious. Although Beth had learned to love and appreciate Don, she realized that he and Eberly were at two very different stages in their lives. At twenty-four, Don was ready to seriously consider marriage, while Eberly was only a senior in high school, who was planning to go to college. Beth feared that their growing attraction to each other might cause them to make unwise decisions, or lead to one or both of them being deeply hurt.

One night as she and Clifford lay in bed, she found that he shared her concerns. "You know, Beth, I've been watching Don and Eberly, and I'm afraid that you were right about the problems that might come from having Don living with us. They're getting altogether too serious about each other! I'm going to have a talk with Don about it tomorrow!" With that settled, he turned over on his side and was soon snoring, but Beth lay awake for a long time, beseeching her Heavenly Father to guide her dear daughter in the way that He wanted her to go, and to keep her from making wrong choices.

The following evening, after Clifford's promised talk with Don, Eberly came running into Clifford and Beth's room, fell onto the bed, and began crying inconsolably. Beth gathered her sobbing daughter close in her arms. "Honey, what on earth is the matter?"

"Don just broke up with me!" Eberly gasped through her tears. "He told me that there is just too much difference in our ages for us to keep going together, and that we should be 'just friends'! And it's all Father's fault," she concluded angrily. "He talked to Don and made him do it!"

Although Beth's heart was flooded with relief that Don had accepted Clifford's wise counsel, and she knew that God would lead Eberly to the man that He had chosen to be her husband at just the right time, she dared not express these thoughts to her daughter!  Her mind flew back across the years to the heartbreak that she had experienced when Dave had broken up with her, and she felt Eberly's pain as if it were her own.  Rather than saying anything, she simply hugged her grieving daughter to her breast and let her cry.

Several weeks later, Don returned to his home in North Carolina.  Although Beth missed the musical companionship which they had shared, she felt assured that he had made the decision that was best for himself and Eberly, even though she realized that her daughter was unable to see it at the time.

One cool night in early 1964, several months after Don had left, Clifford burst enthusiastically through the door, followed by a stocky, white-haired man who was about sixty years old.  "Guess what, Beth!" Clifford cried.  "The Lord has opened the door for us to go back to Alabama and start our church!  This is Leo Davis, and he's offered to go to Alabama with me and build a place for us to live on our property there.  It should only take us a month or so, and as soon as we get it done, I'll be back to take all of you up there!"

Beth's head reeled in shock and amazement at this unexpected announcement.  "But, Clifford, how can we move now?" she protested.  "It would be totally unfair to Eberly!  She's a senior this year, and she'll be graduating in just a few months. She loves playing the violin in the orchestra and taking music theory, and she can never get those courses at Dozier High!"

As Eberly, who was standing openmouthed at Beth's side, realized the implications of what her father had just said, she joined her pleas to her mother's.  "Please, Father, don't make us go to Alabama right now!" she begged.  "I've been looking forward to going to Washington, D. C. this spring with the orchestra. We've been raising money for our trip all year, and we're even going to get to play on the lawn of the White House! Can't we at least stay here until after I graduate?"

In response, Clifford shook his head emphatically. "No, we need to go as soon as Leo and I can get a place built for us to live in. I've been praying for a long time that the Lord would make it possible for us to keep our promise to Mr. Jim and start that church, and now that God has opened the way, we need to take advantage of the opportunity that He's provided!"

A month later, as Clifford pulled into the abandoned cotton field that was now their property and stopped the car in front of their new home, Beth's heart sank. In the midst of a few small, struggling pine saplings and a mass of tall weeds, there stood a dilapidated trailer, an outhouse, and a small, haphazardly-built, one-room structure that could only be described as a shack! "Look at what Leo and I built, Beth!" Clifford announced proudly. "It's great, isn't it? Between the trailer and the house that we built, there will be plenty of room for our whole family! Some of us can sleep in the trailer and the rest of us can sleep in the house!"

Beth sighed wearily as she once again was faced with the daunting task of making a home for her family under such primitive conditions. As she looked at Eberly's forlorn face, her heart ached for her teenaged daughter who had been uprooted from the school, church, and friends that she loved and transplanted to such a totally opposite environment to complete her senior year. Her only consolation was the fact that Clifford would once again be doing the work that he loved, and that together they could reach the needy people of rural southern Alabama with the message of the Gospel.

The year 1964 marked a milestone in Beth's life as she saw her first child graduate from high school in May and then watched her prepare to leave for college that September. Eberly had at first planned to follow in her father's footsteps and attend Moody Bible Institute, but by the time her application was processed, there was

no room remaining at Moody for new students that fall. The same
day that she received this disheartening news, she also received a
letter from Don Warren, telling her about a Christian school which
none of the Frazier family had ever heard of—Bob Jones
University, which was located in Greenville, South Carolina.

"Mother, what do you think I should do?" Eberly questioned in
confusion, handing Don's letter to Beth. "I won't be able to go to
Moody this fall, and I sure don't want to stay here in Alabama! Do
you think that maybe I should go to Bob Jones? Don seems to
think that it's a good school."

Beth took the letter, scanned through it, and then pored over the
information about BJU which Don had enclosed. Though Beth
wasn't familiar with this college, she was impressed with the fact
that BJU offered music lessons to its students at no additional cost
above their tuition. "You know, Eberly," she remarked
thoughtfully, "I don't think that it's a coincidence that you
received both of these letters at the same time. Maybe that's the
Lord's way of showing you His will. Perhaps He is closing the
door for you to go to Moody and leading you to attend Bob Jones.
God has given you a real talent for music, and at BJ, you would be
able to take violin and piano lessons free of charge!"

After carefully considering her mother's advice, Eberly decided
to follow it, and in early September, Beth kissed her daughter
good-bye as she left for college. Although Beth deeply loved her
two sons, she missed the special friendship and companionship that
she shared with her only daughter. Since the Fraziers didn't have a
telephone, Beth's only communication now with her daughter was
by letter. Beth faithfully wrote Eberly every week, sharing the
family news and often illustrating her letters with amusing pencil
sketches of the dogs, chickens, and goats that made up the Frazier
family's current menagerie.

Every day, Beth looked forward eagerly to the coming of the
mailman, hoping that he would bring an envelope addressed in

Eberly's familiar scrawl. If he did, she eagerly tore it open to read the latest details about the busy schedule of classes, work, and activities that now filled her daughter's days. And always after carefully folding up the letter and replacing it in the envelope, she murmured a heartfelt prayer, "Father, please take care of Eberly and help her in all that she is doing. Please lead and guide her and show her Your perfect will for her life!"

The school year of 1964-65 passed rather uneventfully. Beth focused all of her energy and ingenuity on assisting Clifford in the meetings which he held several times each week in various homes in the area, and on making an adequate home for her family under the difficult circumstances in which they were living. This latter task became especially challenging during the late fall, when Clifford decided to leave Beth, Lowell, and Raymond in Alabama and return to Miami and work there for a while. However, this time, instead of coming back and moving them down to Florida, as he had done in the past, he returned to Alabama at Christmas time, remained with them, and resumed his preaching there. As Beth joined with Clifford in his ministry, she rejoiced in the many opportunities that she had to use her musical abilities to help her husband present Christ to souls who desperately needed a Savior.

When Eberly returned home in the summer of 1965, Clifford and Beth were shocked when she announced that she would not be returning to Bob Jones in the fall. "I don't like Bob Jones! They're too strict, and they have too many rules! I think that maybe I'll try to go to Moody after all," she informed them.

However, once again, Eberly found that she had applied to Moody too late to gain entrance for the coming semester. Upon finding out this disappointing news, Eberly decided that she would stay out of college and work for a year, and then return to BJU in the fall of 1966. "I sure do wish that I didn't have to live in the dorm, though," she remarked. "I'd rather be a town student, but of course the only way I could do that would be if you all would move over to Greenville and I could live at home!"

One night in the late summer of 1965, as they sat around the supper table, Clifford announced, "I've got a great idea. I think that we should begin weekly Bible clubs for children in several of the homes where we've been having meetings. Eberly could teach the Bible lesson, since she learned how to do that while she was at Bob Jones."

"That's a great idea, Clifford!" Beth agreed enthusiastically, glad that her daughter was going to have an opportunity to use her talents in their ministry
.

But shortly after they began holding the Bible clubs, the Frazier family was faced with a new challenge. Their car broke down, and since they had no money with which to fix it, they were left without transportation. In spite of this obstacle, however, the Bible clubs and meetings continued throughout the fall and winter, even though the trip to each house involved miles of walking on the dusty, and sometimes muddy, dirt roads. Beth rejoiced in the opportunity to use her artistic abilities to create colorful backgrounds on which Eberly could place the flannelgraph figures that she used to teach the Bible stories, and in the chance to use her cello to provide music for the children as they sang.

One day, as she watched her daughter teaching, Beth thought, "It's so wonderful to have Eberly home with us again! It's sure going to be hard to say goodbye to her when she goes back to school next fall!"

Later that evening, as she and Clifford lay in bed, he remarked, "You know, Beth, I've been thinking about what Eberly said about wishing that she could live at home with us and be a 'town student' at Bob Jones. Maybe we should move over to Greenville so that she can do that."

"Perhaps you're right, Clifford," Beth said thoughtfully. "I've been wondering how she would ever be able to afford going back to college again, but if she lived with us, the only expenses that she would have would be her tuition, books, and fees. She could save a lot of money by not having to live in the dorm!"

"And if she lived with us, she would be able to work in town instead of on campus, and she could make much better wages," Clifford added.

So it was, that in the spring of 1966, Clifford and Eberly moved to Greenville, South Carolina so that they could both get jobs and also find a place to live. This time, to Beth's amazement, Clifford agreed to delay moving the rest of the family until summer, so that Lowell and Raymond could finish their school year in Alabama. By early June, the Frazier family was reunited and settled in their new home in Greenville. It was a great relief to Beth to once again be living under twentieth-century conditions!

# Chapter 14—Traveling Toward HOME!

Not long after Eberly returned to college, she began dating Joe Mehesy, a young man from New Jersey, who was preparing for the ministry. She had met Joe during her freshman year and dated him several times, and they had corresponded sporadically during the year that Eberly was out of school.

One evening in mid-December, Eberly returned home from a concert that she had attended with Joe. "How was your date, Honey?" Beth asked with a smile, as Eberly burst through the door accompanied by a blast of cold wind.

"It was fun!" Eberly huddled close to their small wood stove and rubbed her hands together, trying to warm them. "You know, after Don broke up with me, I thought that I would never be interested in another guy, but I'm really beginning to like Joe. I'm going to miss him a lot when he goes home for Christmas! What do you think of him, Mother?"

"He's a fine young man!  When Joe first wrote to you last year, your father and I were really impressed by his love for the Lord and by how much he cared about you.  And now that we've had the opportunity to get to know him, we really like him!"

One cold, wintry morning in February 1967, Beth, Clifford, and Raymond were coming home from a shopping trip.  As they turned onto Briarcliff Drive, the street where they lived, they were startled to see a fire engine race past them, lights flashing and siren blaring. "Look, Mother!" Raymond pointed to a plume of thick gray smoke which was ascending into the sky, "Someone's house must be on fire!"

Beth glanced over in the direction her son was pointing and cried out in shocked horror, "Why, it's our house that's on fire!"

Instantly, Clifford gunned their car's engine, roared down the street, and screeched to a halt at the curb in front of their burning home.  The three Fraziers jumped out of the car and stood in stunned silence as they watched the firemen labor valiantly to prevent all of their earthly possessions from going up in smoke. Beth breathed a prayer of silent thanksgiving that all the members of her family were safe, since none of them had been home at the time of the blaze.

However, she couldn't help thinking of the precious and irreplaceable belongings that would be gone forever if the fire won its battle to consume them.  Her precious cello, her portfolio of paintings which dated back to her art school days, their family pictures, and Eberly's century-old violin, which had been passed down to her from Clifford's grandfather, would all be lost!  The next few minutes felt like hours as the firemen sprayed the flames with their high-pressure hoses.  At last the fire was brought under control, but as Beth surveyed the charred shell of what had once been their home, she knew that the structure was damaged beyond repair.

A few moments later, a weary fireman trudged toward them. He removed his hat and wiped the sweat from his sooty face with a grimy bandanna. "Are y'all the people who live here?"

"Yes, we are!" Clifford replied. "How soon can we go in there and see what can be salvaged?"

"Well, you'll have to wait until things cool down, and that probably won't be till late this afternoon. But I'm afraid you'll find that there's not much that's worth saving. We did the best we could, but even the things that didn't burn up are badly damaged by smoke and water."

"Could you tell how the fire started?" Beth questioned.

"As far as we can tell, it was ignited by your wood stove, ma'am. We think that it may have started as a chimney fire and then spread to the rest of the house."

Beth groaned inwardly, as she remembered that earlier that morning, she had been concerned about the safety of their heating stove, because after she had started a fire in it, the stovepipe had glowed red-hot. After the fire had died down a bit, the stovepipe had returned to its normal black color, and Beth had thought that the danger had passed. However, she now realized that this excessive heat had probably started the chimney fire which had eventually spread to the rest of the house.

Several hours later, the Frazier family was finally allowed to enter the charred skeleton of their house and sift through the rubble. As the fireman had warned them, there was not much worth saving. All of their furniture and their clothing had either been destroyed by the flames or ruined by smoke or water. However, miraculously, their most precious possessions had been spared. Their family photographs, Beth's portfolio of art work, and their musical instruments had all been stored in one bedroom—the room that had been least affected by the fire, and they had suffered only minor damage! How Beth rejoiced that the Lord had preserved these priceless treasures for her!

For the next few days, Beth and her family stayed in a motel room that was provided for them by the Salvation Army. The local news media broadcast their plight, and the generous people of Greenville showered them with donations of money, clothing, and furniture. Within a week, the Fraziers were settled in a new home and all of their needs had been met!

Several weeks after they had moved into their new home, Clifford remarked, "I'd like to visit that church that is just down the road from here. Let's go there next Sunday."

"That sounds like a great idea, Clifford!"

As she sat in the pew beside her family the following Sunday, Beth was thrilled to see that this church had a small instrumental ensemble that joined with the pianist and organist in providing music. She could hardly wait to meet the musicians, especially since one of them played the cello and another played the violin!

When the service was over, Beth hurried to the front and introduced herself to them. "I enjoyed your music so much! You play beautifully! I am a cellist myself, and my daughter Eberly plays the violin."

"Well, why don't you and Eberly join our little orchestra? We'd love to have you!" invited the man who played the cello. "I'm George Mulfinger, and this is my wife Joan," he added, indicating the violinist who was standing beside him. "We teach music at the university."

So it was that Beth and Eberly joined the Mulfingers in playing for the services each week at Boulevard Baptist. Beth rejoiced at the opportunity to blend the deep, rich tones of her cello in harmony with these talented musicians, who soon became two of her dearest friends.

From that time on, each Sunday provided a musical feast for Beth! She felt as if her creative soul was once again receiving the nourishment that it craved, after having endured a long famine! In addition to her participation in the ensemble at her church, she eagerly looked forward to attending Bob Jones University's Sunday afternoon vespers service, which was a creative, colorful presentation of music and drama that was centered around a different theme each week. And she also often spent part of those Sunday afternoons wandering through the university art gallery and letting her artistic soul drink in the beauty of the world-renowned masterpieces that graced its walls.

One Sunday evening, as Beth was putting her cello back into its case following the church service, Joan Mulfinger turned to her. "Could you and your family come over to our place for some pie and coffee tonight?"

"We'd love to!"

As they sat around the Mulfingers' table enjoying thick wedges of Joan's homemade apple pie and sipping steaming mugs of coffee, George said, "It's so much fun teaching music to our kids. Each of them plays a different instrument. By the time they all grow up, we should have quite a musical ensemble in our family!"

"That's great!" Beth exclaimed. "It's wonderful that your kids have inherited your talent, and that you and Joan are so good at teaching them!"

"I just wish we knew something about teaching art, though," Joan remarked. "Our son Mark seems to have real artistic ability, but neither George nor I are gifted in that area. We've been looking for a teacher for him, but so far, we haven't been able to find one."

"Well, I'd be glad to give him lessons if you want me to," Beth offered.

"Why, Beth, we didn't realize that you are an artist as well as a musician!" George said in amazement.

"She certainly is!" Clifford exclaimed. "Beth graduated from art school, and before we were married, she worked as a greeting card designer in New York City!"

"We'd love to have you teach Mark!" Joan cried joyfully. "I can't think of anyone that I'd rather have as our son's art teacher!"

The following Wednesday, Beth began giving weekly art lessons to Mark Mulfinger, and she was delighted to find that her young pupil had great talent. One afternoon, as she was packing up her art supplies and preparing to leave, she remarked to Joan, "I've never seen a child learn as quickly as Mark does! He is unusually gifted, and I believe that he can have a career as an artist someday, if he chooses to do so!"

She turned to see Mark looking up eagerly into her face. "Oh, do you really that I could do that, Mrs. Frazier?" he asked breathlessly. "I've always dreamed of being an artist when I grow up!"

"You certainly could, Mark!" she encouraged with a smile, as she reached to give her young pupil a hug.

That spring and summer flew happily by in a flurry of activity, and soon a new school year began. Eberly was still dating Joe, and Beth could see that their relationship was becoming more and more serious. On a cool, crisp evening in late October 1967, Eberly and Joe walked into the kitchen of the Frazier house, their faces beaming with joy. "We have an important announcement to make!" Joe exclaimed excitedly. "Tonight, I asked Eberly to marry me, and she said yes! We're engaged!"

"Congratulations, Son!" Clifford cried, taking Joe's hand and shaking it heartily.

"We're so glad that you're going to be a part of our family, Joe!" Beth added enthusiastically.

"When are you going to get married?" Lowell inquired curiously.

"We're planning to be married sometime in the summer of 1970," Eberly replied.

"Why are you waiting so long?" Raymond asked.

"It's because we've decided that we're both going to finish college before we get married," Joe explained.

As Beth watched the happy couple accepting their congratulations, her heart filled with a silent prayer of thanksgiving to the Lord. "Thank You, Father, for giving Eberly such a godly young man to be her husband!"

Early on the morning of New Year's Day, 1968, before anyone else in the Frazier family had awakened, Beth sat alone at her kitchen table. As she closed her Bible, following her daily devotional time, her mind drifted back over all that had happened since they had moved to Greenville. "It's hard to believe that we've actually lived in the same city for a year and a half—even if we have lived in five different houses during that time!" she thought in amazement. As she thought of the friends that she had made and the activities that she had become involved in, she realized that, for the first time in many years, she was beginning to feel settled and "at home". Bowing her head, she murmured a prayer of thanksgiving to her Heavenly Father for His goodness in leading them to this place.

However, even in the midst of Beth's joy, her heart was filled with a deep concern for Clifford's health. Shortly after they had moved to Greenville, he had begun experiencing pain throughout his entire body and a growing weakness which had caused him to begin using a cane to steady himself as he walked. Clifford had been to the doctor several times, but so far, no one had been able to identify the cause of his mysterious ailment. For more than a year now, he had been unable to work, and the Frazier family had been subsisting on the meager salary that Eberly earned in her part-time job as a long-distance telephone operator, plus the fifty dollars per month that Beth received as her inheritance from her parents. As Beth thought once again about her husband's need, she whispered imploringly, "Lord Jesus, You are the Great Physician, and You know exactly what's wrong with Clifford! Please bring healing to his body!"

That night, shortly after Beth had fallen asleep, she was startled awake by her husband's moans of pain. "Clifford, are you all right?" she asked anxiously.

"Oh, Beth," he groaned. "I have the worst toothache that I've ever had in my life! I've got to go to the dentist tomorrow morning and get that tooth pulled!"

As Beth was making sandwiches for lunch the following day, she heard her husband's car pull into the driveway. Wiping her hands on her apron, she hurried out the door to meet him. "How are you feeling, Clifford?" she questioned, as he hobbled up the sidewalk toward her. "Did the dentist pull your tooth?"

"Yes, he did, and I feel much better. And the dentist told me that I need to get all the rest of my teeth pulled as soon as possible."

Beth's mouth dropped open in shock. "Well, I'm glad that your toothache is gone, but why on earth does he want to pull all of your other teeth?"

"When the dentist examined me, he found that I have pyorrhea, a gum disease that has been spreading poison throughout my whole body. I've finally found out what's been making me so sick! The dentist said that the toxin from this infection has caused the pain and weakness that I've had for the past year, and he says that after I get my teeth out, I'll be well again!"

"Oh, Clifford, that's wonderful! Praise the Lord that we've finally found out what's been wrong with you!"

Clifford followed the dentist's advice and had all of his teeth pulled, and not long afterward, his pain vanished, his strength returned to normal, and he was able to throw away his cane! How Beth rejoiced in the renewed health that God had given to her husband in answer to their prayers!

That spring, Lowell began "going steady" with Sandra Jack, a girl whom he had met at school. As spring turned into summer, Beth became concerned as she realized that Lowell and Sandra were spending every available moment together. Since they were both only eighteen years of age, and they still had one more year of high school to complete, she felt that their relationship was becoming much too serious for young people of their age.

Then, in early August, shortly after Sandra's nineteenth birthday, she had to undergo heart surgery to correct a congenital defect. Although Sandra came through the operation well, and her problem was alleviated, Beth could see that this time of crisis had further cemented the young couple's bond with each other.

One morning, as they sat at the breakfast table, Beth asked gently, "Lowell, do you think that it's wise for you and Sandra to be spending so much time together? I know that you care a lot about each other, but even if the Lord should lead you to marry each other someday, you both need to finish school first. It would be quite a while before you could afford to get married."

"Mother, I <u>love</u> Sandra!" Lowell replied emphatically. "When I realized that I could have lost her when she had her surgery, it showed me just how much she means to me, so it's just natural that I want to be with her whenever I can!"

Beth said no more to her son about the subject, but she spent much time in earnest prayer for him and Sandra, that the Lord would guide them concerning His will for their lives.

One sunny morning in mid-September, Lowell didn't come downstairs for breakfast. Thinking that he had overslept, Beth hurried upstairs and knocked at his bedroom door. "Wake up, Lowell," she called through the closed door. "If you don't hurry, you'll be late for school."

She waited for a moment, and then, since she had received no answer, she turned the doorknob, opened the door, and entered his bedroom. She gasped in shocked surprise as she saw that the room was empty and that the bed had not been slept in! Lowell was gone!

At that moment the phone rang. Beth hurried out into the hall to answer it, hoping that this call would solve the mystery of Lowell's disappearance. "Hello," she said eagerly, hoping to hear the voice of her son, explaining the reason for his absence from home.

Instead, she heard the concerned voice of Sandra's mother demanding, "Mrs. Frazier, do you know where Sandra is? When I went to wake her up for school, she wasn't there! And she didn't sleep in her bed last night!"

"No, I don't know where she is," Beth replied in consternation. "Lowell isn't here either!"

"Well, I'm afraid that our two kids have run away together!" Sandra's stepfather, who had been listening to the conversation on their other phone, concluded angrily. "And I'll tell you one thing—if they've been away from home overnight together, they're going to get married!"

Beth spent the rest of the morning calling the homes of various friends of Lowell's, but no one had seen either him or Sandra or knew of the young couple's whereabouts. Her questions were finally answered when Lowell burst through the door late that afternoon. "Lowell, where have you been?" Beth cried. "And where is Sandra? We've all been so concerned about both of you!"

"We tried to elope, but we couldn't get a marriage license without having our birth certificates to prove that we're both at least eighteen and that we didn't need our parents' consent. I came home to get mine, and Sandra has gone home to get hers, and as soon as we get them, we're going to get married. We stayed at a friend's house last night."

Beth opened her mouth to protest, but remembering the comment that Mr. Drummond, Sandra's stepfather, had made, she closed it again. "Perhaps the best thing for them to do now would be to get married," she thought reluctantly, "And anyway, there's nothing that I can do to stop them. They're old enough to make this decision for themselves." Aloud she merely said, "All right, Son, I'll get your birth certificate for you."

So it was that, suddenly and unexpectedly, the older of Beth's two sons left the nest, and Beth welcomed a new daughter into her family. The following Saturday evening, Lowell and Sandra's families and friends joined together in celebrating the young couple's recent marriage by giving them a household shower to help in furnishing the small apartment that they had rented. Both of them dropped out of high school to fulfill their new responsibilities as a married couple. Lowell was able to get a full-time job at the nearby Bi-Lo supermarket where he had previously worked part-time after school, and Sandra began her new role of being a wife and homemaker.

One warm spring evening in May 1969, Joe Mehesy, Eberly's fiancé, joined the Frazier family for dinner. As they enjoyed a meal of juicy roast chicken together, Joe announced, "I got some wonderful news today!"

"What is it, Joe?" Eberly asked eagerly.

"Remember how I asked you all to pray about my application to be a summer missionary on the Navajo Reservation? Well, I've been accepted, and I'll be spending the entire summer at the Navajo Bible School and Mission in Window Rock, Arizona! It will be wonderful preparation for the time when you and I will be missionaries to the Navajos after we're married, Eberly! It will give me a chance to learn about the people and see what the conditions are like before we move out there permanently!"

"That's wonderful, Joseph!" Clifford replied enthusiastically. "How will you be getting out there?"

"By train, I guess, since I don't have a car."

As they finished their meal, Beth let her thoughts drift back over the past several years. How thankful she was that the Lord had brought Joe and Eberly together. From the time that she was a small child, Eberly had always had a special interest in Indians because of her Cherokee heritage. "How wonderful it is that You led her to a young man who feels called to be a missionary to the Indians!" Beth prayed silently, lifting up her heart to the Lord in thanksgiving. "Only You could have given Eberly a husband who is such a perfect partner for her!"

Later that night, as Clifford and Beth lay in bed, Clifford remarked, "Beth, I've been thinking. Why don't you and I take a trip out West this summer? We could give Joseph a ride out to his mission station in Arizona, and then go on out to the West Coast and visit my brothers and sisters and their families and your sister Dot and her family. After all, we haven't seen any of them for years, and most of them still aren't saved. It would give us another chance to give them the Gospel! It would be great to get away and take a trip—just the two of us—and I bet that we would have lots of chances to give out tracts and win souls all along the way too!"

"But what about Raymond? We can't just leave him by himself! Eberly is a grown woman now, and she'd be fine on her own, but Raymond's not quite fourteen yet!"

"Why, he could stay here with Eberly! Like you said, she's an adult now—almost twenty-three years old—certainly old enough to be responsible for him! And besides, we'd only be gone for the summer!"

"I suppose that would be all right," Beth agreed doubtfully, "but I'm really concerned that Raymond might not want Eberly telling him what to do. After all, she's only his sister—not his mother!"

"Aw, they'll be fine!" Clifford dismissed her worries. "It will be a real help to Joseph too! Now he won't have to take that long train trip! I can hardly wait to tell him about it!"

"Yes, I'm sure that he'll be glad to hear it." After a moment of silence, she continued hesitantly. "Clifford, why do you always insist upon calling Joe 'Joseph'? You know that he prefers to be called 'Joe'."

"Because that's his name, and it's a good Bible name too!" Clifford retorted. "You know that I hate nicknames!"

Beth sighed. She had been extremely embarrassed that her husband had refused to honor their future son-in-law's wishes in this matter, and she had hoped that she might be able to convince him to change his mind. However, she knew that it was useless to argue with Clifford once he had made up his mind about something.

When Clifford offered to provide Joe with transportation to Window Rock, Joe gratefully accepted his offer. So it was, that on a stiflingly hot day in the middle of June, Clifford, Beth, and Joe drove out of Greenville and headed west, leaving Eberly and Raymond behind. Beth was thankful that Eberly had been able to find two housemates to share her expenses. Both Erlene and Elle were students at Bob Jones University who were staying in town for the summer and needed a place to stay. However, Beth couldn't restrain her concern about Raymond's being left at home under Eberly's supervision. Although she knew that her daughter would do her best, she still wondered how well her fourteen-year-old son would listen to his twenty-three year old sister! "Father, please take care of my children while I'm away from them!" she implored silently.

After several grueling days of hot, exhausting travel, the Fraziers and their future son-in-law finally reached their destination—a small mission compound located on the eastern edge of the vast Navajo Indian Reservation. To Beth's eyes, accustomed as they were to the abundant vegetation of the eastern United States, the Southwest seemed extremely barren. The landscape of hardened dirt and bare rock formations was broken only by an occasional clump of sagebrush, pine, or cedar.

However, after being there for a few days, Beth began to realize that this area of the country, with its multi-colored rocks molded into a myriad of shapes, had its own stark beauty. She was thankful that she had brought her art supplies with her, and decided that she would try to capture some of these unique vistas on paper. One afternoon, she painted a watercolor picture of the mission station, whose buildings were perched on the edge of a thirty-foot cliff of red rock, with an even higher cliff rising above and behind it. At the bottom of the cliff was an old red barn, which had been converted into living quarters, and which had been jokingly dubbed "The Garden Apartments" by Joe and the other two young men who had come to help at the mission during the summer.

As she was putting the finishing touches on her painting, she was startled to hear a voice behind her. "Well, Mrs. Frazier," a tall, attractive, dark-haired woman remarked, as she looked over Beth's shoulder, "you're quite an artist! We're having Vacation Bible School at our church here next week, and I was wondering if you would be willing to do some chalk talks for us. The children would really enjoy it. By the way," she continued, "I'm Lois Harper. My husband Larry is the director of KHAC, the mission radio station. Your future son-in-law, Joe Mehesy, has been working at the station, and he has told us a lot about you and your husband! We'd love to have you folks stay here at the mission and help out for a while if you can."

"Why that sounds wonderful, Mrs. Harper! Let me talk to my husband about it!"

Clifford was just as excited as Beth was about the opportunity to minister to the Navajos. The next few weeks flew by in a whirlwind of activity as Beth did chalk talks, Clifford preached at the mission's outstation church in beautiful, mountainous Crystal, New Mexico, and both of them used their musical talents to provide special music for several church services. Beth soon felt quite at home among the quiet, reserved Indian people, who gradually responded with shy friendliness to her gentle, loving personality.

One warm, windy day in early July, as Clifford and Beth sat around the lunch table with Joe and the other summer volunteers, Clifford announced, "It's been great being here with you all, but I believe that it's time for Beth and me to be hitting the road. We'll be leaving tomorrow morning and heading for California and Oregon to see our relatives."

"I'll really be praying for you folks, Rev. Frazier, that the Lord will help you to witness to your family, and that they'll soon be saved," Joe said heartily. "You know, I have an aunt and uncle who live in Oregon. They're Catholics, like all the rest of my family, and I sure wish that someone could give them the Gospel. Do you suppose that you would have time to stop by and visit them when you go to Oregon? I could give you their address."

"Why, of course, we would!" Clifford exclaimed enthusiastically. "We're always glad to have the chance to tell people about the Lord!"

The following day, Clifford and Beth left Window Rock and began the long trek across the scorchingly hot, desolate desert to California. The next evening, they arrived at the home of Clifford's brother Earl and his wife Mildred. As usual, Clifford had not notified his relatives that they were coming, and remembering the reception which they had received from Earl the last time that they had visited—fifteen years before—Beth was filled with trepidation.

However, she was pleasantly surprised when Earl welcomed them with open arms. "It's great to see you, Brother!" Earl enfolded Clifford in a tight bear hug. "And you too, Beth!" He reached out an arm to include her in his embrace. "A lot has changed in my life since I saw you last. Most important of all, I've found the Lord Jesus as my Savior!"

"Praise the Lord!" Clifford cried joyfully.

"What a wonderful answer to prayer!" Beth rejoiced. "We've been praying for you for years!"

Thus began several enjoyable weeks of visiting, reminiscing, and fellowshipping with Earl and Mildred. However, one night, as Clifford and Beth lay in bed, Beth asked timidly, "Clifford, don't you think that it's time for us to be moving on? We certainly don't want to wear out our welcome here!"

"Aw, that could never happen! We're <u>family</u>, remember? But I do think you're right about moving on. We still have a lot of people to visit!"

The next day, Clifford and Beth drove to the home of her sister Dot's son, Stuart, and that evening found them sitting around the supper table with Dot, Stu, his wife Nancy, and their three children—Scott, Kim, and Eric. "It's so good to see you again, Stu," Beth beamed. "Why, I haven't seen you since you were just a teenager, about Scott's age. What a lovely family you have!"

"Thank you, Aunt Beth! It's great to have you here with us!"

As Beth savored the delicious meal of pork chops and scalloped potatoes, her mind drifted back across the years to the one time that Dot had allowed her to take Stuart and his sister Nancy to Sunday School. How she wondered if Stu still remembered that day, and more importantly—if he recalled the decision that he had made to accept Christ as his Savior. "Stuart," she said hesitantly, "do you remember the day that I took you and Nancy to Sunday School?"

"Yes, I certainly do!" Stu assured her with a smile. "It was right before Nancy died!"

"And do you remember how you prayed and asked the Lord Jesus to save you?"

Instantly, Stuart's smile changed to a frown, and his face reddened with embarrassment. "Oh, no, that wasn't me, Aunt Beth! I never did that. You must be thinking of Nancy. She prayed that day, but I didn't!"

Without answering, Beth lowered her eyes to her plate, her appetite suddenly gone. "Well, it's just as I've feared all these years," she thought sadly. "Stu just said a prayer to please me, but he didn't really mean it. He's still not saved!"

Although Clifford and Beth had a pleasant visit with the Baker family, they were always met with either a cold, stony silence or a quick, but polite, change of subject whenever they tried to speak to them about the Lord. Also, after staying with them for a week, Beth sensed that they had overstayed their welcome, and she insisted to Clifford that they must leave the following day.

From her nephew's house, Beth and Clifford traveled to visit his sister Betty and her husband Walter. Although his sister and brother-in-law were happy to see them, they made it emphatically clear that they had no interest in the Gospel! "I'm a good woman, Clifford!" Betty maintained firmly, when Clifford tried to show her that she needed Jesus. "I do the best I can, and I try to be kind and help those who are in need, and I'm sure that God will be pleased with that. So just drop the subject! I don't want to hear any more about it!"

Clifford and Beth stayed with Betty and Walter until late August. Once again, Beth worried that her in-laws would feel that she and Clifford were taking advantage of their hospitality, but she also had another concern. School would be starting soon, and they had promised Eberly that they would be home by the end of the summer. "Clifford," she remarked one afternoon, "don't you think it's time for us to be heading home now? Raymond and Eberly will both be going back to school in a few days, and this semester Eberly won't be able to work, because she'll be doing her student teaching!"

"But we're not done visiting all of my family yet, and we promised Joseph that we would visit his aunt and uncle and witness to them too! And besides, everywhere we go, we've had lots of chances to give out tracts, and I've had quite a few opportunities to preach! This is a missionary trip, Beth, and the Lord will provide for our kids while we're gone. We're not going home until we've reached all of the people that God wants us to!"

Beth's heart sank. She knew how Clifford loved to travel, and how long he would stay in each home that they visited, and she realized that it could still be months before they returned home to Greenville. "Lord, please take care of our kids and meet their needs while we're gone!" she breathed.

Their next stop was at the home of Charles and Maxine Koczan, Joe's uncle and aunt, where they were warmly welcomed. "What a pleasant surprise—to be able to meet my nephew Joe's fiancé's parents!" Charles enthused, as Clifford and Beth introduced themselves and explained that Joe had suggested that they stop by for a visit. "We haven't seen Joe and his family in years, and it's hard to believe that he's a young man of twenty-four, who is engaged to be married. You'll have to show us a picture of your daughter!"

However, although the Koczans were glad to see them, they soon let Clifford and Beth know that they were staunch Catholics who had no desire to change their religion. "I was born a Catholic, and I'll die a Catholic!" Charles Koczan declared emphatically one day, as Clifford tried to share the Gospel with him.

"But, Charles," Beth replied gently, "the important thing is whether or not you know Jesus as your personal Savior—not what church you go to!"

"Well, my mother always told me to stay away from discussing either politics or religion, and I think that that is very good advice," Maxine said firmly. "Let's just change the subject!'

After they had been staying with Charles and Maxine for about a week, Beth began to notice a distinct difference in Maxine's attitude toward them. One morning at the breakfast table, she remarked, rather icily, "Well, Clifford and Beth, it's been just delightful having you here, but I know that you must have other people to visit! Where do you plan to go from here?"

"Oh, we're in no hurry to leave. We can stay here as long as you'd like us to!" Clifford replied, totally oblivious to her polite hint that it was past time for them to move on.

"Dear, don't you think that we should get on the road today?" Beth suggested, her cheeks burning with embarrassment at the knowledge that they had already imposed on the hospitality of these total strangers for far too long. "You know that we still want to visit your sister Ione and your brothers Roy and Murray and their families before we head back East!"

"Well, I guess you're right, Beth! We do have a lot of people that we want to see!"

Clifford and Beth's visits with his remaining siblings were similar to the time that they had spent with his sister Betty. None of them were the least bit interested in hearing the Gospel, and in spite of Clifford's assuring Beth that since they were family, it was impossible for them to wear out their welcome, Beth felt certain that in each home they had stayed, they had done just that!

After they had finished visiting Clifford's family in the West, they began the long trip home to South Carolina. However, since they stopped in Illinois and Alabama to visit more friends and relatives, and stayed several weeks with each one, it was not until early March of 1970 that they finally returned to Greenville! Although Beth had enjoyed the many opportunities she had on their trip to tell others about the Lord, and to use her artistic and musical talents, she was appalled that their "summer trip" had turned into an extended absence of nine months from their children! She was thrilled to be home with her family again at last!

One night a few days after they returned home, Clifford remarked to Beth, "I think that the time has come for us to leave Greenville. After all, we only moved here so that Eberly could save money by living at home and being a town student while she was at BJ. Now she's almost ready to graduate, and then she and

Joseph will be getting married. I believe that we should move back to Miami. I just can't find any work here, and I've always been able to get a job down there."

"But what about Raymond? We've lived here for five years now, and he considers this his hometown. He's almost done with his freshman year in high school, and he's got lots of friends here!"

"Aw, he'll be fine! He'll make new friends down in Miami."

"Couldn't we at least stay here until school is out?" Beth pleaded, "It would only be a couple more months. In fact, why don't we wait until after Joe and Eberly get married in July? I'd like to be here to help her get ready for the wedding!"

"No! I've been praying about it for several days, and I'm convinced that now is the time that the Lord wants us to move!"

Several days later, in spite of vehement protests from both Raymond and Eberly, the Frazier family headed south to Florida. As Beth, her husband, and their youngest son drove out of Greenville, Beth's heart was filled with sadness as she left her only daughter behind. How she longed to spend the last few precious months before Eberly's marriage in doing all of the special things that a bride's mother is supposed to do in helping her daughter prepare for her wedding, but now she would be hundreds of miles away from her! "Usually, when children grow up, they 'leave the nest'," she thought ruefully, as she considered their present situation and remembered their long trip of the previous year, "but only in this family does the nest take wings and leave the children behind!"

When the Fraziers reached Miami, they were shocked to see how dramatically the city had changed in the six years since they had left. Everywhere, signs were printed in both English and Spanish, and as they walked down the street, the majority of the people were dark-haired, dark-skinned Cuban refugees, who had fled from Fidel Castro's oppressive regime that had taken over the government of Cuba in 1959. As Beth listened to the babble of voices around her, chattering away in Spanish, she recalled that in the early sixties, shortly before they had left Florida, a trickle of Cuban immigrants had begun coming into Miami, but now that trickle had increased into an overwhelming flood! "Why, this place is like a foreign country now!" she thought in amazement. "I don't even feel like I'm in the United States anymore."

Clifford also soon found out that the Miami of 1970 was drastically different than the city that he remembered from 1964. One night, several weeks after they arrived, he sat dejectedly at the supper table, exhausted from another fruitless day of searching for work. "I've looked and looked, Beth," he sighed, "but everywhere I go, it's the same. None of the hospitals need a male nurse or an orderly. All of the jobs have been taken by the Cubans. And besides that, they won't hire you unless you speak both English and Spanish!"

"But what about private-duty nursing, like you used to do when we lived here before? Remember Mr. Schonfeldt, the Jewish man that you used to care for? If you were taking care of a patient like that, you wouldn't need to know Spanish."

"That kind of work isn't available either." Clifford leaned back wearily in his chair. "All of the wealthy people who used to live in this area and who could afford to hire a personal attendant have moved to other parts of the state."

"Perhaps I should try to find a job, then, so that we'll have some income until you find work," Beth suggested hesitantly.

To her surprise, her husband agreed with her. "Yes, I guess you should," he replied reluctantly. "We're almost out of money, so we need to have someone bringing home a paycheck!"

The following day, Beth bought a paper and began painstakingly searching through the help-wanted ads, trying to find any kind of work that would utilize her skills as either an artist, a secretary, or a waitress. Finally, just as she was about to give up, she spotted a promising lead at the very bottom of the page! "Secretaries Wanted!" she read. "Apply at the United States Government Cuban Refugee Administration Office in the Federal Building. All applicants must be United States citizens. Knowledge of Spanish helpful, but not required."

"Well, I've had secretarial training and experience!" she thought excitedly. "And since these jobs are only available to citizens of the U. S., most of the Cubans won't qualify for them. I might actually have a chance to get a job there."

Beth hurried out of the house and down the street to the address listed in the paper. Fortunately, it was only a few blocks away. After turning in her application and being interviewed by the office manager, she returned home and eagerly awaited the results of her first attempt in many years to find employment.

Two days later, the phone rang. "Is this Mrs. Beth Frazier?" inquired a female voice on the other end of the line.

"Yes, this is she."

"This is Ellen Sheffield from the Cuban Refugee Administration. I'm pleased to inform you that we have decided to hire you for one of our secretarial positions. Could you be at work at eight o'clock tomorrow morning?"

"I certainly could!"

The following morning, as she got ready for work, Beth thought, "I'm so thankful that my dad insisted that I go to business school as well as art school! My secretarial training has been such a help to me throughout the years!"

At work, Beth found that her assignment consisted of recording the results of interviews that Spanish-speaking employees conducted with Cuban refugees who came into the office seeking financial assistance from the U. S. government. She found it to be a fascinating task, because each case history represented a different individual with his or her own unique story. And how thankful she was to have found a job that would provide a good income to support her family!

One sunny day, Beth left the building on her lunch hour, walked to a nearby park, and found a comfortable spot to sit on a bench under the shade of a large tree. As she was munching on an egg salad sandwich, a young Cuban woman came and sat down beside her. With a smile, Beth reached into her purse, pulled out a Christian tract, and offered it to her companion. "Here's something that you might enjoy reading! It tells how you can know for sure that you're going to heaven!"

A puzzled look crossed the young lady's face, and she shook her head, holding her hands palms up in an expression of helpless confusion. "No hablo Ingles!" Then she got up and walked away.

"How I wish I knew Spanish!" Beth thought in frustration. As Beth finished eating, she watched as a steady stream of Cuban men, women, and children passed by on the sidewalk in front of her. As she listened to their unintelligible snatches of conversation, she mused, "Why, the Lord has plopped me down right in the middle of a tremendously needy mission field, but I'm not even able to communicate with these people! I've got to learn how to speak Spanish so that I can give them the Gospel, and I'm going to buy a supply of Spanish tracts and Gospels of John to hand out to them too!"

Later that afternoon, after Beth had finished typing her last report for the day, she turned to Maria Hernandez, who worked at the desk next to hers and asked, "Maria, I was wondering if you could do me a big favor? I'd like to learn to speak Spanish. Would you be willing to teach me?"

"Si, Senora Frazier!" the attractive young brunette replied, her brown eyes sparkling. "I would be glad to help you!"

From that day on, Beth spent most of each lunch hour with Maria, who patiently instructed Beth as she tried to learn the Spanish language. And each evening, Beth pored over a Spanish-English dictionary and a Spanish New Testament, comparing it with her own English Bible, and endeavoring to comprehend the meanings of the foreign words.

As the weeks went by, Beth was amazed at the speed with which she was learning to speak, read, and comprehend Spanish. As she hesitantly conversed with Maria in Spanish one day, her tutor cried enthusiastically, "Bueno, Senora Frazier! Muy bueno! I've never seen anyone learn my language as quickly as you have, and your accent is so good too! Before long, you will be able to say anything you want to!"

True to Maria's prediction, Beth was soon able to use her knowledge of Spanish to share the good news of salvation with many of her Spanish-speaking friends and co-workers. And often during her lunch hour, Beth found herself surrounded by a crowd of children who left their play in the park to listen as she used a "wordless book" to tell them the story of Jesus in their own language. But the most wonderful moment of all came on the day that her friend Maria bowed her head and asked the Lord Jesus to save her! "Gracias, Beth! Muchas gracias!" Her friend's eyes glistened with joyful tears. "If it had not been for you, I might never have come to know El Senor Jesu Cristo as my own personal Savior!"

The spring and summer months of 1970 sped by, and soon it was almost time for Joe and Eberly to be married. Beth rejoiced that Eberly was able to come to Miami shortly before her wedding for a visit. One afternoon, as Beth and Eberly walked down the street, they paused in front of a bridal shop. As they looked at the display in the window, Eberly pointed to a lovely veil decorated with iridescent beads, pearls, and lace. "Isn't that beautiful, Mother? That's just the kind of veil that I would like to wear at my wedding!"

Beth studied the veil closely, until its image was fixed in her artistic mind. "Well, I believe that I could make you a veil just like that, Eberly. All we would have to do is buy the materials!"

"Oh, Mother, that would be wonderful!" Eberly gave Beth a grateful hug.

True to her word, Beth made not only Eberly's bridal veil, but also the headpieces for her three attendants and her flower girl, and the pillow that her ring-bearer carried. How thankful she was that she was able to have at least a small part in helping her daughter prepare for her wedding! And on the afternoon of July 11, 1970, Beth's eyes filled with joyful tears as she watched Clifford escort Eberly down the aisle to be joined in marriage to Joe Mehesy. "Thank You, Father, for giving Eberly such a fine man for her husband!" she breathed gratefully, "and thank You for giving us such a wonderful new son!"

On September 15, 1970, Clifford and Beth reached another milestone in their lives when they became grandparents for the first time, with the birth of Lowell and Sandra's daughter Jennifer Faye. How Beth wished that they lived closer to this precious little one, so that they could enjoy watching her grow, develop a close, loving relationship with her, and be an important influence in her life. Instead, they had to be content with only occasional visits. Each time Beth saw Jennifer, she was amazed at how much she had changed since the last time they had come to Greenville.

One sunny morning in the early spring of 1971, Clifford, Beth, and Raymond were seated at the kitchen table eating their usual breakfast of oatmeal. Suddenly, Clifford laid down his spoon and announced, "Beth, I've been praying a lot recently about what we should do, since I haven't been able to find any work here in Miami, and today I believe the Lord has shown me what His will is!"

Beth looked over at him with interest. "Really? What do you think He wants us to do?"

"I think He wants Raymond and me to go back to Alabama and work on starting a church there, but I think that you should stay here. You know, one of the problems that we've had each time that we've moved to Alabama is that we haven't had enough money to live on, but now that you have this job, that won't be a problem anymore. It will be like we're going there as missionaries and you're supporting us while we do the Lord's work, just like people are going to be supporting Joseph and Eberly when they go to the Navajo field!"

Beth's mouth dropped open in surprise and dismay. "But that will mean that we'll have to be separated from each other! I think that our family needs to stay together."

"Well, we won't be separated all the time. Raymond and I will come down and see you as often as we can, and we'll take you up there with us whenever you can get any time off from work. And besides, just as soon as we get the ministry going good, you can quit your job and you can move there permanently. This is just a sacrifice that we're going to have to make if we're going to do the Lord's work!"

At that moment, Raymond spoke up. "You can move to Alabama if you want to, Father, but I don't see why I have to go with you! I'm not a preacher or a missionary, and besides I like it down here in Florida. It seems like every time that I make friends someplace, I have to move away and leave them!"

"I need you to help me build the church building on the land that Mr. Jim gave us. You're going with me, and that's final! I don't want to hear any more arguments about it!"

So it was that Clifford and Raymond moved to Alabama, leaving Beth alone in Florida. The next few months passed uneventfully, with Beth working hard at her office job and faithfully sharing the Gospel with her Cuban friends and co-workers and Clifford holding evangelistic meetings in rural Alabama, with Beth joining him and Raymond occasionally, whenever she was able.

For Beth, the highlight of the year 1971 came on December 19th, when her second grandchild, Joe and Eberly's daughter Carol Ruth, was born. Although Beth longed to be with her only daughter for the birth of her first child, her work schedule prevented her from doing so. Clifford was able to be in Greenville at the time of Carol's birth, but it was not until the early spring of 1972 that Joe and Eberly were able to come for a visit and Beth was able to hold little Carol in her arms for the very first time!

On a warm evening in the late spring of 1972, as Beth was seated at the kitchen table eating her solitary supper, the door burst open and Clifford and Raymond walked in. Clifford pulled Beth into his arms. "Start packing, Beth. It's time for you to join us in Alabama! We'll leave as soon as you can get ready!"

"That's wonderful, Clifford! It will be great to be together as a family again!"

"Yes, it certainly will! You know, during the time that we've been apart, I've realized that you were right. It isn't good for us to be separated. In fact, it was a hindrance to the ministry. Everywhere I went to preach, people would ask me, 'Where's your wife?' I think that they thought that we must have had problems in our marriage that caused us to separate from each other. I finally realized that I can't do the work that God has called me to do in Alabama without you by my side!"

"Well, the Lord may have called you and Mother to Alabama," Raymond broke in angrily, "but He didn't call me! And this time I'm not going with you! I hate Alabama, and I won't go back there! I'm staying here!"

"But Raymond, you're only sixteen years old, and you haven't even finished high school yet!" Beth protested.

"That's right," Clifford yelled angrily. "Whether you like it or not, you're moving to Alabama with us!"

"I'm old enough to live on my own!" Raymond maintained stubbornly. "I'm not going with you, and you can't make me!"

In spite of Beth's pleas and Clifford's tirades, Raymond remained adamant in his decision to stay in Florida. Tears filled Beth's eyes and spilled down her cheeks as she and Clifford headed north to Alabama the following day, leaving their youngest son behind. "Father, please take care of Raymond," she prayed fervently, "and please bring him back to us soon."

The hot, muggy days of the summer of 1972 seemed to drag on endlessly. Although Beth was glad to be with Clifford again, and she rejoiced that they were able to blend their talents in reaching people with the Gospel, her heart was filled with continual sorrow and concern because Raymond was not with them.

One stormy afternoon in early fall, the front door swung open, and Raymond suddenly appeared, soaked to the skin. Unmindful of his wet clothes, Beth ran to him and enfolded him in her arms. "Son, it's so good to see you! How did you get here?"

"I hitchhiked. I decided that you were right, Mother. I need to finish high school, and there's no way that I can do that and support myself at the same time, so I figured that I'd better come home."

"Praise the Lord!" Beth's tears of joy mingled with the water dripping down from Raymond's hair.

The rest of 1972 and most of 1973 passed uneventfully, with Clifford and Beth throwing all of their energy into evangelistic meetings among the people of rural southern Alabama, while Raymond completed his junior year of high school.

In August, they were all thrilled to receive a surprise visit from Lowell, Sandra, and Jennifer. Beth rejoiced at the chance to see her son and daughter-in-law again, and she marveled at how much little Jennifer, who was almost three years old now, had grown and changed since the last time that she had seen her.

As they sat around the supper table visiting one night, Lowell turned to Raymond. "Why don't you come back to South Carolina with us, Ray? You could live with Sandra and me and finish school there, and you'd be able to find a part-time job in Greenville too. I know it's really hard to find work here!"

Raymond's face lit up. "That's a great idea, Lowell! I'd love to do that! We lived in Greenville for so long that it has always seemed like home to me! I can hardly wait to get back over there and see all of my old friends again!"

So it was decided that Raymond would move to Greenville and live with Lowell and Sandra. Although Beth hated to see Raymond leave, she was thankful that this time he would be living with his older brother, rather than by himself. As Beth watched their car pull out of the driveway several days later, she realized that Raymond would never again be coming back to live with her and Clifford. Since Joe, Eberly, and Carol had moved to Window Rock, Arizona the previous year and were busily involved in their work among the Navajo Indians, and Raymond had now joined Lowell, Sandra, and Jennifer in Greenville, South Carolina, she knew that her nest was truly empty at last. "Lord Jesus, I commit all my children to You!" she whispered, "I've done the best I could to raise them for You, but now they're on their own, and they're in Your Hands!  Please take care of them!"

On a cold blustery morning in early February 1974, as Clifford and Beth sat at the breakfast table sipping steaming hot coffee, Clifford turned to Beth and remarked, "I think that we need a little break from the ministry here in Alabama.  Let's go to the Founder's Week Bible Conference at Moody Bible Institute in Chicago.  It's next week, you know."

"That would be great, Clifford!  It will really be encouraging to hear some good messages from God's Word, and I'm sure that we'll get to see some of our old friends there too!"

The following week found Clifford and Beth sitting together in the huge auditorium of Moody Memorial Church and listening to the teaching of the prominent Christian leaders who had been chosen to preach at that year's conference.  In addition to Beth's enjoyment of the excellent sermons, her musical soul reveled in the beautiful music that was an important part of each meeting.  "How wonderful it would be to live here in Chicago, and to be able to attend Moody Church all the time!" Beth thought wistfully.

On the second night of the conference, immediately following the congregational singing, a tall thin man walked across the platform and up to the microphone.  "I am the director of personnel for Moody Bible Institute," he said.  "I'm sure that in a group like this there are some people who are looking for a place to serve our Lord.  I would just like to let you know that we at Moody always have a need for more staff members to join with us in our work of preparing young people for God's service.  One of our special needs at this time is for a secretary to work in the records office.  Would you please pray that the Lord will supply this need, and also pray about the possibility that He might want you to serve Him in some way here at Moody?"

"A secretary?" Beth thought excitedly. "Why, I could do that! I'd love to be on staff here at Moody! But of course I can't. Clifford needs me to help him in his ministry in Alabama." With that, she dismissed the thought from her mind.

However, later that night, as they were lying in bed, Clifford said, "Why don't you go in tomorrow and apply for that position in the records office? You're well qualified for the job!"

Beth gasped in surprise. "But what about the work in Alabama, Clifford? I thought we had agreed that you needed me to work with you in the ministry there, and that we shouldn't be separated anymore."

Clifford sighed regretfully. "Well, the work in Alabama seems to have come to a standstill. I really don't know what more we can accomplish there right now. If you got this job, it would give us a source of income, as well as giving you a wonderful opportunity to serve the Lord! Moody is the best Bible school in the country, and if you work there, you'll have a part in training pastors and missionaries who will be proclaiming the Gospel all over the world!"

The following morning found Beth at Moody Bible Institute filling out an application for employment. After turning it in, she returned to the hotel where she and Clifford were staying. However, just as she walked in the door, the phone rang. "Who could be calling us here?" she wondered.

Clifford answered the phone, listened for a moment and then handed it to her. "It's for you, Beth. It's Leonard Rascher, the man who's in charge of the records office and of the practical Christian work department at Moody! Maybe you've got the job!"

"I've been looking over your application, Mrs. Frazier," Mr. Rascher said after she had greeted him, "and your qualifications for the job in the records office look superb!  I was also especially interested in the fact that you are an artist.  We could really use someone with artistic talent in the practical Christian work department!  Could you come in this afternoon at two o'clock for an interview?"

"I'd love to!  I'll see you then!"

That afternoon, when Beth met with Mr. Rascher, she was hired, with the understanding that she would be dividing her time between working in the records office and in the practical Christian work department.  She was to begin the following Monday.  Beth could hardly wait to tell Clifford that she was now on the staff of Moody Bible Institute!

"It will be a wonderful opportunity to use my artistic ability as well as my secretarial training!" she told Clifford excitedly as they sat in their hotel room.  "Mr. Rascher says that each student at Moody has a practical Christian work assignment and that they have to turn in a report about it each week.  One of the things that he wants me to do is to design some eye-catching posters that will remind the students to turn in their reports!  And he says that he has lots of other ideas for using my art ability there too!"

"That's wonderful, Beth!  Now the next thing that we have to do is to find ourselves a place to live!"

The next few days flew by at whirlwind speed for Clifford and Beth.  In between attending the remaining services of the Bible conference, they were able to find a small studio apartment that was located several blocks down the street from Moody Bible Institute and to move their belongings into it.  Founder's Week ended on Sunday night, and on Monday morning Beth was in the office at Moody for her first day of work.

Going to work each day was a joy for Beth.  She was thrilled to be using her talents for the Lord again at last, and she deeply enjoyed the fellowship of her Christian coworkers. Just as Mr. Rascher had promised, there were many opportunities for Beth to do artwork, as well as to use her secretarial skills. And when she learned that Moody also had an orchestra that was open to any student or staff member who wished to join it, her joy was complete. One evening, at orchestra rehearsal, as she drew the bow over the strings of her beloved cello, and listened as its rich tones blended in beautiful harmony with those of the other instruments, Beth's eyes welled up with tears of joy. "Thank You, Father!" she breathed in gratitude, "Only You could so perfectly give me all the desires of my heart!"

However, although Beth was supremely happy, she noticed that Clifford seemed to be getting more restless by the day. Although he spent many hours each day looking for employment, he had not been able to find a job. One night after supper he announced, "I can't keep on living here like this, Beth! I'm glad that you've found a place to serve the Lord, but I need to find a ministry too!"

"But you do have a ministry! Everywhere you go, you hand out tracts and witness to people about the Lord! You've seen lots of people saved too! The Lord has really given you a gift for evangelism!"

"I know, but that's not enough! I miss preaching! I've been praying about it, and I think that you should keep your job at Moody, and I should become a traveling evangelist!"

"But if I'm not with you, won't you run into the same problem that you had before—with people wondering where your wife is?"

"Naw. That's only a problem if I stay in one place, like I did in Alabama. There are lots of evangelists who travel and hold meetings by themselves, while their wives stay at home."

So it was settled. From then on, Clifford divided his time between preaching in various parts of Illinois, Alabama, and Florida and spending time in Chicago with Beth. Although Beth missed him deeply, her life was filled with many activities. In addition to her participation in the orchestra, she joined a group of musicians who went weekly to a local nursing home and held services for the residents. And she also began attending evening Bible school classes several times a week at Moody, since these were provided free of charge to staff members. She found her studies fascinating, and her soul feasted on the rich spiritual food that she was receiving.

The remainder of 1974 sped by in a flurry of joyful activity. However, to Beth, the most special events of that year occurred when she and Clifford welcomed two new grandchildren into their family. On April 12th, their first grandson, Paul Andrew Mehesy, Eberly and Joe's son, was born, and their second grandson, Lowell Jason Frazier, was born to Lowell and Sandra on July 26th!

Once again, because of her work schedule, Beth was unable to be with her daughter for the birth of her baby, even though Clifford was able to go. So she was thrilled when, by June of 1975, she had accumulated enough vacation time to allow her and Clifford to make a trip to Arizona to visit Joe, Eberly, Carol, and Paul. How she marveled at how Carol had grown from the tiny three-month-old baby whom she had held in her arms in Florida into a lively three-and a half-year-old who was already beginning to show signs of a budding artistic talent! And how she rejoiced as she held one-year-old Paul on her lap for the first time, and watched him smile contentedly up at her!

Beth found an added joy in the fact that they happened to arrive during the same week that Joe and Eberly were teaching Vacation Bible School classes. Once again, Beth was able to do chalk talks to present the Gospel to the Navajo children. And, as the kids were working on their handwork each day, Beth quietly pulled out her sketchpad and filled it with beautiful pencil portraits of her students.

347

The remainder of 1975 passed uneventfully, and the new year of 1976 brought both sorrow and joy to Clifford and Beth. One evening in late summer, the phone rang, and when Beth answered, she heard Lowell's voice on the other end of the line. "Mother, I'm sorry to have to tell you this," he began hesitantly, "but Sandra and I have separated, and we're planning to get a divorce. You know that we've had problems in our marriage for a long time. We've tried our best to work them out, but we just can't! It's impossible for us to stay together any longer!"

"But, Lowell," Beth sobbed in protest, tears streaming down her cheeks, "when you marry someone, you promise to stay together for as long as you both shall live! Don't give up on your marriage! The Lord is able to help you, if you will let Him! All things are possible with Him!"

"I'm sorry, Mother," Lowell repeated firmly. "I know that this is hurting you, but I felt like I had to be honest with you and let you know what is going on in our lives. Sandra and I just don't see any other way out! Besides, it's not good for Jennifer and Jason to be in an atmosphere of constant fighting!"

Beth and Lowell talked for a while longer, as Beth tried to persuade her son to reconsider his decision, but when she hung up the phone, she knew that nothing that she had said had made any change in Lowell and Sandra's decision to end their marriage. Dropping to her knees, she pleaded through her tears that her Heavenly Father would somehow intervene in her beloved son and daughter-in-law's lives and save their marriage, and also that He would protect her precious grandchildren from being hurt by the situation.

But it was not to be. Several months later, Lowell and Sandra's divorce became final. Jennifer and Jason remained in Sandra's care, although they also spent much time with Lowell. However, Beth continued to pray faithfully for the entire family, that the Lord would draw each of them into a close relationship with Himself, in spite of all that had taken place in their lives.

A welcome respite from the past few sorrowful months came when Joe, Eberly, Carol, and Paul came to Chicago to spend Thanksgiving with Clifford and Beth. Once again, Beth was astonished to see how much Carol and Paul had grown and changed in the year and a half since she had seen them. And as she looked at the newest examples of Carol's artwork, which Eberly had brought along to show her, Beth was amazed to see such evidence of talent in a child who was not yet five years old! Though they were only able to stay for a few days because they were traveling to the East Coast where they would be speaking in churches and telling about their missionary work, it was a time of joyful fellowship! And an added highlight of their visit was their surprise announcement that a new little Mehesy would be joining the family in early May, 1977!

"Wouldn't it be great if this baby is born on your birthday, Mother?" Eberly asked, when she called Beth on the phone one night in early 1977. "It could be, you know, because it's due on May 9th—the day after your birthday!" However, on the evening of April 19th, 1977, Clifford and Beth received a phone call from Joe and Eberly informing them that their third granddaughter, Sharon Joy, had just made her entrance into the world--three weeks early!

As the rest of 1977 passed, Beth noticed that each time Lowell called, he talked more and more about Debbie Wade, a young woman whom he had met at work and had begun dating. Although there was a difference in age of more than eight years between them, since Debbie was only nineteen years old and Lowell was now almost twenty-eight, Beth sensed that their relationship was becoming increasingly serious. So she was not surprised when one evening, Lowell called and exclaimed enthusiastically, "Guess what, Mother! I've got great news! I asked Debbie to marry me, and she said 'yes'! We're going to be married next spring—on

May 27$^{th}$! And we're hoping that after we're married, Jennifer and Jason will be able to come and live with us!"

As Beth's sixty-second birthday approached in May, 1978, she knew that she was facing a major decision. "Should I retire from Moody now, or should I continue to work until I'm sixty-five?" she wondered one night. As she thought and prayed about it, she realized that although she loved her job, she longed to be free to travel with Clifford and aid him in his ministry and also to be able to visit her children and grandchildren more often. Another thing influencing her decision was the fact that, during the four years that she had attended evening Bible classes, she had completed all of the courses necessary to earn a diploma! "There's nothing holding me here anymore," she finally decided. "I'll give my notice tomorrow."

Clifford was overjoyed at her decision. "It's wonderful the way the Lord has worked all of this out!" he exulted. "Now you'll not only be free to travel with me, but we'll have your pension from Moody and your social security check, as well as mine, to help pay our expenses!"

So it was that on the evening of May 26, 1978, Beth graduated from the Moody Bible Institute Evening School, while Clifford watched proudly from the audience. As the dean of the school shook her hand and gave Beth her diploma, he signaled her to remain beside him on the stage for a moment. He turned and faced the audience and announced, "I want to extend my special congratulations to this dear lady--my good friend, Beth Conrad Frazier, who has accomplished the amazing feat of completing our entire evening Bible school course at the same time that she worked fulltime in the records office. She will be retiring and leaving us soon, and she will be greatly missed! Congratulations, Beth, and may the Lord richly bless you, as you and your husband Clifford continue to serve Him together!"

As Beth descended from the platform amid a thunder of applause, she thanked the Lord for the many blessings that He had showered upon her during her time at Moody. However, although she had enjoyed her graduation tremendously, she fervently wished that it could have been scheduled for some other time. Since Lowell and Debbie were to be married the very next day in Greenville, South Carolina, attending the graduation had made it impossible for her and Clifford to go to their wedding!

In July 1978, after Beth had retired, she and Clifford once again made the trip to Arizona to visit Joe and Eberly and their family. While they were there, they had the joy of seeing their new granddaughter Sharon, who was now a bubbly, active one-year-old, for the very first time! And they were greeted with the glad news that a new little brother or sister would be joining Carol, Paul, and Sharon in November!

However, on the evening of October 6th, when the phone rang and Beth answered it, she was surprised to hear the voice of her son-in-law on the other end of the line. "Mother, Eberly began hemorrhaging today, and the baby had to be delivered by emergency Caesarean. You have another granddaughter—Janet Faith! Even though she was born five weeks early, she seems to be doing well, and Eberly is doing fine too!"

"Praise the Lord that they're both all right!" Beth sank into a chair, her knees weak as she considered the myriad of things that could have happened.

But it was only twenty days later, on October 26th, that Beth answered the phone and heard the weeping voice of her daughter. "Oh, Mother," Eberly sobbed into the phone, "we almost lost Janet today, and we may still lose her! Please, please be praying for her, and ask everyone else you know to pray too!"

"What happened, Honey?" Beth cried, rooted to the spot in shock.

Eberly's words burst forth like a torrent. "I was nursing Janet this afternoon, and she went to sleep, and when I tried to wake her up to nurse some more, I realized that she wasn't breathing and that her heart had stopped beating. She died in my arms, Mother! Her skin got really pale, and she was just as limp as a rag doll, and then her eyes opened up, but there was no expression in them, and I knew that I had lost her! I was holding her little body, but she wasn't there anymore! I cried out, 'Jesus, help Janet! Jesus, help Janet!' and then I ran outside carrying her and looking for someone to help us! There were two young women nearby who gave her CPR, and they revived her, but she was clinically dead for at least five minutes! She's in the infant intensive care ward at the hospital now, but every time that she goes to sleep, she forgets to breathe again, and her heart slows down. There's a nurse standing beside her crib and watching her constantly, and every time her heartbeat gets slower, the nurse has to wake her up so that she'll start breathing again. The doctor says that the condition she has is called apnea, and that it's common in premature babies. He also says that if she had died today, he would have said it was a 'crib death', and that she could have this problem again anytime during the first two years of her life! So we may still lose her!"

"Try to calm down, Sweetheart, and remember that Janet's life is in the Lord's Hands!" Beth tried to soothe her heartbroken daughter as her own tears fell unheeded to the floor. "Right now, let's just praise the Lord that He allowed Janet to be brought back to life this afternoon, and let's trust Him to take care of her. He must have a very special purpose for her if He intervened so miraculously to save her from dying!"

"All right, Mother, I'll try to do that, but it sure is hard!" Eberly responded in a tearful whisper.

"I know it is, Honey, but the Lord will give you the strength that you need," Beth encouraged her. As Beth hung up the phone, she sank to her knees and implored her Heavenly Father to spare the life of her precious granddaughter, if it was His will to do so!

The very next morning, Eberly called back to tell her the joyful news that about two-thirty that morning, Janet had stopped having apnea and her breathing had returned to normal. "Of course, the doctor still says that it could happen again at any time," Eberly concluded, "but like you said, Mother, we're just going to have to trust the Lord to protect her!"

The last two months of 1978 passed by uneventfully. And in the summer of 1979, Beth and Clifford had the unspeakably great joy of holding little Janet, who was now a healthy eight-month-old, in their arms for the first time, when Joe and Eberly and their four children came to see them in southern Illinois. While the Mehesy family was there, Raymond, who had just been discharged from the army after completing his time of enlistment, was able to join them for a visit also!

As Beth enthusiastically thanked the Lord for this added blessing, she couldn't help but wish that Lowell, Debbie, Jennifer, and Jason could be there too. "If only they were here, our family reunion would be complete!" she sighed wistfully, "It would be so wonderful to have all of our children and grandchildren with us at the same time!"

But as soon as this thought crossed her mind, she mentally shook herself. "How can I be ungrateful when You've already given me so much, Father?" she whispered contritely. "Please forgive me!" And dismissing all such wishful thinking, she threw her whole being into wholeheartedly enjoying this precious time that she was able to share with Raymond and with Eberly and Joe and her grandchildren.

The following year flew by, as Clifford and Beth continued the evangelistic travels that they had begun after Beth had retired from Moody in the summer of 1978. They divided their time between the four areas in which they owned property—the Gulf coast of

Florida near Fort Myers, southern Alabama, southern Illinois, and the tiny town of Lostant, Illinois, where Clifford had recently been able to purchase the house that was his birthplace. Everywhere they went, they passed out tracts and gave the Gospel to anyone who would listen, and Beth often taught impromptu Bible lessons and did chalk talks for the groups of children that they encountered in various parks along their journeys. In addition to all of these opportunities, they held numerous evangelistic meetings, in which Clifford proclaimed God's Word and they utilized their musical talents to share God's love with others. And of course they made frequent trips to Greenville, South Carolina to visit Lowell, Debbie, Jennifer, and Jason, and also Raymond, who was now attending college there.

On the morning of May 14, 1980, just six days after her sixty-fourth birthday, Beth sat leisurely eating breakfast, as she gazed out the window at the tall pines that grew on their property in Alabama. Her mind drifted back over the previous two years since she had retired from Moody and joined Clifford in his evangelistic travels. "They've been good years—probably the best years of our married life!" she mused thankfully. "We seem to be able to work together as a team better now, and I think that we're finally beginning to achieve some of the closeness and harmony that I've always longed for in our relationship. Thank you so much for all of your blessings, Father!"

A moment later, however, her dreamy reverie was abruptly brought to an end, as she suddenly experienced the worst indigestion that she had ever had in her life. Rising from the table, she hurriedly mixed some baking soda into a glass of water and drank it, hoping to relieve her gas pains. However, in spite of her continued efforts to burp and alleviate her heartburn, her discomfort grew steadily worse! Soon she felt a suffocating pressure in her chest that left her gasping for breath, and then, as the room spun crazily about her, she sank down into a chair, afraid that she was going to faint. "Oh, Clifford, help me!" she cried weakly through the open window. "Something is terribly wrong with me! I'm so sick!"

A moment later, the front door burst open and Clifford hurried into the room, his face filled with concern. "I heard you calling me, Beth! What's the matter, dear?" Then, as he saw her pale face, beaded with sweat, and heard her labored efforts to breathe, he helped her up from her chair and guided her out the door toward the car, supporting her with both of his arms. "Beth, we're getting you to a hospital as quickly as we can! I'm afraid that you're having a heart attack!"

The long ride to the hospital was a nightmarish blur of pain and near-suffocation for Beth. She felt herself fading in and out of consciousness and she felt that at any moment she might leave earth behind and go to be with her Lord! Although she hated the thought of leaving her family, she was filled with inexpressible joy at the prospect of at last seeing face-to-face the One Whom she had loved supremely for so many years! "My life is in Your Hands, Father!" she thought, for she was far too weak to pray audibly. "I commit myself to You! May Your will be done!"

As their car raced down the highway toward the hospital, she was vaguely aware of Clifford's voice in the background. It sounded like it was far away—at the end of a long dark tunnel. "Hang on, Beth!" he implored. "We're almost there now! Please don't leave me!" Then she heard him pleading in prayer, "Lord Jesus, please spare her! Please save my precious Beth's life!" Then everything went black.

Beth awakened to find herself lying in bed in a hospital room. The pain had abated somewhat and it was a bit easier to breathe, but she felt terribly weak and weary. She looked up and saw a doctor standing by her bedside. "Well, Mrs. Frazier, you gave us quite a scare earlier today. We almost lost you! Your husband got you to the hospital just in time! We're glad that you're still with us, but the tests that we have done show that you have suffered a major heart attack."

"A heart attack?" Beth echoed weakly in disbelief. "But I've always been so healthy!"

"Unfortunately, something like this often strikes suddenly without any warning."

"Am I going to get better?" Beth questioned. "How long do I have to stay in the hospital?"

"Well, with lots of rest and the proper medication, you should improve somewhat," the doctor said soberly. "However, I'm afraid that your heart has been damaged so extensively that you will never completely recover from the effects of this heart attack, and if you should ever have another one, you probably won't survive it."

After the doctor left the room, Beth lay quietly in bed, stunned by the enormity of what she had just heard. Then she whispered, "Father, this bed is an altar and I present myself to You on it as a living sacrifice. May Your will be done in my life—whatever it is!"

Throughout the next few days Beth experienced several episodes of irregular heart rhythm and sudden drops in blood pressure, and there were several times when the doctors were unsure if she was going to survive. However, at last her condition stabilized, and several weeks later she was finally strong enough to leave the hospital and return home. But just as the doctor had said, she was far from well. The slightest exertion, even engaging in an animated conversation, drained her strength to the point that she felt short of breath and overwhelmed with weakness, forcing her to stop whatever she was doing and lie down to rest.

Over the next few months, Beth's condition improved enough that she was able to do some traveling with Clifford, but she never again regained her full strength. As she faced the possibility that she could have another heart attack at any time, and that if she did, it would probably take her life, her heart was filled with a deep longing to see her daughter Eberly just one more time. "Please,

Father, let me see Eberly and Joe and their children again before you take me Home to be with You!" she whispered one night as she was feeling especially weak.

That prayer was answered in July 1981 when Joe and Eberly and their family came to visit Beth and Clifford in Lostant, Illinois. To Beth's great joy, they were able to stay for an entire week! It was a time of wonderful fellowship. How Beth enjoyed her four precious grandchildren—Carol, who was now nine and a half years old, Paul who was seven, four-year-old Sharon, and Janet who was almost three. Beth's heart overflowed with thanksgiving as she saw how strong and healthy Janet had grown to be and realized that she was now old enough so that apnea no longer threatened to take her life! But the most special highlight of the week was the opportunity that Beth had to teach art to Carol, who was thrilled to receive art lessons from her "artist grandma."

Sunday, September 13, 1981was a perfect fall day—bright and sunny, with a slight chill in the air. The day before, Clifford and Beth had driven from Lostant to Chicago, and that morning they attended Moody Church together. Beth felt that the music in the service that day was some of the most beautiful that she had ever heard, and the sermon was a special blessing to her too.

After a delicious dinner with friends, Beth and Clifford went to a nearby nursing home and spent the afternoon visiting the patients there and sharing the Gospel with them. Just before they left, Beth played several hymns on her cello and then blended her soft alto voice in perfect harmony with Clifford's melodious tenor as they sang one of their favorite songs,"No One Ever Cared For Me Like Jesus", together.

Later that evening, after they had returned to the home of their friends to spend the night, Beth suddenly felt overcome by a feeling of total exhaustion and weakness. "I'm really tired,

Clifford," she sighed wearily. "I think I need to go to bed right now."

"Well, you go ahead, but I'd like to stay up and visit a while longer. I'll be there in just a few minutes. But before you go to sleep, why don't we have prayer together and you can say a psalm."

"All right." Beth sank heavily down into a chair. After Clifford had led in prayer and thanked the Lord for the many blessings He had showered upon them, Beth recited from memory one of her favorite portions of Scripture—Psalm 91. "He that dwelleth in the secret place of the Most High shall abide under the shadow of the Almighty. I will say of the Lord, 'He is my Refuge and my Fortress: my God; in Him will I trust'," she began softly. She then proceeded to quote the rest of the psalm, ending with the last three triumphant verses, "Because he hath set his love upon Me, therefore I will deliver him; I will set him on high, because he hath known My Name. He shall call upon me, and I will answer him: I will be with him in trouble; I will deliver him and honor him. With long life will I satisfy him, and show him my salvation!"

As Beth rose from her chair and walked out of the room, she gave a tiny gasp of surprise and delight as she suddenly looked up and saw for the first time the lovely Face of the One Whom she had loved and longed to see for almost fifty years! With a radiant smile, she entered the bedroom and lay down on the bed. She breathed one last quiet sigh, and then her soul stepped from her weary body and ran into the welcoming Arms of Jesus, her beloved Savior! As He enfolded her in His tender embrace, she looked up into His smiling Face and heard Him say joyfully, "Welcome Home, Beth, my precious child! Well done, My good and faithful servant!"

## The End

# About the Author

Eberly was born in Chicago, Illinois and was raised in the United States, but she is now proud to call herself a native of Colorado, since she has lived there for the past 37 years. Eberly and her husband Joe have been missionaries to the Native American people for the past 44 years. They have 4 children and 5 grandchildren. Eberly began writing stories as a young child, as soon as she was able to read and write. As a young woman, she had a story published in the magazine "Young Ambassador". She is also the co-author, with her daughter Sharon, of A Likely Story, a book which tells of Sharon's miraculous recovery from a severe traumatic brain injury.

In her spare time, Eberly enjoys reading, writing stories, poems, and songs, singing and playing music, swimming, and spending time with her children and grandchildren. She can be found most days either spending time with her grandchildren or curled up somewhere with a good book.

Eberly may be contacted at eberlymehesy@gmail.com

Made in the USA
Las Vegas, NV
27 December 2024

15486147R00203